The
Written
Image

The Written Image

Japanese Calligraphy and Painting from the
Sylvan Barnet and William Burto Collection

MIYEKO MURASE

With contributions by Sylvan Barnet and William Burto,
Karen L. Brock, Sondra Castile, Maxwell K. Hearn,
Tadayuki Kasashima, Denise Patry Leidy, Masako Watanabe,
and Yūji Yamashita

The Metropolitan Museum of Art, New York
Yale University Press, New Haven and London

This publication accompanies the exhibition "The Written Image: Japanese Calligraphy and Painting from the Sylvan Barnet and William Burto Collection," held at The Metropolitan Museum of Art from October 1, 2002, to March 2, 2003.

The exhibition and its accompanying catalogue are made possible in part by the Toshiba International Foundation.

Additional support for the exhibition has been provided by the Japanese Chamber of Commerce and Industry of New York, Inc.

Additional support for this publication has been provided by the Roswell L. Gilpatric Fund for Publications.

Published by The Metropolitan Museum of Art, New York

John P. O'Neill, Editor in Chief
Kathleen Howard, Editor
Bruce Campbell, Designer
Sally VanDevanter, Production
Minjee Cho, Desktop Publishing
Penny Jones, Bibliographic Editor
Robert Palmer, Indexer

Photography by Bruce Schwarz, The Photograph Studio, The Metropolitan Museum of Art
Charts by Anandaroop Roy

Set in Galliard and Diotima
Color separations by Professional Graphics Inc., Rockville, Illinois
Printed on NK New Espel
Printed and bound by CS Graphics PTE Ltd., Singapore

Jacket illustration: Jiun Onkō (1718–1804), *Sukuna Hikona no Mikoto (God of Medicine and Wine)* (cat. no. 51)
Frontispiece: Detail of Daigu Ryōkan (1758-1831), *Poem about a Crazy Monk* (cat. no. 54)
Illustrations for section openings: p. 2, detail of Musō Soseki (1275-1351), *Poem on the Theme of Snow* (cat. no. 36); p. 10, detail of Jiun Onkō (1718-1804), *Like a Dream* (cat. no. 52); p. 24, detail of Sesson Yūbai (1290-1346), *My Thatched Hut* (cat. no. 38)

Cataloguing-in-publication data is available from the Library of Congress.

ISBN: 1-58839-068-3 (The Metropolitan Museum of Art)
ISBN: 0-300-09689-5 (Yale University Press)

Contents

Director's Foreword

For forty years Sylvan Barnet and William Burto have pursued a passion for Japanese art. Like many collectors, they began their odyssey with a single object: a Korean celadon bowl. Significantly, after acquiring the piece, they immediately turned to a museum to search out comparative examples. Discovering a similar bowl in the Museum of Fine Arts, Boston, they felt a sense of excitement and affirmation—they had acquired a work of art worthy of a museum collection. The desire to learn more about their piece and find others like it opened a new world for them, an ever-widening circle of contacts and friendships: dealers, curators, professors, collectors, and students. What began as an instinctive response to a beautiful object became a study, a commitment, and an abiding part of their lives.

Two landmark exhibitions of private collections of Japanese art—the Powers Collection, shown at Harvard's Fogg Art Museum in 1970, and the Burke Collection, exhibited at the Metropolitan Museum in 1975—provided early inspiration and much needed scholarship. These exhibitions both presented encyclopedic collections of Japanese art. But Messrs. Barnet and Burto found that their own interest centered on a uniquely Japanese aesthetic, often summed up in a single word: Zen. "Zen Painting and Calligraphy," an exhibition organized in 1970 by the Museum of Fine Arts, Boston, and featuring major loans from Japan, played a key role in broadening their taste.

While ceramics served as an entry point into the world of Asian art, Messrs. Barnet and Burto rapidly discovered a far more challenging and ultimately more engrossing passion: Japanese calligraphy. Moved by a work by the eighteenth-century master Jiun seen at a New York dealer's, they acquired three more examples a short time later on their first trip to Japan. This incident highlights a pattern in their collecting: a preference for depth over breadth. Eschewing the impulse to "fill gaps," they have acquired only what they could not resist. This principle led them to gradually expand their collecting horizons to include paintings and calligraphies by *zenga* artists, the writings of early Zen monks, secular poems and letters, and Buddhist sutras, as well as several major Buddhist and Shinto paintings and objects.

It is this intensely focused passion that we celebrate here. That two American professors of English literature have achieved distinction in an area that most Japanese collectors and scholars find daunting bespeaks a remarkable spirit of curiosity and tenacity. Their collection, virtually unique outside Japan, not only embodies a fundamental aspect of Japanese culture but also testifies to the growing sophistication of Americans' engagement with other cultures.

The Metropolitan Museum's identity and its strength as an institution are defined primarily by the vision of such private collectors. Since 1987 loans from the Barnet and Burto collection have significantly augmented our presentation of Japanese art. Their gifts and promised gifts will not only fill major lacunae in our holdings but will also make our display of Japanese calligraphy and religious icons one in which any Japanese institution would take pride. An encyclopedic museum where visitors may encounter and compare representative works from every major world culture, the Metropolitan Museum is dedicated to presenting each artistic tradition through works of the highest possible caliber. Thanks to the generosity and vision of Sylvan Barnet and William Burto, American audiences will gain a richer understanding of Japanese art. This catalogue celebrates that achievement.

We are most grateful to members of the curatorial and conservation staff of the Metropolitan's Department of Asian Art—Miyeko Murase, Maxwell K. Hearn, Denise Patry Leidy, Masako Watanabe, and Sondra Castile—who selected the objects for the exhibition and prepared this catalogue. Thanks are also due to Karen L. Brock, Professor Emerita, Washington University, and two scholars from Japan, Tadayuki Kasashima, Idemitsu Museum of Arts, Tokyo, and Yūji Yamashita, Meiji Gakuin University, Tokyo.

The Metropolitan Museum extends its sincere thanks to the Toshiba International Foundation for its generosity toward this exhibition and its accompanying catalogue. Our sincere gratitude also goes to the Japanese Chamber of Commerce and Industry of New York, Inc. for its contribution toward the fruition of this project. We are also indebted to the Roswell L. Gilpatric Fund for Publications for its support of this volume.

Philippe de Montebello
Director
The Metropolitan Museum of Art

Contributors

Miyeko Murase (MM) is Special Consultant for Japanese Art at The Metropolitan Museum of Art. Other members of the Museum's staff who contributed to this book are Sondra Castile, Conservator of Asian Art; Maxwell K. Hearn (MKH), Curator of Asian Art; Denise Patry Leidy (DPL), Associate Curator of Asian Art; and Masako Watanabe (MW), Senior Research Associate in Asian Art. Karen L. Brock (KLB) is an independent scholar; Tadayuki Kasashima (TK) is Curator at the Idemitsu Museum, Tokyo; and Yūji Yamashita (YY) is Professor at the Meiji Gakuin University, Tokyo. Sylvan Barnet and William Burto live in Cambridge, Massachusetts.

Chronology

Protoliterate era	ca. 10,500 B.C.–A.D. 538
Jōmon period	ca. 10,500 B.C.–ca. 300 B.C.
Yayoi period	ca. 4th century B.C.–ca. 3rd century A.D.
Kofun period	ca. 3rd century A.D.–538
Asuka period	538–710
Nara period	710–794
Early Heian period	794–ca. 900
Late Heian period	ca. 900–1185
Kamakura period	1185–1333
Nanbokuchō period	1336–1392
Muromachi period	1392–1573
Momoyama period	1573–1615
Edo period	1615–1868

The Written Image

Collectors' Foreword

Sylvan Barnet and William Burto

The early 1960s were a good time for beginners with only moderate financial means to collect Japanese art. On the East Coast, where we were and still are, two dealers, Mathias Komor and Nat Hammer, had museum-quality objects that were remarkably affordable even for college teachers. They were affordable because in those days there were 360 yen to a dollar; today the rate is about 120 yen to a dollar, but even today's rate is much better than it was a decade or so ago, when it dipped to below 100 yen to a dollar. Having written these words, we are suddenly overcome with embarrassment because we are talking about money when we should be talking about art, and we recall Willa Cather's high-minded words, "Religion and art spring from the same root and are close kin. Economics and art are strangers." But of course Cather is mistaken: Art has always been tied to money (just as a collector's money is tied up in art). Museum directors know this today, hence museums have development offices. Artists have always known it, hence they have sought patrons — in the past, the Church and the aristocracy and in more recent years the bourgeois collector and (for artists desperate for regular income) the university, which provides teaching positions. The university also supports art historians, many of whom seem more interested in the relatively new subject of the history of art patronage than in the traditional subjects of iconography and formal analysis.

Collectors are regularly compared to bowerbirds, magpies, and pack rats, and probably most collectors uneasily sense the accuracy of these comparisons as the objects pile up and the space for living in one's living quarters diminishes. Howard Mansfield (1849–1938), a trustee of the Metroplitan Museum and the donor of some three hundred Japanese prints, was that rare exception, the collector who puts a limit on the size of his collection. It is said that at a certain point every time he acquired a print he sold one. (But is this true? Or was Mansfield like the collector who said he limited his collection to one hundred objects. One day when a visitor asked where the lavatory was, the collector told him to go down the hall and to open the second door on the right. The visitor mistakenly opened the second door on the left, saw what must have been a thousand objects, and returned, saying, "You told me your collection is limited to a hundred objects." "Oh," was the imperturbable reply, "those are not part of the collection.") Even the most passionate collectors (those who have too many objects) and the most carefree collectors (those who no longer feel guilty about having paid too much) rationalize their activities with elevated thoughts about the spiritual qualities of art, the benefit to the public, and so on. But all of these collectors must feel a twinge when they accept that a passion equal to theirs is felt by persons who collect barbed wire or Barbie dolls.

We can easily distinguish a high view of collecting and a low view. The high view (advanced by museum curators and development officers, dealers, and the collectors themselves) says that collecting requires intelligence and sensitivity and that giving works of art to museums is an act of public spiritedness. The low view (advanced by many sociologists and psychologists) says that collecting is an attempt to achieve social approval by means of exhibiting objects that allegedly testify to the collector's wealth and sensitivity.

Our own view, higher than the low view but lower than the high view, is that works of art give a distinctive kind of pleasure and that, good as some reproductions may be, even the best cannot give the pleasure of the originals. One might at first think that calligraphy, essentially black and white, reproduces very well in books, but in fact the ink has ranges of hue that the printing process can't catch, the silk or paper has a distinctive texture, and certainly a work of calligraphy is not at all like a reproduction of the same calligraphy in a book. Perhaps we are kidding ourselves, perhaps we are confusing ownership with aesthetic appreciation, but this is how we see it.

To return to high and low views of collecting: in *The Art of Art History: A Critical Anthology* (1998), the editor Donald Preziosi says that collecting is "The practice of constructing identity and forging allegiances" (p. 578). Preziosi uses the language of professors; Brenda Danet and Tamar Katril, in an essay in *Interpreting Objects and Collections* (edited by Susan M. Pearce, 1994), put the matter more bluntly: "There is often competition among collectors as to who has the best collection of a given type. Collections are also meant to demonstrate or to claim high social status. . . . The pinnacle of achievement is to have one's collection displayed by a museum" (p. 222).

The grave can end one's efforts to display a collection, but it can also harbor a collection or some portion of it. The Tang emperor Taizong (r. 626–649), who owned thousands of pieces of calligraphy, commissioned experts to evaluate them. It was agreed that one of the greatest pieces was a work by Wang Xizhi (ca. 303–361), and it is this piece that the emperor ordered be buried with him. Apparently no one told him that he couldn't take it with him, so at his death his wish was granted.

The odd thing about the psychological interpretation, most fully seen at its most insulting in Werner Muensterberger's *Collecting: An Unruly Passion, Psychological Perspectives* (1994), is that collecting supposedly involves relieving anxiety and tension. Our own experience has been that collecting creates tension. A visit to a dealer generates such questions as: Is the piece right? (In our experience American and Japanese dealers in East Asian art are thoroughly honest, but even the best dealer may make a mistake.) Can we afford this? It's very nice, but is it really something that will continue to give pleasure?

To repeat, the 1960s were a good time to begin collecting Japanese art, at least on the East Coast. It all began by accident, in the spring of 1962, when we were in the gallery of Mathias Komor, a Hungarian who had been an art dealer in Peking (that is what we called it before we learned to call it Beijing) and who set up in New York, first as a dealer in Chinese art but soon as a dealer in all sorts of things — among them antiquities, small medieval sculptures, and drawings. We were there with Sylvan's brother and sister-in-law (Howard and Saretta Barnet), who were looking at antiquities, when we noticed a green bowl on a shelf. We admired it from a distance, then Komor took it down and handed it to us, and we admired the incised phoenixes on the inside. He told us it was a Korean celadon — we had never heard the word celadon — and that the Museum of Fine Arts, Boston, had a notable Korean collection. Although we live in Cambridge and we had often been to the MFA, we had never set foot in the Korean galleries. The bowl was not expensive, it felt good in the hands, it had those beautiful incised phoenixes, so we bought it. The next day, back in Boston, we hurried to the MFA, saw that indeed they had a substantial Korean collection, and were pleased to see that our bowl — said to be twelfth or thirteenth century — was as old as theirs. Astounding! How could we be the owners of something that was eight hundred years old! Something we could actually handle! With those beautiful birds incised on the inside. We did not notice that the color on the outside of ours (unevenly brownish) was not nearly so attractive as the color of theirs (uniformly pale green), but live and learn. It's a nice piece, still with us — how could we ever sell or trade the piece that started us on this delightful madness? — and it really is not at all bad. In fact, the shape is good, the color on the inside is good, and the incised drawing is excellent. It's just that the color on the outside, well. . . . In two years we bought two additional Korean celadons of much better color from Komor and two from other New York dealers, Howard Hollis and William Wolff.

The Fogg Museum, at Harvard, also had some celadons on view, and after a few more trips to New York, each of which was marked by a purchase, we came to know people at the Fogg and at the MFA. Max Loehr was teaching Chinese art and John M. Rosenfield was teaching Japanese art; both (as well as Jan Fontein of the MFA) were extremely encouraging to these two naive teachers of literature who were captivated by East Asian ceramics. Through them, especially through John, we got to meet curators and graduate students in what now seems to be the Golden Age of the study of East Asian art — especially Japanese art — at Harvard. Later we will mention the names of the people who were kind enough to respond to our enthusiasm and who often helped us to learn more about the objects we were acquiring. In those early days, the mid-1960s and 1970s, we learned not only from Fontein, Loehr, Rosenfield, and their associates but also from exhibitions, exhibition catalogues, and books — although there were very few English-language books on Japanese art in those days. The volume in the Pelican History of Art series was deadly, but some books were exciting to the neophytes, especially Langdon Warner's *The Enduring Art of Japan* (1952), Roy Miller's *Japanese Ceramics* (1960), Terukazu Akiyama's *Japanese Painting* (1961), and Dietrich Seckel's *The Art of Buddhism* (1964). Although books were few, important exhibitions were increasing, and these exhibitions, especially from about 1970, were accompanied by excellent catalogues, which in our view remain indispensable works. Among the earliest scholarly exhibition catalogues are two based on the two most important American private collections of Japanese art: John M. Rosenfield and Shujiro Shimada, *Traditions of Japanese Art: Selections from the Kimiko and John Powers Collection* (1970), and Miyeko Murase,

Japanese Art: Selections from the Mary and Jackson Burke Collection (1975). In more recent years John Rosenfield and Fumiko Cranston—who have given us invaluable help and encouragement—did a three-volume catalogue of the Edo material in the Powers collection, and Miyeko Murase has written several additional catalogues of the ever-growing Burke collection. The exhibitions and their handsome, readable, informative catalogues have taught us much of what we think we know about Japanese art.

Another great exhibition during our early years was *Zen: Ink Paintings and Calligraphy* (1970) at the Museum of Fine Arts, Boston, with an important catalogue by Jan Fontein and Money Hickman. (Some years later, to our amazement and delight, in Japan we found that one of the paintings from the Boston exhibition was on the market, so we bought it; see cat. no. 40 in the present publication.) And in New York, Rand Castile brought important exhibitions to the Japan Society Gallery, for instance a tea ceremony show with a catalogue by Seizo Hayashiya and others, *Chanoyu: Japanese Tea Ceremony* (1979), and a show of treasures from Hōryūji, one of the greatest temples, with a catalogue by Bunsaku Kurata, *Hōryūji, Temple of the Exalted Law* (1981). We remember these exhibitions with immense pleasure, and we often find ourselves leafing through the informative catalogues that accompanied them.

While we are in this nostalgic mood, we will mention the catalogues of a few other exhibitions that have been especially significant for us: John M. Rosenfield and Elizabeth ten Grotenhuis, *Journey of the Three Jewels* (1979); Miyeko Murase, *Emaki: Narrative Scrolls from Japan* (1983); Yoshiaki Shimizu and John M. Rosenfield, *Masters of Japanese Calligraphy, Eighth–Nineteenth Century* (1984); Stephen Addiss, *The Art of Zen* (1989); Museum of Fine Arts, Boston, *Courtly Splendor: Twelve Centuries of Treasures from Japan* (1990); Anne Nishimura Morse and Samuel Crowell Morse, *Object as Insight: Japanese Buddhist Art and Ritual* (1995); Michael R. Cunningham, *Buddhist Treasures from Nara* (1998); and Miyeko Murase, *Bridge of Dreams: The Mary Griggs Burke Collection of Japanese Art* (2000). Clearly this list is highly selective; it omits great exhibitions that we missed (for example, a 1993 exhibition of Zen art in Zurich, which has a superb catalogue by Helmut Brinker), and it omits excellent exhibitions and catalogues that happen to fall outside the areas of our chief interests. For a fairly complete bibliography (to 1997) of material in English on Japanese art, see our "A Reader's Guide to the Arts of Japan," a bibliography available on the website of the Asia Society. A somewhat earlier version appears in Penelope Mason, *History of Japanese Art* (1993).

We have gotten ahead of our story. We had been collecting Korean and Japanese ceramics for almost three years before we became interested in calligraphy, and then it was more or less by chance. Nat Hammer showed us a large piece by Jiun Onkō (cat. no. 51), and it simply hit us. Then, a few months later, on our first trip to Japan, we visited Soshiro Yabumoto in Tokyo— Komor had generously given us his name—and asked if by any chance he knew of a calligrapher named Jiun and if by some remote possibility he had an example of Jiun's calligraphy. No expression crossed his face but he said something in Japanese to an assistant, who briefly disappeared, returned with half a dozen boxes, disappeared again, returned with another half a dozen, and then opened the boxes and hung the scrolls they contained—all by Jiun.

Mr. Yabumoto explained that his father had written a book on Jiun, and he himself owned many dozens of pieces. We were staggered by the works. One piece, with a minimal drawing of Daruma (cat. no. 49), however, was twice the price of the others. Clearly this piece was exceptional; we loved the one calligraphy we already owned, and we loved most of what Yabumoto showed us, but the Daruma was a knockout, in a class by itself, so we unhesitatingly bought it. We wished we could buy another half a dozen, but our resources were limited, and if we went for the Daruma we really were going about as far as we could or should go. Still, in a fit of enthusiam that we have never regretted, we bought two other works by Jiun. That added up to four, nothing compared to what Mr. Yabumoto was showing on his walls, but four was a good beginning. When we were back home and hung the Daruma on the wall, we stopped feeling guilty about spending money for ink on paper. Our enthusiasm for Jiun has not diminished, and in later years we bought several other pieces by him.

It's our impression that New York dealers did not carry much calligraphy when we were beginning. More precisely, the calligraphy they carried was for the most part inscriptions on paintings by later Zen monks such as Sengai and Hakuin. Still more precisely, it now occurs to us that Nat Hammer probably carried almost no calligraphy, but Mathias Komor did indeed sell a fair amount to Philip Hofer, a Cambridge book collector. The Hofer material, with material from the collection of his friend Mary Hyde, was exhibited at Harvard, with a marvelous catalogue by John M. Rosenfield, Fumiko E. Cranston, and Edwin A. Cranston, *The Courtly Tradition in Japanese Art and Literature* (1973). The works in the present catalogue are chiefly sutras (eighth through the seventeenth century) and literary texts (chiefly sixteenth through the eighteenth century). Komor had shown us a very few of these kinds of things, but we blush to say that when we saw our first sutra, with its regular characters in neat rows, one of us mumbled to the other that it looked like a laundry ticket. Somehow the literary texts that Komor showed us seemed a bit too elegant for our (undeveloped) taste.

We did buy some late Zen pictures—such material, in distinction from early Zen art, is called *zenga*—and these did include calligraphy (examples are the pieces by Nobutada [cat. no. 55] and Taiga [cat. no. 57], though it happens that neither artist was a monk). *Zenga*—ink paintings with simple forms quickly executed by Zen monks who were amateur painters and by laymen who imitated their style—was very popular at the time. Indeed one might almost say that for the general public Japanese culture was raw fish, harakiri (more properly seppuku), flower arranging, woodblock prints, and Zen. Daisetz Suzuki had written many popular books about Zen, including *Zen and Japanese Culture* (1959) and *Sengai, the Zen Master* (1971). Other immensely popular works of the period were Alan W. Watts, *The Way of Zen* (1957), Nancy Wilson Ross, *The World of Zen* (1960), and Yasuichi Awakawa, *Zen Painting* (1970). We don't know what sorts of works of Japanese art Hammer and Komor bought in Japan to sell to places like the Freer Gallery and the Cleveland Museum of Art (the Met, we think, was not purchasing much Japanese art in the 1960s and 1970s), but we do know that these dealers always showed *zenga,* and we bought a few pieces, chiefly for the pictures, not for the calligraphy.

From Jiun, who was not a Zen priest but is often grouped with *zenga* painters, we moved to calligraphy by earlier Zen monks, chiefly from the fourteenth and fifteenth centuries (cat. nos. 27–29, 36–42), and then to sutras, chiefly from the twelfth through the fourteenth century (cat. nos. 1–13). In "Some Western Thoughts on *Shodō*" below, we try to explain what qualities we find of special interest in *bokuseki* ("ink traces," early Zen writing) and in sutras. In our earliest years as collectors, when we were chiefly buying Korean ceramics, we may once or twice have thought of buying a piece because we thought it would fill a gap in the collection, but we never yielded to this temptation. We bought only what we intensely liked. This self-indulgence is a luxury that private collectors of moderate means can easily afford and that wealthy museums cannot. The encyclopedic museum, we gather, recognizes the need to acquire representative examples of all sorts. Museums must fill gaps — although as our friend John M. Rosenfield astutely pointed out, buying a work never fills a gap; far from filling a gap, every new purchase creates two gaps, one on each side. Private collectors of art are not stamp collectors seeking to complete a series. Rather, they buy what they can't resist, and in due time they find they are living with a group of objects that for the most part coheres but that also includes some items whose presence can be explained only on the grounds that they exerted an irresistible appeal. How else, in the present exhibition can we account for such things as one Esoteric Buddhist mandala (cat. no. 19), one landscape painting (cat. no. 23), and one portrait (cat. no. 35)?

Will people come to see an exhibition that consists chiefly of Japanese calligraphy? Maybe not. After all, as Yogi Berra said, "If people don't want to come out to the ball park, nobody's going to stop them." But perhaps there is an audience out there; even chance museum-goers may wander into the galleries and find something that captures them.

We want to end by again thanking our friends, acquaintances, and commercial contacts (some of whom are now friends) for helping us to understand and enjoy East Asian art. We have already named Fumiko Cranston, Jan Fontein, Nat Hammer, Mathias Komor, Max Loehr, John M. Rosenfield, and Soshiro Yabumoto, but there are many others. At Harvard we first met Susan Bush, Louise Cort, Edwin Cranston, Christine Guth, Richard Mellott, Anne and Sam Morse, Robert D. Mowry, Julia Murray, Stephen Owyoung, Elizabeth de Sabato Swinton, Elizabeth ten Grotenhuis, and Yutaka Mino. Japanese art in the Cambridge-Boston area also received a boost from Arts Asia, a gallery run by Nitza Rosovsky and Linda Abegglen, where one could see excellent contemporary ceramics and calligraphy. At the Museum of Fine Arts, Boston, the late Yasuhiro Iguchi was immensely helpful.

In later years we had the good fortune to exchange thoughts with many collectors, conservators, curators, and scholars: Stephen Addiss, Qianshen Bai, Helmut Brinker, Karen Brock (a contributor to this catalogue), Sidney Cardozo, John T. Carpenter, Sondra and Rand Castile, Willard Clark, Michael Cunningham, Peggy and Richard Danziger, Jacki Elgar, Betsy and Bob Feinberg, Felice Fischer, Kurt Gitter and Alice Yelen, Patricia Graham, Maribeth Graybill, Peter Grilli, Marilyn and Robert Hamburger, Andrew Hare, Hirose Mami Asano, Anne Rose Kitagawa, Yukio Lippit, H. Christopher Luce, Andrew Maske, Julia Meech, Constance and Sanford Miller, Bob Moore, Alexandra Munroe, Akira Nagoya, Amy Poster, Audrey Seo, Yoshiaki Shimizu, Melinda Takeuchi, James Ulak, Nayda and David Utterberg, Victoria Weston, Richard Wilson, Dorothy Wong, Yūji Yamashita (a contributor to this catalogue), Mimi Hall Yiengpruksawan, and Ann Yonemura, all of whom helped us to understand and enjoy East Asian art. At the Metropolitan Museum we greatly profited from conversations with Barbara Ford (who has been borrowing some of our things since 1987), Maxwell K. Hearn, Miyeko Murase, Takemitsu Oba, Judith G. Smith, and Masako Watanabe, as well as with two curators whom we first met when they were at the Museum of Fine Arts, Boston, Denise Patry Leidy and James C. Y. Watt.

And then there are the dealers; without them there could be no collection. We have already mentioned Nat Hammer, Howard Hollis, Mathias Komor, and William Wolff—all of New York and all deceased—but we have not mentioned other dealers to whom we are indebted, not only for works of art but also for information and even for friendship. Sometimes it is easy to be friends with a dealer, sometimes not. In fact, we have met an occasional dealer whose manner was so forbidding that we feared to make a second visit. On this issue we received excellent advice from the late Harry Nail, himself a dealer: "It is your job to build the best collection possible, even if it means having to do business with . . . ," and here he named an American dealer whose difficult manner was legendary. This man would bring out a box, place it on a table before us, undo the ribbons, take out a Japanese or Korean object, place it on the table, remove the box, draw back from the table, solemnly announce it was the finest example of such-and-such that had ever come his way, and strongly imply that we were privileged to have it offered to us. He would then wait for us to make an appreciative remark and to ask about the price. Alas, sometimes the best we could do was to say, "Oh, yes, that's very nice indeed. Thank you for showing it. Very nice, indeed. But, er, uh, er, do you perhaps have something else?" On these occasions the object was popped back into its box, our unworthiness was clearly conveyed to us, and the session was over. But he sometimes did have things that greatly appealed to us, so following Harry Nail's advice, a few months later we would summon up the courage to visit him again, perhaps to be again humiliated, perhaps to be again rewarded by seeing an object that indeed was for us.

Many dealers have put up with us even when we foolishly neglected to see the merits of a marvelous piece that we now realize we should have bought. Among them are: Fred and Joan Baekeland, Carol Davenport, Shirley Day, Jim Freeman, Sebastian Izzard, Andreas Leisinger, Leighton Longhi, Mary Ann and Howard Rogers, and Hiroshi Sugimoto (although today Hiroshi is internationally famous as a photographer, a couple of decades ago he supported his photography by dealing in *mingei* [folk art] and other kinds of Japanese art—in fact, we bought our first sutra from him). In Boston we are indebted to Judith Dowling. In Tokyo we always visited the late Junkichi Mayuyama, Tajima Mitsuru, Sasazu Etsuya, Setsu Isao, and the late Setsu Iwao, Setsu Kippei, Setsu Takako, Ueno Takeshi, Yabumoto Shun'ichi, the late Yabumoto Sōshirō, Yanagi Hiroshi, and Yanagi Takashi.

Things have changed in Japan since 1965, when we first went there, and a taxi was ninety yen (about twenty-five cents) and a room at the Imperial Hotel was about twenty dollars, but the dealers remain immensely helpful, even when we don't buy. Again, talk of money, but in talking about collecting it can't be helped.

We have learned an immense amount from our associations with these people. Oscar Wilde said, "Nothing that is worth knowing can be taught," and for more than three decades, as teachers of literature, we almost believed him, but as students of Japanese art we soon learned that he is mistaken.

An Introduction to Japanese Calligraphy in the Barnet and Burto Collection

Miyeko Murase

The works of art presented here from the collection of Sylvan Barnet and William Burto include more than forty examples of Japanese calligraphy as well as more than fifteen paintings and sculptures representing various aspects of Buddhist and Shinto imagery. They reflect the taste and personal aesthetics of their owners rather than presenting a chronological survey of Japanese religious art and calligraphy.

Calligraphy in particular has been a primary focus of the Barnet and Burto collection. Among the most difficult of all East Asian art forms to comprehend and appreciate, it is regarded in China, Korea, and Japan as the supreme form of artistic expression and achievement. Ancient belief holds that calligraphy is the purest visual manifestation of the artist's inner character and level of cultivation; it is the medium by which the artist's soul, thoughts, and feelings are best communicated. This is not to say, however, that a viewer can take on the role of palm-reader in examining a single work of calligraphy. As stated in *The Tale of Genji*,[1] not only calligraphy but also poetry manifests personal character, and all the arts express — to a greater or lesser degree — the inner nature of their creators. To grasp the many aspects of a calligrapher's personality, it is also necessary to know something about his or her background, education, and social identity.

What we can expect to find in a calligraphic work — even in the absence of information about the artist — is a chance to relive the creative experience during which a calligrapher manipulates a brush to create an object of beauty whose rhythmic energy is conveyed through strokes and dots in ink. It is often asserted that textual content should not influence one's aesthetic judgment of a calligraphic work, yet it is undeniable that the text plays a role in determining the artist's state of mind as he or she inscribes it. The text can also determine the calligrapher's choice of script. In fact, calligraphy can never be completely dissociated from the message conveyed by the written characters. It is widely assumed that full appreciation is denied to viewers lacking knowledge of the Japanese or Chinese written language and thus unable to read or understand the text. However, aesthetic appreciation of a calligraphic work is certainly available to the viewer who endeavors to discover the secrets of a master's brushwork. Even without linguistic proficiency, one can follow the creative process in which the brush traveled across the silk or paper surface to form a character or appreciate the ability of the brushwork to convey every nuance of emotion or self-expression. A thoughtful viewer can discern the beauty of individual brushstrokes, as well as the changes in ink gradation, and the organic relation of both in a single written character. The viewer can also appreciate the internal space within the structure of each character, and the way in which that space is related to the surrounding space formed by the character's shape. Likewise, the spatial relationship of the character to other characters in the text, and their relation to the work as a whole, can be admired without any knowledge of what the letters themselves mean.

Among the three major script types still in use, *kaisho* (C: *kaishu*; cat. no. 1), or regular script, is the easiest to read, allowing the viewer a straightforward glimpse of the creative process. Although *kaisho* is the most clearly written of the three scripts, it was systematically standardized much later than the two other scripts, the cursive *sōsho* (C: *caoshu*; cat. no. 54) and the semicursive *gyōsho* (C: *xingshu*; cat. no. 35). The earliest of the three to evolve, *sōsho* developed from a simplified archaic form called *reisho* (clerical script; C: *lishu*; cat. no. 58). *Sōsho* is the most abbreviated form of writing and is therefore the most difficult to decipher. Among the three scripts, *gyōsho* is the most graceful and offers the greatest artistic potential. Both *gyōsho* and *sōsho* emphasize movement and rhythm, while *kaisho* has a symmetrical beauty, clarity, and an architectonic appearance. Finally, although *kaisho* achieved its final state only during the Sui and early Tang dynasties (late sixth and seventh centuries), it is correct to state that calligraphy in Japan only began with its introduction to the imperial court soon after.

The sophisticated viewer is expected to recognize the source of the artist's style and to admire his or her ability to make personal contributions to an established tradition. To achieve this level of expertise, the viewer can rely on an enormous number of books and articles, replete with references to a superabundance of calligraphic schools and with lengthy scrutinies of the styles of famous individual artists. Much of this material is not helpful to a general audience, however, and in fact differences among various schools of calligraphy are not always easily discerned or understood even by specialists. A discussion of different schools and the artistic lineages of individual masters is therefore omitted here, in the belief that it is entirely possible to enjoy the beauty of calligraphy without such knowledge.

What may be more meaningful to the general audience is a point that Sylvan Barnet and William Burto have emphasized in their collecting activity: that a piece of calligraphy should be viewed not as an isolated object but as an aesthetic microcosm, consisting of the work itself and the mounting—usually a hanging scroll—of silk or paper. Konoe Nobutada's calligraphy and painting (cat. no. 55) depicts the ninth-century Japanese scholar Sugawara Michizane (later deified as Tenjin). It is mounted as a hanging scroll on fabric ornamented with a design of plum blossoms, Tenjin's favorite flowers, perhaps an almost too facile example of the relationship between object and setting. On the other hand, a simple, intentionally modest scroll containing a letter by Rikyū (cat. no. 30) mounted on paper and coarse silk is a visual reminder of the aesthetics of tea taste. Here a moment in the life of an historical personage, a renowned tea master, is preserved: Rikyū's writing is presented against materials that epitomize the deliberate simplicity (*wabi*) he championed.

Many pieces in this catalogue were separated in the past from a larger whole. The fragments were mounted with the greatest of care as hanging scrolls and have been treasured as works of art. It is not uncommon for calligraphic works to exist in a fragmented state; apart from the vandalism or greed that sometimes led to the cutting up of a lengthy scroll, the centuries-old Japanese aesthetic that views a damaged piece as a viable work of art resulted in the preservation of many an incomplete object. A damaged piece — or an incomplete piece — is suggestive of an existence beyond the boundaries of the physical object. The fragment, in other words, can provide the viewer with a sense of the whole or in some instances be even more satisfying aesthetically than the original intact piece.

SACRED TEXTS

It is not known precisely when the Japanese, or at least their aristocracy, came to value literacy in the Chinese written language. There are indications that some form of literacy existed in Japan prior to the introduction of Buddhism in 538, when sacred scriptures, small iconic sculptures, and a royal message in Chinese characters were delivered to the imperial court from the Korean kingdom of Paekche. Members of Japan's elite must have made an heroic effort to learn to read, understand, and copy difficult Buddhist texts in an astonishingly brief period of time, for by the early seventh century courtiers like the prince regent Shōtoku (574–622) were conversant enough in Chinese to read sutras and compose commentaries. Shōtoku's commentary on the Lotus Sutra[2] was inscribed in his own hand in standard, or *kaisho*, script, a form of writing that had only just achieved its fully evolved form in China. Although lacking somewhat in calligraphic refinement, the commentary confirms that both the comprehension of Buddhist doctrine and the ability to handle brush and ink had reached a fairly high level in Japan by the early seventh century. In the half century that followed Shōtoku's time the level of literacy in Japan continued to rise: according to the first documented record of sutra copying, a large group of scribes was assembled at the Asuka-period temple of Kawaradera in 673 to copy the texts of the Daizōkyō (the compendium of all Buddhist sutras, which is also called the Tripitaka, or Issaikyō), a work consisting of more than five thousand handscrolls.

Records of ambitious sutra-copying projects have been preserved from the Nara period, when the government sponsored most such projects, with occasional programs undertaken by influential temples. Approximately twenty projects dedicated to copying the Daizōkyō, with its records of sermons delivered by the Buddha, monastic rules, and philosophical treatises, were carried out. It has been calculated that for each such project about ten thousand workers, including scribes, proofreaders, mounters, inspectors, and others, were engaged for a period of roughly twelve months.[3] Evidently one Daizōkyō project was carried out every three and a half years during the seventy-four years that the court resided at Nara. Both the act of copying scriptures and the copied texts themselves were known as *shakyō* and were regarded as a form of prayer of such importance that an official Buddhist scriptorium was established within the imperial palace compound sometime before 727. High-ranking scriptoria employed numerous specialists who worked in an assembly-line fashion. Among them were copyists, proofreaders who also polished the gold letters, and mounters whose job included dyeing paper and drawing ruled lines. Their working conditions were well documented in various records preserved in the Shōsōin, the imperial repository at the temple of

Fig. 1. Detail of *Section of "Ananda's Perfect Memory,"* *chapter 45 of the Sutra of the* *Wise and the Foolish* (cat. no. 1)

Tōdaiji in Nara. Quotas set for the number of scriptures copied daily were strictly enforced, and payment was reduced according to the number of errors made. The scriptoria calligraphers executed an enormous number of sutra scrolls under these severely regulated circumstances, and more than one half of the calligraphic works that have survived from the Asuka and Nara periods are Buddhist scriptures. The scribes were professional craftsmen, not to be regarded as inspired masters of the art of the brush, but their works helped to improve Japanese awareness of calligraphy as an artistic medium.

Sutra-copying projects undoubtedly gave the aristocracy of Japan an appreciation of quality in calligraphy, for compared to the somewhat undistinguished handling of the brush that appears in Shōtoku's work, sutras copied by professional scribes of the Nara period demonstrate an enormous leap forward in terms of style and assurance (cat. nos. 1–4). These eighth-century works are often described as "following the style of Wang Xizhi (ca. 303–ca. 361)," the most revered of Chinese calligraphers, although none of their stylistic features finds parallels in Wang's distinctive writing. Nara-period sutras are for the most part characterized by squat and squarish letters; each brushline is carefully conducted, with a sharp angle wherever the brush changes direction. The characters are robust, solemn, and regular in shape and have an austere and dignified beauty as well as a sense of fervent devotion to the text and to the actual work of copying the sacred scriptures (fig. 1).

The very enormity of sutra-copying projects hints at the urgency that may have seized the Nara court when faced with the need for a large number of complete sutra sets. Each province throughout the country was to be given a monastery and nunnery, and each of these institutions would need a copy of the Daizōkyō. The contents of the Daizōkyō formed the basic canon of Mahayana Buddhism, and these sacred writings were the principal means of transmitting the faith. Mahayanist teachings also emphasized the spiritual value of worshiping the books themselves. The act of copying sutras and the commissioning of sutra copies were among the most meritorious of acts. The value accorded to writing out the texts was doubtless behind the proliferation of hand-copied sutras, although printing techniques were already in use.[4] The sutras themselves were not used every day. Large sets of sutras were often placed in sutra repositories, from which some were removed for special functions; others were deposited in pagodas or enclosed within statues. Much later, in the eleventh and twelfth centuries, sutras were interred in sutra mounds as a means of countering the approach of *mappō*, the anticipated decline of Buddhist law, due to commence (according to one count) in the year 1015. Interred sutras were meant to preserve records of Buddha's words and teachings until the coming of the Buddhist messiah, Miroku (S: Maitreya).

The actual copying of a sutra was most often regarded as a prayer for the spiritual welfare of the deceased; the work also atoned for various transgressions, ensured peace within the nation, and invoked protection against calamities. In addition, the sutras themselves instructed the faithful to copy them — or commission their copying by others — to guarantee their personal welfare. Folklore accounts also promoted the merits of sutra copying; one recounts the rebirth of a man who died after copying a sutra.[5]

Most large-scale sutra-copying projects were commissioned by the government or members of the imperial or noble families, but provincial governors and even people of less exalted status were also caught up in this practice. The calligraphic style of sutras copied in the provinces or by members of lower social classes was reminiscent of that favored in metropolitan areas.[6]

A document in the Shōsōin collection, dated 753, refers to a sutra whose text was copied onto dyed paper. References to papers dyed in different colors—purple, pale green, pale blue, or pink—with texts inscribed in either gold or silver ink were often included in Nara-period records. Later, during the eleventh and twelfth centuries (Late Heian period), the use of colored papers for sutra texts became enormously popular.[7] A deep indigo-blue paper dyed to simulate the color of lapis lazuli—a precious mineral mentioned frequently in sutras but not readily available in Japan (cat. nos. 6 and 7)—became especially favored. On this indigo paper texts were inscribed in gold, silver, or other precious minerals; on rare occasions columns of gold characters alternated with columns of silver. Ruled lines were also drawn in gold or silver ink, as in the example included here (cat. no. 4); an even more lavish example (cat. no. 10) shows *kirikane* (thin strips of cut gold) used for these lines. Sutra scrolls of this type, clearly expensive creations, were usually inscribed by superior calligraphers.

The dignified and solemn style of the Nara-period *shakyō* gradually gave way to more relaxed brushwork with less tightly structured characters, which was a precursor of Heian-period style. This change was an inevitable outcome of the radical shift in the court's policy toward increasingly intrusive ecclesiastics. The court escaped the all-pervading influence of the powerful Buddhist temples by removing itself from Nara in 784 and establishing a new capital city, Heian-kyō (Capital of Peace and Tranquillity), now Kyoto, in 794. Buddhist institutions were excluded from the city compound of the new capital. The abolition of official scriptoria and rising popularity of the recently introduced Esoteric Buddhism (Mikkyō) contributed to a decline in the number of large-scale sutra-copying projects in the ninth century. Early Japanese Mikkyō lacked official court patronage, and the once strictly observed rules established by the old scriptoria were noticeably loosened during the late 800s. Although no example is included in this publication, sutras from this period did not always contain the same number of characters per line, and the erstwhile high standard of *kaisho* writing was no longer followed. Also apparent in sutras copied during the early Heian years is the frequent omission of characters. Most such sutras have been preserved in provinces where they seem to have been produced.

The increasing popularity of the Lotus Sutra (J: *Hokekyō*; S: *Sadharmapundarika*) ushered in a new phase of *shakyō* production in the mid-tenth century. Among the thousands of Buddhist scriptures, none proved to have the appeal and long-lasting influence of the Lotus. Many passages from the twenty-eight chapters that make up this sutra promise salvation through the practices of reciting and copying the text (with double merit offered). During the eleventh century the Lotus Sutra became the focal point of a near craze, and Lotus Sutra handscrolls of the twelfth century, many decorated in an unprecedentedly lavish manner, are unique in the history of Japanese *shakyō*. A number of works included here testify to the unmatched quality of Late Heian sutra copying, especially those of the Lotus Sutra, often copied on paper dyed a deep indigo (fig. 2).

Indigo-dyed sutras usually feature decorative covers and frontispieces with painted narrative scenes. The three examples in this publication, however, belong to a different genre, also

Fig. 2. Detail of *Section of "Simile and Parable," with Pagoda Decoration, Chapter 3 of the Lotus Sutra* (cat. no. 6)

popular during the Late Heian period. They are ornamented with miniature stupas (pagodas) printed or drawn in mica, each of which contains a single character inscribed in gold or black ink. This practice of encasing a character within a stupa seems to have its basis in the sutra's proclamation of the merit of making offerings to stupas. In a well-known episode from chapter 4 of the Lotus Sutra, two buddhas, Shaka (the Historical Buddha; S: Shakyamuni) and Tahōbutsu (the Buddha of the Past; S: Prabhutaratna), share a seat within a stupa. Since each letter of the Lotus text was venerated as a buddha, each was placed within a stupa. In a variation a Lotus Sutra from the early Kamakura period (cat. no. 12) displays four characters placed between a canopy and a lotus pedestal printed in silver ink. Such designs endow written characters with a divine quality, treating them as images of the Buddha.

A second group of decorated sutras in this publication (cat. nos. 8–11) is ornamented in a more conventional manner, with painted designs often combined with sprinkled gold and silver particles or larger pieces of gold and silver foil scattered to create random patterns (cat. no. 10). The most lavish example of this type of decorated sutra is the renowned *Heike Nōkyō*, the most sumptuous assemblage of sutra handscrolls in Japan.[8] These scrolls have beautifully decorated paper, exquisite paintings and roller ends set with semiprecious stones, placed in delicate open metalwork. Woven ribbons, of subtle colors and designs, fasten the rolled-up scrolls.

Another distinctive feature of Heian-period sutras is that some were inscribed in fluid *gyōsho* or *sōsho* script, revealing the distinctive personal style of the calligrapher (cat. nos. 5 and 6). Even in the examples of written *kaisho* there are a noticeable softening of the brushlines and a loosening of the structure of individual characters as well as the use of rounded rather than angular corners. Some changes in calligraphic style no doubt resulted from the widespread use of kana, especially for secular literature, during the Heian period (see below). However, by the close of the twelfth century a growing fascination with a new cult of Amida Buddha that promised salvation through the mere recitation of his name — a most appealing practice to the less-educated and less-privileged believers — contributed to a decline in sutra copying, as did the introduction of Zen Buddhism, which attracted the warrior rulers. In addition, large numbers of printed sutras from China became available, and the production of printed Japanese copies led to an irreversible decline in sutra copying.

KANA SCRIPT AND CORRESPONDENCE

The Japanese of the Asuka through the Early Heian period struggled to express their thoughts and words using Chinese scripts, suitable for a language fundamentally different from that of Japan. As early as the eighth century some form of syllabic writing was beginning to evolve.[9] This system, known as *man'yōgana*, used some Chinese characters (kanji, literally "Han letters") for meaning and some for their phonetic value without regard for their ideographic significance. *Man'yōgana* represented Japan's first attempt to devise a writing system in which native words, names, thoughts, and sentiments could be recorded. It was slowly replaced by the simpler and more practical kana (literally, temporary or unofficial [*ka*] name [*na*]. Two types of kana writing developed: katakana (partial or fragmentary kana), which derived from parts of Chinese characters, and hiragana (easy and rounded kana), a drastic

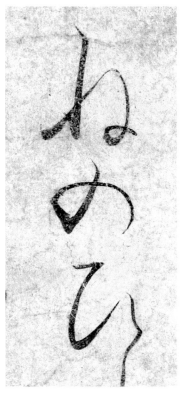

Fig. 3. Detail of *The Poet Fujiwara Kiyotada* (cat. no. 25)

Fig. 4. Detail of Myōe Kōben (1173–1232), *Dream Record with Painting of Mountains* (cat. no. 27)

simplification of selected Chinese characters written in *sōsho*. Both forms of kana are in common use today. Katakana, which first developed as a mnemonic aid for the pronunciation of difficult Buddhist texts, was widely used in the mid-tenth century for secular literature, including waka (indigenous poetry). Today it is used primarily for loanwords of Western origin. Angular in design, its letters retain remnants of their original Chinese forms, although katakana was never accepted as an artistic form.

Hiragana, which was once called *on'na-de* (woman's hand) because of its cursive feminine look, is used today for grammatical particles and inflected verb endings, in conjunction with Chinese characters that express meaning. By the ninth century hiragana was used by both men and women and played a major role in the development of waka and narrative prose. Well suited for the expression of spontaneous thoughts, the fluidly brushed hiragana evolved into a highly refined form of calligraphy. Its thin threadlike brushstrokes glide from one letter to the next, sometimes combining five or six letters in a continuous rhythmic flow of curved lines (figs. 3, 4; cat. nos. 25, 27, 28). When combined with kana, Chinese characters provide visual accents and breaks in the rhythmic flow of the brush. Some of the finest examples of kana calligraphy from the twelfth century, especially those written on beautifully decorated paper like the Selection of Thirty-six Immortal Poets in Nishi Honganji, Kyoto,[10] stand as unique monuments in the history of world calligraphy.

Among the examples included here, the Kasuga Shrine *kaishi* (cat. no. 24) of the thirteenth century and inscriptions on portraits of poets from the Kamakura and Muromachi periods (cat. nos. 25 and 26) exemplify the strength and rhythmic speed of kana works from the thirteenth through the fifteenth century. The beauty of this delicate script can also be appreciated in much later works, like the nineteenth-century artist Rengetsu's poetic inscription on her own painting (cat. no. 33).

While katakana is relegated to limited use today, its original function as mnemonic device, used primarily by scholarly monks, was never completely abandoned, and it became a popular form of writing among both scholars and monks. Two records of dreams kept by the monk Myōe (cat. nos. 27 and 28) were written primarily in Chinese characters, sprinkled with katakana for inflected verb endings. One reason for Myōe's use of katakana may have been his role in preaching Amidism (devotion to Amida Buddha who presides over the Western Paradise or Pure Land) to the masses. Katakana was apparently the preferred method of written communication for less-educated followers of Pure Land Buddhism, and he may have become accustomed to using this script.

Included in this publication are examples of kana writing executed for formal occasions or for commissions (cat. nos. 25, 26, 31) and spontaneously written pieces such as Myōe's dream memoirs. It also includes examples of correspondence (cat. nos. 29, 30, 32). As with all other types of written text in Japan, correspondence was first conducted only in Chinese, although women began using hiragana in their letters soon after its creation.[11] Men also wrote in hiragana when addressing women, but gradually a mixture of kanji and hiragana came into use, and it remains the norm for correspondence today. *The Tale of Genji*, written in the early eleventh century, is replete with references to the exchange of letters: letters written on colored papers were invariably tied to long blades of grass or branches of flowering trees. This elegant practice was eventually replaced by the use of plain white paper in the Kamakura period, at which time short letters were written on paper folded in half, top to bottom, leaving the lower half blank (cat. no. 30). When more space was required, the paper was turned around for writing on the lower portion. Consequently, when the folded paper was opened, the writing on the side that formed the lower portion was literally upside down.

Personal letters were not originally intended for posterity. Some missives contain postscripts asking that the addressees "throw them into a fire." In any case many of these letters are greatly treasured today not only as specimens of refined and unique writing but also as historical documents. Correspondence by masters like Rikyū and Kōetsu (cat. nos. 30 and 32) are now viewed as works of art, and accordingly are mounted as hanging scrolls for display in tea rooms. They are treasured not only because of the prominence of these calligraphers in the history of Japanese art but also because of their highly personal brushwork and calligraphic style. Spontaneity is the most appreciated feature of letter writing, and some connoisseurs believe that the calligraphy of personal correspondence best reveals the intrinsic nature, character, and individual style of the person wielding the brush. Two examples of Kōetsu's writing (cat. nos. 31 and 32) testify to differences in calligraphy style, depending on the purpose and nature of the text. One is a formal, commissioned work, the other a piece of personal, intimate correspondence.

Like all aspects of Japan's religious and cultural activities, the art of calligraphy was profoundly influenced by Zen (C: Chan; S: Dhyana), a form of Buddhism emphasizing contemplative meditation, mental self-discipline, and self-reliance. In Zen two practices assist the individual to break the chain of conventional thinking and to attain a deeper intuitive awareness of reality: zazen, or seated meditation, and the use of *kōan*, or questions and answers of an enigmatic or paradoxical nature. First brought to Japan from China during the late twelfth century, Zen grew in influence during the late Kamakura and Muromachi periods when it was adopted enthusiastically, especially by the military class.

A popular misconception holds that Zen Buddhism is iconoclastic. In fact, in its pristine form it has no need for scriptures, temples, icons, or other paraphernalia associated with religious institutions. In practice, however, it encouraged various arts to flourish in its name. Thus, in connection with the widespread adoption of Zen, Japan returned to a deep dependence on Chinese artistic models after more than two centuries of cultural self-assertion. Learned monk-scholars of this time, many of them prominent abbots at notable Zen temples, regarded painting or calligraphy in the Chinese mode as a means of assistance in the quest for a firmer grasp of Zen doctrine. In their artistic endeavors they emulated Chinese scholar-officials. Japanese monks who were trained in both Zen and Chinese literature composed poems in the Chinese style, inscribing their verses on their own paintings or on works by others. These paintings, usually executed in ink, depicted typically "Chinese" images of birds, plum blossoms, orchids, bamboo, and landscapes (cat. no. 40).

Paradoxically, Zen, which is theoretically not dependent on the written word, used calligraphy as the most eloquent supplementary vehicle to express what was not stated orally. Writings by Zen monks are known as *bokuseki*—literally, traces (*seki*) of ink (*boku*). The same word in Chinese (*moji*) was originally applied to the art of writing in general, but in Japan *bokuseki* is used exclusively for the writing of Zen monks. Already in use in early fourteenth-century Japan,[12] the term *bokuseki* referred to works by both Chinese and Japanese calligraphers. This genre encompassed works from the Kamakura and Muromachi periods (fig. 5; cat. nos. 34–42) as well as pieces by later Zen practitioners of the Edo period like Hakuin and his pupils (cat. nos. 48 and 57) and writings of monks belonging to the Ōbaku (C: Huangbo) sect, founded by Yinyuan Longqi (1592–1673) of Ming China, who came to Japan in 1654 (cat. nos. 44–46). The term is sometimes extended to include the works of individuals like Daigu Ryōkan (1758–1831; cat. no. 54), who did not have firm ties to the established Zen community. In a similarly broad fashion there are no rigid rules governing content or brushwork in *bokuseki*.

Bokuseki also include the official and private correspondence of Zen monks as well as their personal wills and last testaments. The most important of the monks' "ink traces," however, were Zen masters' certificates of the transmission of their teaching to pupils, their expositions on the words of the Buddha, and records of the ecclesiastic names bestowed on pupils or the names given to temple buildings. To this list may be added poetic inscriptions added to *chinsō*—portraits of Zen masters—written either by the sitter (cat. no. 35) or by an acquaintance who expressed the sitter's inner spirit eloquently and succinctly.

Fig. 5. Gukyoku Reisai (ca. 1369–1452), one of *Two Buddhist Maxims* (cat. no. 42)

During the Kamakura period numerous Chinese monks visited or settled in Japan to escape political turmoil on the continent. At the same time many Japanese monks began traveling to China to study Zen. Some returned home with superior examples of classical Chinese calligraphy in the form of rubbings of engraved stone steles. Because of these circumstances, Japanese Zen calligraphy was deeply influenced by Chinese calligraphic style, and the Muromachi period was a golden age of Chinese-style calligraphy in Japan.

Using Chinese works as their models, Japanese practitioners of Chinese-style calligraphy underwent long years of rigorous training to attain a high level of proficiency. However, it is also clear that the works of these Japanese calligraphers exhibit a wide variety of styles. Especially impressive are highly idiosyncratic works by masters like Hakuin Ekaku (1685–1768; cat. no. 48), Jiun Onkō (1718–1804; cat. nos. 49–52), and Ryōkan (cat. no. 54), which consciously ignore established rules of classical calligraphy. Although attempts have been made to categorize the stylistic features of writings by Zen masters, these efforts are futile in the context of Zen teachings. Zen stresses the discovery of truth outside and beyond the established orthodox path. Therefore the writings of Zen masters are and should be the expression of their own individual characters. Their works may not display a refined technique, but they are uniquely expressive of the inner workings of the writers' minds. It is probably for that reason that *bokuseki* represent an independent trend within the history of Japanese calligraphy, exerting little influence on calligraphy outside of Zen circles.

Very few *bokuseki* by Chinese Chan monks have been preserved in China, because the Chinese of later periods did not appreciate works that disregarded classical canons. Many Chinese examples have, however, been treasured in Japan. Both Chinese and Japanese *bokuseki* were preserved in Zen temples, but an almost equal number were acquired for secular purposes, notably for use in the tea ceremony. *Bokuseki* — especially pieces mounted as hanging scrolls using old textiles or otherwise treated with special care — were prized for display in tearooms. Tea masters who had received Zen training, like Sen no Rikyū (1522–1591; cat. no. 30), had particular insights into the contents of the texts inscribed by great Zen clerics. In later periods fewer tea masters underwent the same degree of rigorous Zen study, and the texts of *bokuseki* were shortened: a single line of writing, or simply two or three words excerpted from famous poems or well-known Zen passages, came to be preferred items for tearoom display (see, for example, cat. no. 39).

While the large-lettered bold calligraphy of Ōbaku monks and some others (cat. nos. 46–49) was not considered suitable for a standard tea ceremony (chanoyu), such works found numerous admirers among the practitioners of *sencha*, a special form of tea preparation and drinking that uses steeped tea.

ECCENTRIC MASTERS

During the flamboyant Momoyama period a spirit of unfettered freedom existed even outside Zen circles, reflecting the bold expansive mood of the warrior class and the sudden shifts of power and wealth that occurred during this short but brilliantly productive era. Works by such artists as Konoe Nobutada (1565–1614; fig. 6; cat. no. 55) and Hon'ami Kōetsu (1558–1637; cat. nos. 31, 32) convey a sense of the innovative and vigorous spirit of the time. Of high aristocratic birth, Nobutada was a rather undistinguished student of Zen, but his calligraphic works display an extraordinary virtuosity. His shorthand images, one thousand of which purported to be of "Tenjin Returning from China," are succinct expressions of his unshackled individuality. Nobutada, Kōetsu, and Shōkadō Shōjō (1584–1639; cat. no. 56) are often called the Three Brushes of the Kan'ei Era (1624–44), although they worked in totally different social circles and calligraphic styles. Strictly speaking the designation is not accurate, as Nobutada died long before the Kan'ei era was so named. However, it does reflect the deep affection that even present-day Japanese have for three outstanding masters of the early seventeenth century, whose classically rooted calligraphy expressed each artist's unique, highly cultivated individual style.

Scholar-artists of the Edo period — of whose work only two examples are included here (cat. nos. 57 and 58) — represent a spirit somewhat akin to that of learned Zen monks of the Muromachi period, albeit unconstrained by religious doctrine. The *bunjin* artists, collectively known as members of the Nanga school, were totally committed to art; Ike Taiga (1723–1776; cat. no. 57) and Uragami Gyokudō (1745–1820; cat. no. 58), two of the most prominent Nanga painters, are also revered as great calligraphers. In his pictorial reference to the most well-known pair of eccentrics in Zen lore (cat. no. 57), Taiga depicted the broom-wielding Jittoku (C: Shide) in a most uninhibited manner, endowing him with an amorphous shape and no discernible facial features, while his constant companion Kanzan (C: Hanshan) is said in the accompanying text to have "not yet arrived." Taiga himself was an unusually well-educated member of Edo's lower classes, but Gyokudō was a patrician and had an orthodox education in Chinese literature, arts, and music. He inscribed colophons on almost all of his paintings in ancient *reisho* (clerical) script, indicating renewed interest in a form of writing that had fallen into disuse.

Literati artists like Taiga and Gyokudō had ample opportunity to study Chinese calligraphy and could rely on a tightly organized network of scholar-artists with access to imported Chinese models. Even when Chinese originals were unavailable, there were abundant rubbings from engraved stone steles. Artists and calligraphers of other schools, who preferred the Japanese classics to Chinese works, could turn to models in the textbooklike assemblages of calligraphy samples, known as *tekagami* (*te* means "hand" [as in "handwriting"], and *kagami* means "mirror"). This generic name, used for accordion-fold albums of calligraphy specimens, reflects the long-held Chinese belief that one's calligraphy mirrors one's character, education, and upbringing. *Tekagami* were also referred to as *kohitsu tekagami*, as *kohitsu* literally means "old [hence superior] brush"— in other words, an album containing samples of superior old calligraphy, created to express admiration for past accomplishments in this art. Pages from books or small fragments of handscrolls were pasted into these accordion-fold books, a format that seems to have come into use in the late Muromachi period and to have become increasingly popular in the Momoyama period, when ownership of *tekagami* signified education and sophistication. *Tekagami* were often displayed during the tea ceremony; still later, in the Edo period, such albums formed part of the well-born young woman's dowry. Unfortunately the rising popularity of *tekagami* resulted in the willful fragmenting of complete manuscripts, handscrolls, and even historical correspondence that might otherwise have survived intact. Examples of small fragmented pieces included here (cat. nos. 9, 12) were most likely taken from *tekagami*.

Fig. 6. Detail of Konoe Nobutada (1565–1614), *Tenjin Returning from China* (cat. no. 55)

The contents and format of *tekagami* became more or less standardized by the late sixteenth century. The usual album consisted mostly of fragments from poetic anthologies and sections of Japanese — and occasionally Korean — Buddhist sutras (cat. no. 12). Specimens of documents, narrative tales, and personal letters were sometimes included, although examples of these genres were fewer in number. By the mid-seventeenth century the arrangement of the fragments seems to have been codified in the following manner: writing by members of the imperial family, noblemen, and high court officials were pasted on the obverse side of the accordion folds, while pieces by famous calligraphers, eminent priests, and warriors were placed on the reverse side. Examples by women were included at the very bottom of the reverse side.

By the mid-seventeenth century the demand for *tekagami* had become so great that a printed reproduction of an original album was published in 1651 under the title *Keian Tekagami* (Album of the Keian Era [1648–1651]). *Tekagami*, with their many examples of *kohitsu*, allowed classic calligraphy styles to be widely disseminated.

EPILOGUE

Although there are calligraphy collections in most important Japanese museums, some of which employ curators specializing in its study, calligraphy itself seems to be of little concern to the Japanese today. With the onslaught of Americanization, which began in 1945, and the widespread use of computers and computer-generated texts, interest in the art of the hand-written word appears to have diminished. Few private collectors in Japan focus specifically on calligraphy, and it is therefore heartening that devoted connoisseurs like Sylvan Barnet and William Burto have concentrated their collecting efforts on this most abstract of all art forms. It is also reassuring to observe that children, attending New York schools for Japanese language, enter their first attempts into annual competitions. The level of proficiency and artistry found in some of these youthful works puts many members of the adult generation to shame. The future of Japanese calligraphy may thus lie with American cognoscenti and those Japanese youngsters who have been baptized into Western culture yet remain intrigued by their own country's ancient traditions. Perhaps Westerners will help open the eyes of the Japanese to an appreciation of past achievements, as the American orientalist Ernest Fenollosa did at the close of the nineteenth century. It is sincerely hoped that this exhibition of a collection lovingly assembled by two scholars of English literature will awaken Japanese and Americans alike to an interest in and an appreciation of Japan's calligraphic legacy.

1. For example, in chapter 17 (A Picture Contest). See Murasaki 1987, pp. 307–17.

2. This work, the oldest extant example of calligraphy on paper in Japan, is in the Imperial collection. See Tokyo National Museum 1980, no. 1.

3. Tokyo National Museum 1980, p. 9.

4. For example, around 767, one million copies of darani (S: *dharani*), magical Buddhist incantations, were printed and placed in miniature wooden stupas. See Murase 2000, no. 7.

5. *Nihon ryōiki* (A Record of Miraculous Tales from the Asuka and Nara Periods), compiled around 822, Endō and Kasuga 1967, vol. 70, pp. 191–93.

6. Ōyama et al. 1987, p. 173.

7. Tokyo National Museum 1980, p. 16.

8. Sutras donated in 1167 by the Taira family, which are housed in the Itsukushima Shrine near Hiroshima.

9. For example, the scribblings found under the ceiling of the pagoda of Hōryūji. See Horie 1977, fig. 15.

10. Parts of this work are also in Japanese museums and private collections. Shimizu and Rosenfield 1984–85, nos. 9, 10, 11.

11. Zaitsu 1973, p. 17; the oldest extant letter in *hiragana* is dated 905.

12. Entries in the *Butsunichian* of 1363.

Some Western Thoughts on Shodō: The Way of Writing*

SYLVAN BARNET AND WILLIAM BURTO

More than twenty-five hundred years ago Laozi wrote, "Those who know do not speak/And speakers do not know."

Can we speak usefully about Japanese art, specifically about Buddhist art and about calligraphy? Anyone who has read a fair amount of critical writing has read a good deal of unintelligible talk ("If we problematize the Althusserian notion of ideology as interpellation . . ."), and a good deal of simple talk that, however heartfelt, means almost nothing to the reader ("beautiful," "moving," "highly imaginative"). We will try to be clear and helpful, but we are not scholars of the history of Japanese art, and we are keenly aware that we may misinterpret what we think we see. A cautionary anecdote comes to mind: in the 1920s Paul Éluard talked eloquently with Joan Miró about what Éluard took to be a solar symbol in one of Miro's paintings. After a decent interval Miró replied, "That's not a solar symbol. It's a potato."

WHAT CAN ONE SAY?

Given these warnings—Laozi's praise of silence and Éluard's misunderstanding of what was before his eyes—what can we say? We begin with an indisputable fact: the word "calligraphy" comes from Greek words meaning "beautiful writing." From the point of view of the enjoyment of and the study of East Asian writing, it would have been just as well if the word "calligraphy" had never been invented or at least had never been applied to what the Japanese call *shodō*, the way of writing, or the art of writing, or even the ritual of writing. In East Asian thinking calligraphy is not a matter of decorative or of ornamental writing but a matter of conveying one's personality, one's heart and mind, one's true nature. Something of the special esteem in which writing is held can be sensed from the fact that the materials used in writing—brush, ink, paper, and inkstone, which are also the materials used in painting—are called the Four Treasures of Writing. The brush's handle may be ivory or bone but is more likely to be bamboo or reed, and its pointed tuft is made of sheep hair (soft and difficult to control but favored by experts) or of more springy material such as rabbit or deer hair or pig bristles or even mouse whiskers or split bamboo. The ink is usually made of carbon derived from pine soot, mixed with resin or lacquer, heated, and then molded into a stick, to be

*We are grateful to Andrew Hare, Maxwell K. Hearn, John M. Rosenfield, Elizabeth ten Grotenhuis, and James C. Watt for their valuable suggestions.

dissolved later as needed. The paper is made of vegetable fibers (especially from *Broussonetia papyrifera*, or paper mulberry); it may be absorbent or it may be so highly coated that the ink sits on the surface. The inkstone is a stone or ceramic slab with a well: the ink stick is rubbed on the moistened flat surface and the excess water collects in the well.

In the West, when we think of calligraphy — of beautiful writing — we think of Osmiroid nibs, and we envision wedding invitations done in an italic hand with an abundance of flourishes. There are of course alternative ways of shaping the letters in such writing and of joining them into words — some arrangements more pleasing than others — but the emphasis is on an impersonal beauty not on a distinctive personal quality. Indeed in the West before the invention of printing, when relatively few people could write, the chief purpose of writing was communication, which meant that legibility was prized and personal expressiveness was virtually unthinkable. Apparent exceptions, such as the ninth-century Book of Kells, probably are not really exceptions, since the elaborate decorative treatment of the ornamented initials and almost illegible pages is not personally expressive but is presumably meant to suggest the mystery and power of the author, God. Until the invention of the typewriter in the 1870s, documents in all fields were handwritten, again with the emphasis on legibility. The type-writer and then the word processor largely displaced handwriting except for private jottings (these can be almost indecipherable scribbles) and for thank-you notes and letters of condolence (these must be legible), but handwriting has rarely been considered, as it *is* considered in the East, a vital skill for the educated person.

In East Asia, to repeat, calligraphy is valued not for its superficial beauty but for its revelation of a personality; the brushstrokes are seen as expressions of the writer's mind. This idea is not foreign to Western thinking: one of the great commonplaces of literary history and art is a remark by the eighteenth-century French thinker Buffon: after saying that subject matter is external to the artist, he went on, "Le style c'est l'homme même" (The style is the man himself). Another commonplace is that every portrait is a self-portrait. What we value in a Rembrandt portrait of some Dutch burgher is not what this solid citizen is or was, but Rembrandt's particular way of seeing the subject. We say the work is a Portrait of X, but more significantly we also say, "It is a Rembrandt." We do not see X but Rembrandt or more precisely Rembrandt's way of seeing. Consider, too, a remark by Jackson Pollock: when asked why he did not paint from nature, he said, "I am nature. . . . Every good artist paints himself." And because in East Asia until fairly recently painters and calligraphers used the same materials — brush, paper, ink — it is a commonplace in Chinese criticism to say that "Writing and painting have different names but a common body." One can almost say that painters were calligraphers, writing their pictures, writing their selves. Confirmation comes from a curious but authoritative source: seeing a Chinese friend writing characters in the sand on a beach, Picasso said, "If I were born Chinese, I would not be a painter but a writer. I'd write my pictures."[1]

But to return to calligraphy: in our system of writing, words are made up of letters that are associated with certain sounds. For the most part we run our eye over the words purely to get at their meaning; we can hope that the typeface is legible, that we don't have to squint to make out a word such as "ill," which in a poorly designed typeface might at first look like three vertical lines, but for the most part we pay little attention to the visual form. True, advertisers sometimes do call our attention to the form, making words such as "thick" or "thin" resemble what they stand for or making a word such as "speedy" imitative (the letters lean to the right, and some additional horizontal lines are supposed to indicate that the word is in motion). In Shakespeare's *Twelfth Night* the rascally Sir Toby, urging the timorous Sir Andrew to send a challenge, says, "Go, write it in a martial hand," but it is hard to imagine how one would impart a martial look to English words.

Chinese characters—and the Japanese did not have a system of writing until they adopted Chinese characters in the sixth and seventh centuries A.D.—have a strong visual interest. A character, like a Western written or printed word, is a verbal sign, something that we can pronounce and translate, but it is also something we can look at with heightened pleasure. Since some Chinese characters originated in pictographs, it might be thought that the visual interest is in their imitativeness, but the characters that are recognizably imitative (these include the characters for mountain, river, and gate) are very few. One occasionally hears that the alleged essential or original pictorial element somehow makes itself evident to the viewer, thus giving the characters special power, but this is simply untrue. (Comparable misstatements would be the assertion that when we visit a museum we are aware that it is the "seat of the Muses" or that when we see or hear "America" we sense the presence of the Italian voyager Amerigo Vespucci.)

WRITING AND METAPHOR

In our reading of classic treatises on Chinese and Japanese calligraphy—in translation, we quickly add—we notice that writer after writer uses metaphor after metaphor. For East Asian calligraphers and for students of calligraphy, from ancient times to the present, simple direct language is inadequate. The reason is not far to seek: literal language cannot go much beyond the surface—it can tell us how many characters are on the page, the height of each character, perhaps the meaning of the text, but it cannot get at the essence or art of calligraphy. For that, writers regularly turn to metaphor, a kind of language which in Robert Frost's famous words provides "the one permissible way of saying one thing and meaning another."

Almost every Chinese or Japanese treatise on calligraphy speaks of the "bones" and "sinews" of the characters—and the "flesh" too, though it is the bones and sinews that are most admired (figs. 7, 8). The strokes and the characters that are made up of the strokes, in this view, are images of phenomena that occur in the natural world. Thus, "cracks in a wall" is a name for vertical downward strokes of the brush, with zigzag turns, and "traces of a leaky roof" is a name for vertical wriggly strokes. To name the strokes is to see them more fully, to see them as, so to speak, physical presences in our daily experience. Consider this passage from an eighth-century text—Huaisu said: "When I look at the summer clouds . . . and also when I come upon cracks in a wall by the road, [I see that] each of them is natural." Yan Zhenqing said: "What about traces of a leaky roof?" Huaisu rose, pressed Yan's hands, and said: "I get it."[2]

But getting it is not merely noticing visual phenomena; rather, it is essentially a matter of calling attention to the workings of natural forces. The following three passages show the metaphoric language that characterizes most discussions of calligraphy. Such language seeks

Fig. 7. Detail of Seigan Sōi (1588–1661), *Hell* (cat. no. 47)

Fig. 8. Detail of Jiun Onkō (1718–1804), *Daruma* (cat. no. 49)

to convey the action inherent in the execution of the characters, that is, in the brush movements as the writer works with certain scripts and in certain styles. The first example is from *Treatise on Calligraphy* (*Shupu*, 687), by Sun Qianli, also called Sun Guoting (648?–703?):

> Consider the difference between the *xuanzhen* [suspended needle] and *chuilu* [hanging dewdrop] scripts, [and then consider] the marvels of rolling thunder and toppling rocks, the postures of wild geese in flight and beasts in fright, the attitudes of phoenixes dancing and snakes startled, the power of sheer cliffs and crumbling peaks, the shapes of facing danger and holding on to rotten wood which are sometimes heavy like threatening clouds and sometimes light like cicada wings; [consider] that when the brush moves, water flows from a spring, and when the brush stops, a mountain stands firm; [consider] what is very, very light, as if the new moon were rising at the sky's edge, and what is very, very clear, like the multitude of stars arrayed in the Milky Way—these are the same as the subtle mysteries of nature: they cannot be forced. Truly, [fine calligraphy] may be called the result of wisdom and skill achieving joint excellence, of mind and hand acting in harmony. The brush never moves without purpose; when it comes down, there must be direction. Within a single stroke, changes result from alternately raising and lowering the tip; inside a single dot [*dian*], movement rebounds at the very end of the brush. How much more is this true when you combine dots and lines to form characters![3]

Here, from *Sequel to "The Treatise on Calligraphy"* (*Xu shupu*, 1208) by Jiang Kui (ca. 1155–ca. 1221), is a passage on "the bearing of the characters." According to this text, the first requirement for brushing effective characters is the superior character—inner nature—of the calligrapher himself. (Again we think of Buffon's "The style is the man himself.") If the calligrapher himself has a noble character, and if he has mastered the brush, ink, and paper, the written character will itself have a personality:

> The first requirement for the bearing [of the characters] is a noble character [on the part of the calligrapher]; the second is modeling oneself on ancient masters; the third is good-quality brush and paper; the fourth is boldness and strength; the fifth is superb skill; the sixth is moist brightness; the seventh is a suitable internal balance; the eighth is occasional originality. When these requirements are met, long characters will look like neat gentlemen; short characters will be like strong and unyielding persons; skinny characters will be like hermits living in mountains and marshes; fat characters will be like idle rich men; vigorous characters will be like warriors; handsome characters will be like beautiful women; slanting characters will be like intoxicated immortals; correct characters will be like gentlemen of high moral standing.[4]

Our third example is from the treatise A *Diagram of the Battle Formation of the Brush*, purportedly written in 348 by Madam Wei Li (272–349) but widely regarded as from the early seventh century, that is, early Tang dynasty. Using metaphors drawn from nature, it describes seven kinds of strokes:

> Those skilled at imparting strength to their brush have much bone [that is, strong structure], while those not so skilled have much flesh.
> 1. First stroke [horizontal]: like a cloud formation stretching a thousand *li*, indistinct but not without form.
> 2. Second stroke [dot]: like a stone falling from a high peak, bouncing and crashing, about to shatter.
> 3. Third stroke [downward left]: the tusk of an elephant or rhinoceros [thrust into and] broken by the ground.
> 4. Fourth stroke [upward hook]: fired from a three thousand pound cross-bow.
> 5. Fifth stroke [vertical]: a withered vine, ten thousand years old.
> 6. Sixth stroke [ending stroke]: crashing waves or rolling thunder.
> 7. Seventh stroke [left hook]: the sinews and joints of a mighty bow.
> The seven strokes above represent a diagram of the battle formation of the brush, charging in and pulling back, slashing and cropping.[5]

CALLIGRAPHERS AT WORK

The system may appear highly formulaic, but (except for the most circumscribed official forms of writing described below) there is room for personal expression. Think of Plácido Domingo and Luciano Pavarotti as Manrico in Verdi's *Il Trovatore*, where the notes and words are the same but the performances are highly distinctive, or compare Murray Perahia and Glen Gould performing Bach's Goldberg Variations. A final example: Monet and Renoir are both Impressionists, and in 1874 both painted pictures titled *Regatta at Argenteuil*, but viewers who have any knowledge of other works by these artists can immediately tell which man painted which picture, and we value each picture for its particular vision.

Calligraphers learn the rules and then learn to go beyond the rules, producing writing that is valuable not for what it explicitly says but because it has the imprint of their personality. Sun Qianli, in his *Treatise on Calligraphy*, gives the overall pattern:

> When students exert themselves without stopping, they pass through three stages. Each stage changes to the next as its potential is exhausted. When you first learn to structure your writing seek only the level and the straight. At the first stage you have not arrived yet. At the middle stage you have gone too far. At the stage of comprehensive mastery, the person and the calligraphy will be ripe and mature.
>
> Confucius said: "At fifty I knew heaven's will; at seventy I followed my heart." Thus, when one understands what is level and what is precipitous, then one comprehends the rationale of change; when one first plans and then moves, the movements do not lose their proper place; and when one speaks only at the right time, the words hit the mark.[6]

Finally, in the metaphoric language we are now used to, here is a Tang critic describing the calligraphy of Wang Xizhi (303–336):

> Hsi-chih's calligraphy is like a brave warrior unsheathing his sword to dam the waters and stem their flow. A dot he placed at the top is like a rock falling down from a high precipice. A horizontal stroke he made is like a cloud sweeping across a thousand miles. A slanting *na*-stroke he dashed is like the roar of wind and thunder. A vertical stoke he wrote is like a ten-thousand-year-old withered vine . . . and tigers crouching across the phoenix's gateway . . . like dragons leaping through Heaven's door."[7]

In contemporary Western art criticism, where does one find this sort of metaphoric language, with its emphasis on forces of nature? In discussions of Action Painting and of Abstract Expressionism. Here, from a source as staid as *The Dictionary of Art*, is Francis V. O'Connor writing in the entry on Jackson Pollock:

> One of the hallmarks of most of Pollock's large-scale work is that the major design elements flow from left to right, as if written out. The left edge of the work . . . always begins with an elegant pirouette of paint, which then dances across the length of the canvas, until it reaches the terminal right edge, where a suddenly stymied form signifies the artist's frustration that subjective infinity is limited by the objective length of his ground. In the case of Number 2, 1949, after thinking through the overall coherence of its composition from both sides, Pollock felt it "worked" better if the tension in the whites was retained against the freer blacks underneath. This was typical of his way of thinking, akin to the wildness of nature.

Words like "flow," "pirouette," "dances," "suddenly stymied," "wildness," and "nature" are of a piece with the language regularly used for more than a thousand years in speaking of East Asian calligraphy.

Relations between Japan and China declined in the ninth century, partly because of the declining power of the Tang empire and partly because the Japanese apparently felt they no longer needed to learn from China, and in 894 official contact ceased. Relations were renewed in the 1160s, however, and a few decades later Japan was again deeply influenced by Chinese culture, this time by developments that had occurred during the Song period (960–1279). For our purposes the most relevant of these was the emergence of the Meditation School of Buddhism (C: Chan), which we will call by its Japanese name, Zen. Briefly Zen saw itself as originating in an episode when disciples asked Shakyamuni, the Historical Buddha, to preach on the Law. He silently turned a flower in his fingers, and one disciple, Kashyapa, smiled. Shakyamuni then said, "To you, Kashyapa, I give over this most precious treasure," and so the transmission of wisdom went, through the centuries, from mind to mind. Over and over in reading about Zen, one encounters words attributed to Bodhidharma, a sixth-century Indian monk, but probably composed by Nanquan Puyan, an eighth-century Chinese priest: "a special transmission outside the scriptures" and "no dependence on words and letters." In fact, Zen does not dispense with the study of texts, but at least in theory the emphasis is on a silent transmission.

Japanese monks went to China to study with masters, and when they returned to Japan, they often brought back with them writings by the masters, perhaps a poem, or a farewell note, or a certificate of approbation, or a brief essay. Such writings have come to be called *bokuseki*, usually translated as "ink traces," meaning not simply the traces of ink left by a brush moving over paper but the traces of the personality of a Chan or Zen monk of the Kamakura, Nambokuchō, and Muromachi periods (late twelfth through late sixteenth century). Among the examples in this catalogue are a line from a Chinese poem transcribed by the Japanese monk Zekkai Chushin (cat. no. 39) and a poem in Chinese composed by Musō Soseki, whose connections with the shogunate made him the most important Japanese monk of the fourteenth century (cat. no. 36). Such works, often written in a highly personal style, have been assiduously collected in Japan at least since the thirteenth century and have been especially valued for use in the tea ceremony. In China such writings were little valued, with the result that most of the extant writings by Chan priests survive not in China but in Japan.

Bokuseki is written with Chinese characters, kanji, which are signs or ideograms. Kanji stand for meanings, for things or ideas, not for pronunciations. Our arabic numerals are a sort of equivalent to kanji, standing for things, not sounds, whereas the letters of our alphabet stand for sounds, not things.

The Japanese did not have a system of writing until they borrowed Chinese kanji, apparently in the sixth century, but during the Heian period (794–1185) they developed another system of writing, kana, which used highly simplified forms of cursive kanji to indicate syllables, not meanings. Although kana is a syllabary, not an alphabet (its signs combine consonants and vowels), it functions much as our alphabet functions, telling the reader how to pronounce the writing. But the important point is this: the look of kana—asymmetrical, attenuated, sinuous, fluid (as many as five or six characters may be joined), with columns of irregular length (*chirashigaki*, or scattered writing)—is different from the look of kanji, where normally the characters are relatively symmetrical, sturdy, independent, in lines of regular length. After the tenth century Japanese calligraphers could use kanji or kana or a mixture; kanji remained the standard medium for religious, business, and military texts and for literature composed in Chinese styles such as the *bokuseki* by Sakugen (cat. no. 43), whereas kana, or kana combined with some semicursive or cursive kanji, was used for poems in Japanese forms and for other Japanese literature.

Turning to sutras, we must admit with some embarrassment that almost everything we have said thus far about calligraphy (especially about *bokuseki*) as highly personal is irrelevant to sutras, which on the whole are written impersonally—though there are notable exceptions.

Sutras are texts that report the words of the Buddha. (*Sutra* is from a Sanskrit word that literally means "thread"—the Indo-European base gives us the English words *sew*, *seam*, and *suture*—but metaphorically sutra came to mean an aphorism, a string of wise words.) The sutras were originally written in Indian languages, Sanskrit, Prakrit, and Pali, but had been translated into Chinese during the later Han dynasty (first and second centuries A.D.). When Buddhism entered Japan (mid-sixth century), it was these Chinese versions that the Japanese used. In Japan as in China sutras were most often written in the highly legible form called regular script (J: *kaisho*), usually with seventeen characters to each column, or thirty-two or thirty-four if the characters are small. (In regular script the brush is lifted after each stroke, and a single character may be built out of twenty or more strokes.) The earliest Japanese transcriptions of sutras show some variations in the style of writing, but by the middle of the eighth century the writing is highly disciplined and quite uniform. Each stroke is individual and each character stands by itself in an imaginary square. This uniformity may at first seem surprising given the dozens of scriptoria, some quite large, such as that at Tōdaiji in Nara, which employed about two hundred and fifty scribes. There were also scriptoria at other monasteries, at the Imperial Palace, at some twenty state-supported sites, and at some private residences. But the uniformity of style is not surprising when one understands that professional scribes were employed to produce versions of the sacred texts that by their sanctity rather than by any artistic power would benefit the places where they were lodged. The point of a copy of a sacred work is that it is accurate, not that it is original in any way. Its eternal meaning, we might say, is conveyed in part by its uniform and impersonal style, each word of the Buddha being accorded its own space in regularly spaced columns.

Despite this emphasis on accuracy, legibility, and uniformity, the texts were often richly adorned, especially in the twelfth century, in accordance with the idea that so precious a thing as the word of the Buddha ought to be presented in the most elevated manner. The text is sometimes written on paper enriched with bits of gold and silver, or it may be written in gold or silver on dark blue or purple paper. Even these luxurious versions, however, were usually written in regular script with uniform spacing between the characters. In some cases (cat. nos. 5 and 6) each character is enclosed within a pagoda and is written not in the regular hand but in a semicursive hand. (A pagoda is a reliquary, so in these instances each word of the Buddha is treated as a precious relic.) Both of these works are attributed to Fujiwara Sadanobu (1088–1156?), who is said to have copied the entire Buddhist canon of 5,048 scrolls in twenty-three years. Given the magnitude of this task, he may have chosen a system of writing that allowed strokes to be continuous and therefore more quickly executed than those of regular script. But speed was not Sadanobu's only concern; surely he must have seen his elegant writing as itself a way of adoring and adorning the Buddha's words.

Fig. 9. The character *butsu* (Buddha) from *The Heart Sutra* (cat. no. 2)

Fig. 10. The character *butsu* (Buddha) from *Section of "The Emergence of the Treasure Tower," with Pagoda Decoration, Chapter 11 of the Lotus Sutra* (cat. no. 5)

The standard script form of the character *butsu* (Buddha) consists of eight discrete brushstrokes beginning with the two strokes that constitute the left-hand component followed by the six strokes of the right-hand component, as in an example from the Heart Sutra (fig. 9). In the more cursive form of the same character, these strokes are abbreviated and merged in a fluid rendition. In the example from the Treasure Tower Lotus Sutra (fig. 10), the calligrapher has not lifted the brush from the paper in writing out the first six strokes of the character so that the individual strokes are connected by thin ligatures of ink. The final two strokes are similarly linked.

The standard script form of the character is composed of fully articulated strokes arranged in a stable, rectilinear formation that adheres closely to the square grid—only the final vertical stroke impinges on the space of the character below. The cursive form of the same character, however, is dynamically asymmetrical: The left and right components lean away from one another and brushstrokes vary dramatically in width so that the ponderous right side of the character appears as if it were about to fall over. Only the thin connective stroke that ties the two sides together and the final elongated stroke that plunges below the imaginary square grid allotted to the character serve to anchor it in place. MKH

ENJOYING CALLIGRAPHY

Before we talk about enjoying calligraphy, let's enjoy this passage from *A Diagram of the Battle Formation of the Brush*: "The paper is the battlefield. The brush is the sword and halberd. The ink is the helmet and armor. The water in the inkstone is the castle moat. The teacher is the general. The heart is the assistant general. The structure [of the character] is the strategy. The raising of the brush is destiny; its moving to and fro is the command; its bending and curving is the killing and slaughter."[8] Strenuous activity, yes, but surely enjoyable for the calligrapher, and the viewer ought to respond with equal energy and enjoyment.

How can people who cannot read Chinese or Japanese, or who at best know a handful of characters, enjoy what they cannot read? Those of us who do not read Chinese or Japanese can take some small comfort in the fact that many Chinese and Japanese people cannot read texts written in cursive styles. Even if the text is written in the highly legible regular script, they cannot fully understand it if it includes technical Buddhist terms. We can take additional comfort in the fact that as early as the eighth century Chinese calligraphy was regarded as not merely writing, not merely instruction on such matters as morality, ritual, and law, but as a revelation, through the characters, of hidden forces. Zhang Huaiguan (fl. 714–760) says that a superior mind ignores the superficial meaning of the characters: "Those who know calligraphy profoundly observe only its spiritual brilliance and do not see the forms of the characters."[9] We are reminded of the Taoist story of a Jiu Fang Gao, a horse expert, who judged a horse not by its form, its contours and muscles, as most experts did, but by its inner nature. Because externals meant nothing to him, he paid no attention to them. Commissioned by the emperor to find a superior horse, he returned some months later and reported that he had completed his mission. When the emperor asked what kind of horse it was, Jiu Fang Gao said it was a yellow stallion. The horse was brought in, and to the emperor's surprise it proved to be a black mare, but it was a most superior horse which did not raise dust when it galloped or leave footprints behind.

In fact, of course, if we want to know the meanings of the characters we can find out: museum labels often translate or at least summarize the texts, and catalogues usually give full translations. We can then enjoy the sentiments expressed in (for example) a Chinese poem or a thank-you note or a sacred text (we will discuss this point later in a little more detail).

Can we say that characters may be expressive enough to convey meaning even if viewers do not know their literal sense? We have already mentioned that regular writing, a rough equivalent to our block capitals, was commonly used for sutras and official documents and that there was little opportunity for subjective expression in these works. In other writings, notably those of the Zen masters, expressiveness was valued. Can we find "meaning" in personal styles? After seeing a translation, the reader may see something of the meaning in some semicursive or cursive characters — this character may look "dry" or that character may look "angry." But even as we say these things, we know that we are projecting, reading into the character something that we would not have guessed without knowing its literal meaning. Still, in our own experience, one of the pleasures of looking at calligraphy is in discerning forms: here a character seems to "flow," and there a connected group of characters seem to "join in battle." There is no evidence that calligraphers gave their characters mimetic connotations, and readers should probably not regard the characters in this light, but — such is the human tendency to see meaning in things — we do occasionally see characters as significant in themselves, and we enjoy the sight (even if it is an illusion). Which reminds us: some art critics have observed that the public likes Van Gogh for the wrong reasons. This is a foolish comment: there is not one right reason to like a work of art, and anyone familiar with a little art history knows that works valued for many centuries may have been appreciated for a number of different reasons.

A second source of pleasure lies in appreciation of what Walter Benjamin calls the aura of the work, the sanctity a viewer perceives in a sort of secular relic. For Benjamin the aura is not inherent within the object but is bestowed on it from outside, surrounding it with an enlarged importance. Benjamin says that "the collector . . . always retains some trace of the fetishist and by owning the work of art . . . shares in its ritual power," but he might have agreed that even viewers who are not owners may feel that they are participating in a sharing of ritual power. What counts is the document itself, not its philosophic or narrative content. True, the writer—let's say a distinguished monk—may be dispensing lofty (if enigmatic) advice to a disciple, and the text may therefore be esteemed, but even if the work is a trivial letter, for instance a thank-you note by a monk, it nevertheless is esteemed because it comes from the hand of the master. In fact, a document of no great wisdom may be valued especially because it is personal, showing the master in an intimate rather than in a professional situation and revealing a spontaneous play of mind rather than an assumed formal identity.

Third, one of course takes pleasure in the aesthetics of the work, the interesting architecture or shape of a particular character, the interesting linkages between characters, the layout of all of the characters on the sheet, the variations in inking—"See here, where he dipped the brush again, and see here, how the brush is drying out and then is charged again." (Looking at a Jackson Pollock painting, we may retrace the artist's gestures in our imagination.) In addition to seeing the work as something created in time, that is, brushstroke by brushstroke, a viewer enjoys seeing the work as a finished whole, noticing with pleasure the variations in the thickness of individual strokes, the dark and light strokes, the wet and dry strokes, the overall composition. In this view the calligraphy is writing-to-be-looked-at rather than writing-to-be-read. Recalling the words of Madam Wei Li about calligraphy as a battle, we take pleasure in contemplating the victory that is represented on the sheet. We enjoy the thrusts and parries, the energy and the poise, the variety and the complex delicate balance where unity embraces variety. When Zhai Qinian asked Mi Fu (1052–1107), "What should calligraphy be like?" he was told, "Whatever hangs down must turn upward; whenever one goes, one must turn back."[10]

Viewers who contemplate this battle, or this journey of the brush, see it taking place on a particular field or ground, paper or silk that may be white or creamy or yellow (dyed with bark) or even dark blue (dyed with indigo) or purple (dyed with perilla), in which case the writing is done in gold or silver. Each of these variations has its own significance. For example, the paper of a Lotus Sutra (cat. no. 4) has been dyed a dark blue, in imitation of lapis lazuli, one of Buddhism's Seven Treasures or Seven Precious Substances and said to be the material out of which the palaces of a Buddha are built.

Gold characters—gold is another of the Seven Treasures—are sometimes inscribed within mica pagodas (cat. nos. 5, 6, 7), which are almost invisible today because the mica has flaked away. But viewed from a certain angle, the pagodas suddenly appear, magically changing the work and giving the viewer an unexpected delight. Can this delight, based on surprise, be experienced a second time? Not quite, but on a second or third viewing the initial pleasant surprise is replaced by a greater pleasure, the pleasure of suspense ("What must I do to get the pagodas to appear again?") and, when the head is properly tilted, the pleasure of fulfillment ("Ah, there they are!"). The sutras in this publication, written on paper and now mounted as hanging scrolls with fabric borders, are small segments from what were once long handscrolls. Such an extended scroll was fastened at the extreme left to a roller with knobs of ivory, staghorn, metal, or lacquered wood. The scroll was read by unrolling it from right to left: that is, as it was unrolled from the roller with the left hand, it was rolled up by the right. Over the centuries the hue of the writing surface has usually changed, and the mounting was not chosen by the calligrapher, but still the whole is much more than the meaning of the words on the paper or silk. Take, for example, a fragment from a Nara-period sutra (cat. no. 1) written on creamy paper—this paper in itself provides sensuous delight—containing tan flecks. These particles of aromatic wood were thought to be pulverized bones of the Buddha, so for the faithful this scroll preserved not only the Buddha's words but also traces of his body. The largest cloth portions of the mounting are a seventeenth- or eighteenth-century blue silk twill woven with patterns of clouds, an appropriate motif because they symbolize heavenly abundance and are the substance on which deities sometimes stand in paintings (fig. 11). The pattern, a copy of a Nara fabric, is consonant with this Nara document. The fabric, enriched with imprinted gold, probably was part of a monk's *kesa* (surplice) or outer robe, and thus is an appropriately splendid adornment of the Buddha's words.

As a second example, consider the mounting for Musō's Chinese poem on snow (fig. 12). It is very handsome, with its peonies amid arabesques, but why, a Western viewer may wonder, are large peonies used to surround a Buddhist priest's poem about snow. The plum blossoms in the mounting of a portrait of Sugawara Michizane (fig. 13) make sense because Michizane (also called Tenjin) was said to be so fond of plum trees that, when he was exiled, a plum tree magically left his garden and joined him in his place of exile, but this doesn't tell us why peonies are appropriate for a priest's poem about snow. The answer is twofold. First, the peonies are of a size that suits the rather large calligraphy, and so, from a formal point of view, they are aesthetically satisfying. Second, peonies have Buddhist associations: because in China peonies were associated with the nobility and also with the royal status of the Historical Buddha, they came to be a common motif on garments worn by important priests such as Musō. The mounting of Musō's poem is not contemporary with the calligraphy—it is impossible to know what the original mounting looked like—but it makes aesthetic and intellectual sense for today's viewers.

In talking about the physical properties of the paper and mounting, we remind viewers of the joys of looking at the actual object. Walter Benjamin argues that advances in technology eliminated the issue of authenticity, and therefore, when a work is widely reproduced, the original loses its aura. Such is not our experience. One can look at a reproduction in a book or on a postcard, and it can seem pretty good, but when one sees the original, one realizes how different the two objects are. This is true not only of oil paintings, where color and texture play important parts, but also of drawings in pen and pencil and of other works that may be regarded simplistically as merely black and white (calligraphy, for instance). Depending on the paper and the ink, the calligraphic strokes—ranging from silvery gray to blue black and to an almost tactile charcoal or velvet black—can appear soft and moist or hard and dry. Excellent though the reproductions in this catalogue are, they cannot replicate the ink tones, the color of the ground, and the colors and textures of the mountings. Seeing the original work after seeing a reproduction is something of a shock, so different is the power, the aura of the original. The aura can be dismissed only by holding the poststructuralist view that the aura is merely something imposed from outside and that "meaning" is in this factitious aura—for instance, by the spectator's awareness that an object is expensive or that it was

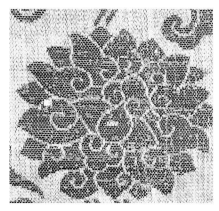

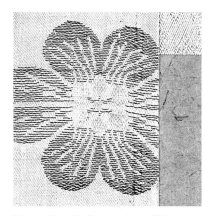

Fig. 11. Detail of mounting of *Section of "Ananda's Perfect Memory," Chapter 45 of the Sutra of the Wise and the Foolish* (cat. no. 1)

Fig. 12. Detail of mounting of Musō Soseki (1275–1351), *Poem on the Theme of Snow* (cat. no. 36)

Fig. 13. Detail of mounting of Konoe Nobutada (1565–1614), *Tenjin Returning from China* (cat. no. 55)

owned by George Washington. In contrast we are talking about an aura created not from without but from within.

In talking about an aesthetic appreciation that is independent of an understanding of the meaning of the words written on the paper or silk, are we deluding ourselves? Perhaps. But people who do not know Latin and who do not know the content of a Christian mass can nevertheless be deeply moved by a Bach mass. Perhaps instead of the word "meaning" we should use "significance" or "import."

If we are interested in *Portrait of a Man and Woman at a Casement* by Fra Filippo Lippi in the Metropolitan Museum, we may learn that the couple are Lorenzo Ranieri Scolari and Angiola di Bernardo Sapiti who were married in 1436. But the picture's significance or import for us is the artist's way of seeing these figures. Does the biographical information—this knowledge of, so to speak, the text of the picture, this contribution to "meaning"—increase our enjoyment of the picture? Probably not. And perhaps, in looking at calligraphy, comprehension of the written text is not essential; what one values is not the text but the execution of the text. For what it is worth, we have heard calligraphers say that they regard the text as an occasion—a pretext, one might say—for their calligraphy; what counts, in this view, is the performance not the explicit meaning of the text.

Finally we return to the question of meaning and enjoyment. As we have already said, translations are usually available, and in many instances even in translation the text is impressive, whether a personal letter, a poem, or a sacred utterance. Consider this Chinese poem (cat. no. 38), transcribed by Sesson Yūbai, an early fourteenth-century Japanese monk who spent more than two decades in China:

> My thatched hut is woven with scattered layers of clouds,
> Already my footprints are washed away with the red dust.
> If you ask, this monk has few plans for his life:
> Before my window, flowing water; facing my pillow, books.[11]

Fig. 14. Detail of Sesson Yūbai
(1290–1346), *My Thatched Hut*
(cat. no. 38)

That the final character (lower left; fig. 14) signifies calligraphy or writing as well as books especially endears the piece to anyone interested in reading and writing.

For a last example, consider a fragment from the third chapter of the Lotus Sutra, recounting in fluent gold writing on indigo paper the Parable of the Burning House (cat. no. 6). Here is the gist of the story. A rich man has a large but decaying house with a single gate. A fire breaks out, but his children, absorbed in play, ignore his cries of warning. To induce the children to leave the burning house, he tells them there are playthings outside that will delight them, specifically carts drawn by a deer, a goat, and an ox. The children run to safety through the gate, and the father then gives each of them a splendid jeweled cart drawn by a great white ox, something far beyond their childish dreams. The parable is interpreted thus: the decaying house is the world of human society, the children absorbed in games are ourselves (that is, persons enthralled by worldly pleasures), the fire is our physical and mental desires (in Buddhist thought the causes of suffering), the father is the Buddha who saves us, the carts drawn by deer, goats, and oxen are stages of spiritual awareness or kinds of teaching that are rightly suited to persons with weak understanding but that in time are replaced by the splendid cart drawn by the white ox, that is, by supreme wisdom, the great vehicle of Buddhism, specifically the Lotus Sutra.

We end by saying this: not every reader of the Lotus Sutra—even when the characters are written in gold and inscribed within mica pagodas on indigo paper—is drawn to the teachings of the Buddha. These writings and paintings can, however, exert a mysterious appeal and can have far-reaching effects on a viewer. One effect is, quite bluntly, to impoverish the collector; a second effect is to enrich the viewer immeasurably.

1. Quoted in Ashton, ed. 1977, p. 131.
2. Chang and Frankel 1995, p. 22.
3. Chang and Frankel 1995, pp. 3–4.
4. Chang and Frankel 1995, p. 27.
5. Quoted in Tseng 1993, pp. 229–30.
6. Chang and Frankel 1995, pp. 11–12.
7. Quoted in Wang 1999, p. 144.
8. Quoted in DeCoker 1988, p. 273.
9. Quoted by Robert E. Harrist, Jr., in Harrist and Fong 1999–2001, p. 6.
10. Jiang Kui, "Sequel to the 'Treatise on Calligraphy' (*Xu shu pu*)," in Chang and Frankel 1995, p. 19.
11. Translation by Stephen Addiss, letter to Sylvan Barnet and William Burto, 1993.

CATALOGUE

SACRED TEXTS

I.

Section of "Ananda's Perfect Memory," Chapter 45 of the Sutra of the Wise and the Foolish

Nara period (710–794), eighth century
Handscroll mounted as a hanging scroll, ink on paper, 10¾ × 17½ in. (27.3 × 44.5 cm)
Literature: London Gallery, Tokyo 2000, no. 124

This scroll is part of a large-character copy of the Sutra of the Wise and the Foolish (*Kengukyō* or *Gengukyō*), attributed to Emperor Shōmu (r. 724–749), a devout Buddhist who unified Japan in the eighth century.[1] Each column in this scripture has twelve or thirteen characters rather than the seventeen found in most sutras. The paper, called *dabishi* (containing relics of Shakyamuni), was made of hemp mixed with white clay and aromatic wood particles and may be of Chinese origin.

Known as the Ōjōmu (Great Shōmu), the sutra was originally dedicated to Tōdaiji, a temple in the ancient capital of Nara that the emperor commissioned in 743.[2] Tōdaiji, with its colossal bronze image of the Vairochana Buddha, served as the national temple, and Shōmu also decreed that branch monasteries (*kokubunji*) and convents (*kokubunniji*) be erected in each province. Although this ambitious scheme was not fully realized, a large number of new temples were established, leading to an increased demand for sutra copies (*shakyō*) and the scriptoria (*shakyōjo*) to produce them.[3] The scriptoria, including the government establishment at Tōdaiji, employed skilled copyists, many of whom were recent immigrants from Korea or descendants of earlier immigrants.

Sutra copies in the Nara period were indebted to early Chinese calligraphic styles of the fourth through seventh century, particularly those of Wang Xizhi (303–361) and Ouyang Xun (557–641), whose characters were admired for their elegance and solid structure. In the Ōjōmu's monumental calligraphy, however, a new influence from China can be seen.

The Ōjōmu writer used a short thick brush with a fine tip. The brush's thick belly created a sense of weightiness, especially at the corners of characters where a horizontal stroke turns into a vertical stroke. The large scale, strong brushwork, and careful balance of each character have much in common with Chinese Tang calligraphic styles, and the scholars Kakui Hiroshi and Higuchi Hideo have suggested that the Ōjōmu sutra copy may have been

imported from China during the Tang period, when standard script became dominant.[4] In particular, Kakui compares the stately calligraphy of the Ōjōmu to that of the great Tang calligrapher Yen Zhenqing (709–785), who set a new standard for bold powerful script. Other Japanese eighth-century sutra copies have a calligraphic style similar to that of Yen Zhenqing: the well-known Lotus Sutra in large characters in Ryūkōin and the Fukū Kenzaku Shinpen Shingon Sutra in Sanbōin, both in Wakayama prefecture, and the Lotus Sutra at Kiyomizudera temple in Hyōgo prefecture.[5] However, none of these sutras can compare with the Ōjōmu in the grandeur of each character and the richness of its brushwork.

Ōjōmu fragments, which were highly prized, were often used as the opening section in *tekagami* (albums of ancient calligraphic fragments), followed by an example of sutra copying by Empress Kōmyō (701–760). The present section comes from "Ananda's Perfect Memory [*Anan Sōjibon*]," chapter 45 of the Sutra of the Wise and the Foolish, in which Shakyamuni Buddha explains that his disciple Ananda had absolute memory because he had amassed "a mountain of virtue" in his previous life.[6]

M W

1. The attribution of the Ōjōmu to Emperor Shōmu is not accepted by all scholars, and neither is there consensus among scholars whether the Ōjōmu was produced in China or Japan. The most reliable example of Shōmu's calligraphy is the *Zasshū,* a compilation of Chinese poems on Buddhism, in the Shōsōin repository at Tōdaiji, Nara, which houses the emperor's personal effects.
2. According to Haruna 1979, p. 369, the Ōjōmu originally consisted of more than thirteen scrolls. Most extant scrolls are registered as national treasures and housed in Tōdaiji, Nara, in the Tokyo National Museum, in the Hakutsuru Fine Art Museum, Hyogo, and in the Maeda Ikutokukai Foundation, Tokyo. Numerous fragments are found in *tekagami* albums, and many are mounted as hanging scrolls.
3. The Greater Sutra of the Perfection of Wisdom (C: *Mahaprajna paramita sutra;* J. *Daihannyakyō*) commissioned by the imperial prince Nagaya no Ō (684–729) in 728, was one of the earliest sutra copies done at a scriptorium in Japan. The organization of the scriptorium followed the Tang

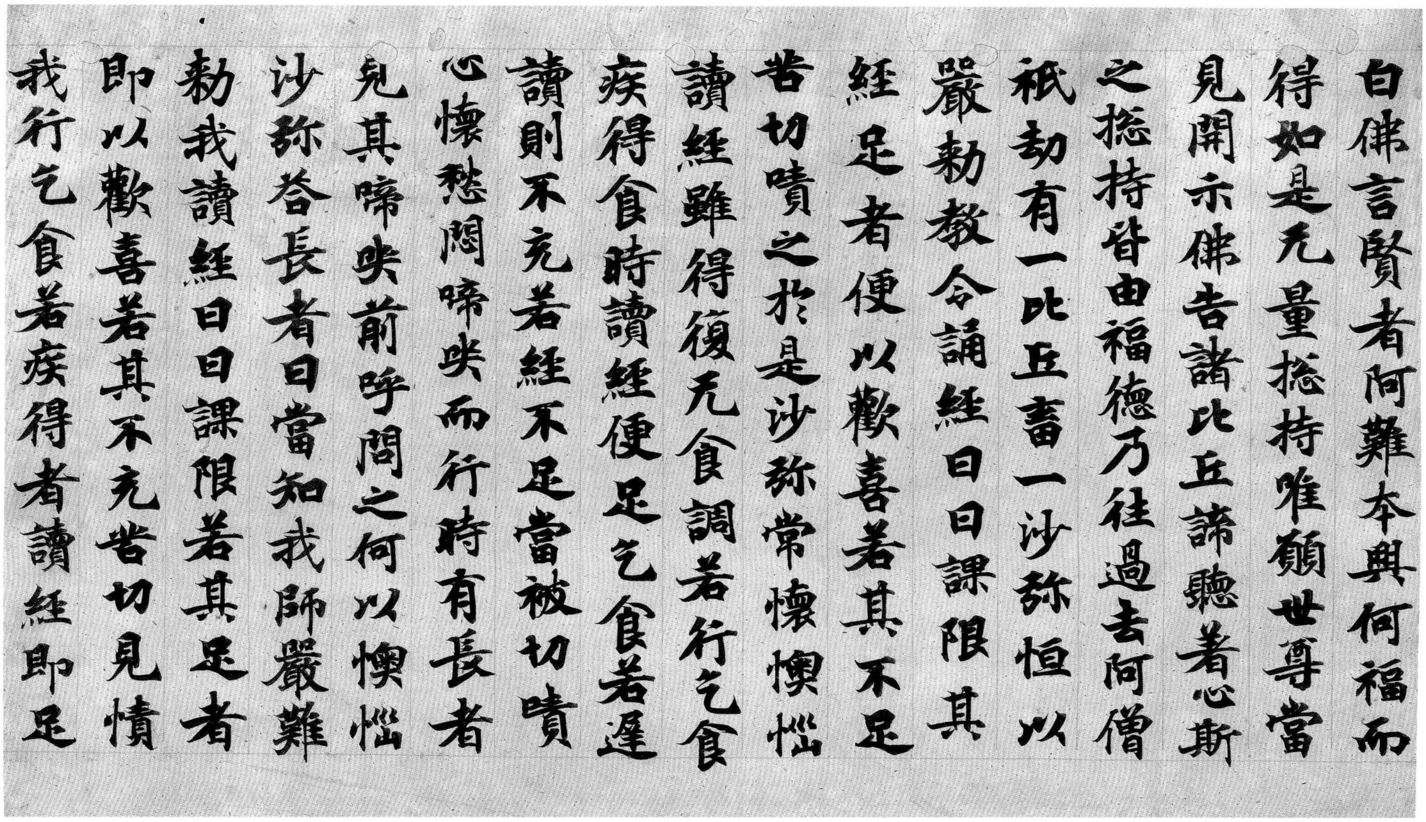

我行乞食著疾得者讀經即足
即以歡喜著其不充苦切見情
勅我讀經日日課限若其足者
沙弥荅長者曰當知我師嚴難
見其啼哭前呼問之何以懊惱
心懷愁悶啼哭而行時有長者
讀則不充著經不足當被切嘖
疾得食時讀經便足乞食著遲
讀經雖得復无食調若行乞食
苦切嘖之於是沙弥常懷懊惱
經足者便以歡喜著其不足
嚴勅教令誦經日日課限其
祇劫有一此丘畜一沙弥恒以
之揔持皆由福德乃往過去阿僧
見開示佛告諸此丘諦聽著心斯
得如是无量揔持唯願世尊當
白佛言賢者阿難本與何福而

dynasty system; see *Shodō zenshū* 1954–68, vol. 9, pp. 23–28, and Harrist and Fong 1999–2001, p. 230, on the Tang government scriptoria.

4. Kakui 1964; Higuchi 1960.

5. For a reproduction of the Ryūkōin Lotus Sutra, see Ōyama et al. 1987, pl. 26. For a reproduction of the Sanbōin Fukū Kenzaku Shinpen Shingon Sutra, see Nara National Museum 1983, pl. 92. For a reproduction of the Kiyomizudera Lotus Sutra, see Suzuki K. 1991.

6. *Daizōkyō* 1924–34, vol. 4, no. 202, p. 202.

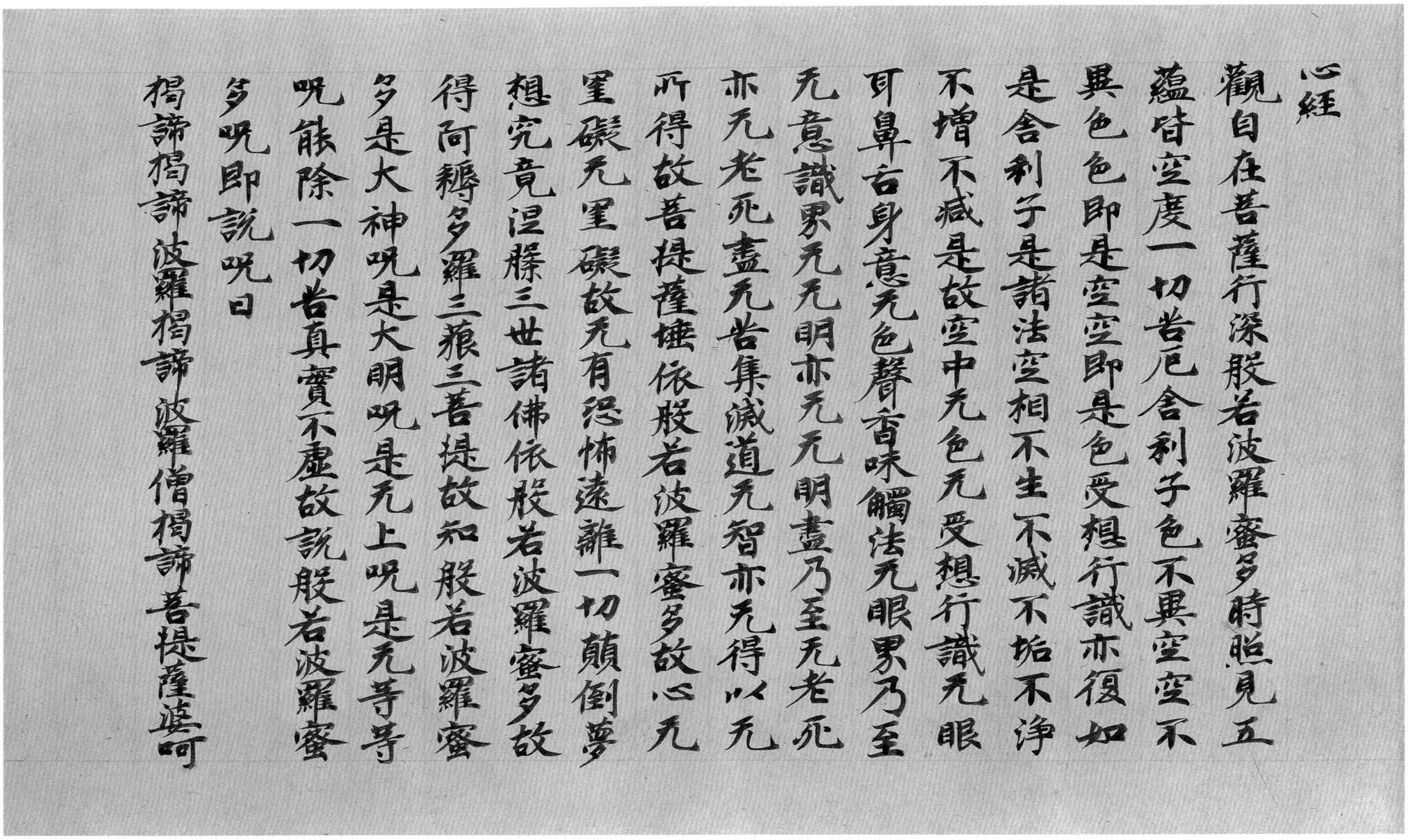

心経

觀自在菩薩行深般若波羅蜜多時照見五
蘊皆空度一切苦厄舍利子色不異空空不
異色色即是空空即是色受想行識亦復如
是舍利子是諸法空相不生不滅不垢不淨
不增不減是故空中无色无受想行識无眼
耳鼻舌身意无色聲香味觸法无眼界乃至
无意識界无无明亦无无明盡乃至无老死
亦无老死盡无苦集滅道无智亦无得以无
所得故菩提薩埵依般若波羅蜜多故心无
罣礙无罣礙故无有恐怖遠離一切顛倒夢
想究竟涅槃三世諸佛依般若波羅蜜多故
得阿耨多羅三藐三菩提故知般若波羅蜜
多是大神咒是大明咒是无上咒是无等等
咒能除一切苦真實不虛故說般若波羅蜜
多咒即說咒曰
揭諦揭諦波羅揭諦波羅僧揭諦菩提薩婆訶

2.
The Heart Sutra

Nara period (710–794), ca. 755
Handscroll mounted as a hanging scroll, ink on paper, 9½ ×
15⅜ in. (24.1 × 39.1 cm)
Literature: *Bessatsu Taiyō* 1999,
no. 25

This is one of numerous copies of the Heart Sutra discovered at Kairyūōji temple in Nara.[1] Since the Heart Sutra is very short, it was common to mount several copies of the sutra in a simple handscroll.[2] Over time, however, most of the Kairyūōji copies were separated and have been dispersed among various collections and museums.

Kairyūōji flourished during the eighth century. Located in the northeast corner of Nara (thus its nickname, Sumidera), this temple was once part of the estate of Fujiwara no Fuhito (659–720), the most influential aristocrat of his time and the father of Empress Kōmyō (701–760). After his death his mansion became the empress's palace and in 731 was converted into a major monastery.

Documents in the Shōsōin repository record sutra copying at Tōdaiji temple in Nara. For example,

768 copies of the Heart Sutra were produced at Tōdaiji's scriptorium in the year 746. This number is twice the number of days in that year (384 in the lunar calendar) and suggests that the copies were meant as daily prayers for the peace of Emperor Shōmu and Empress Kōmyō. The Kairyūōji copies were traditionally attributed to the famed Japanese monk Kūkai (774–835), but this attribution is not accepted by scholars.[3] The evidence of a large number of Heart Sutra copies at Kairyūōji suggests they were produced as part of this annual practice at Tōdaiji.[4]

There are three types of Heart Sutra copies from Kairyūōji, which vary slightly depending on the Chinese model that the copyist followed. In the first type, to which this example belongs, the sutra text is followed by a one-line verse. In the second the text is followed by a three-line verse telling the benefits of the virtuous deed of copying the Heart Sutra. The third type is the same as the second, except that it omits the last four characters of the three-line verse.

The strong austere brushwork of the present copy reveals a well-trained hand. Each tightly structured character is written in regular script (*kaisho*), typical of Japanese sutra copies of the mid-eighth century. At the same time, a subtle fluctuation of thick and thin brush lines can be observed, presaging elements of softness and rounding that appear in the Heian period. (See the appendix for a discussion of this scroll's mounting.)

The two-character title at the upper right of the present sutra reads *Shingyō* (Heart Sutra), the abbreviated name of the formal title *Maka hannya haramitta shingyō*. Some copies of the Heart Sutra bear its full title, Greater Sutra of the Perfection of Wisdom (S: *Mahaprajna paramita sutra*; J: *Daihannya haramittakyō*). This important Buddhist sutra deals with the realization of perfect wisdom (prajna), that is, the attainment of enlightenment. The state of mind required to reach prajna is described as sunyata, a term that has been translated as the "void, emptiness, and nothingness."[5] Well-known paradoxical phrases in the Heart Sutra, such as "form is emptiness, and the very emptiness is form; emptiness does not differ from form, form does not differ from emptiness," have been the object of great study by Buddhists and non-Buddhists alike.[6]

M W

1. Another Heart Sutra found at this temple is in the United States; see Rosenfield et al. 1973, pp. 36–37.
2. The Kairyūōji temple, the Shōchiin subtemple on Mount Koya, and the Nezu Institute of Fine Arts in Tokyo each own a handscroll consisting of ten copies of the Heart Sutra.
3. This attribution was based on Kūkai's daily visits to the temple for lessons before leaving for China in 804. However, the Kairyūōji's Heart Sutra copies were done before Kūkai's time.
4. Nishigami 1999. One of the copies, in the Yasuda Bunko, bears the date 755.
5. Rosenfield et al. 1973, p. 30.
6. Conze 1958, p. 81.

3.
Section of Chapter 21 of the Medium-Length Agon Sutra

Nara period (710–794), 759
Handscroll mounted as a hanging scroll, ink on paper, 10¼ × 29¾ in. (26 × 75.5 cm)

The large red seal "Zenkō," lower center, identifies this scroll as part of a set of sutras known as "Zenkō shuinkyō" (sutras with a red seal of Zenkō). More than twenty fragments with this seal have been found, and several of them have been registered as important cultural properties. These fragments are mostly from the Agon (S: Agama) sutras, the earliest Buddhist canon, reflecting the fundamental teachings of the historical Buddha.[1] The text of this scroll is the last section of the *Sesshokyō* (Sutra of Teaching the Ayatana Twelve Sense Fields), the 86th sutra, which is one of three sutras in Chapter 21 from the so-called Medium-Length Agon Sutra (J: *Chūagongyō*). It was translated by the Indian monk Samghadeva into Chinese in 397–98, during the Eastern Jin dynasty.[2] This sutra concerns the important disciple Ananda who with other young monks was staying in the Jatavana monastery in Shravasti,[3] where they have listened to Shakyamuni Buddha's sermons. In this chapter, Shakyamuni, in closing his sermon, encourages the constant effort of faithful practice to free oneself from suffering and to achieve complete fulfillment.

At the end of the scrolls of the Zenkō shuinkyō group is often found a record of the participants who copied the sutras, which suggests a project coordinated in a scriptorium.[4] To the left of the sutra section on the present scroll is an inscription that records the date of copying and the names of those who produced Chapter 21.

On the fifteenth day of the ninth month of the first year of the Tenpyō Hōji era [757], the sutra text was examined by Kaminoge no Kimi Taiga.

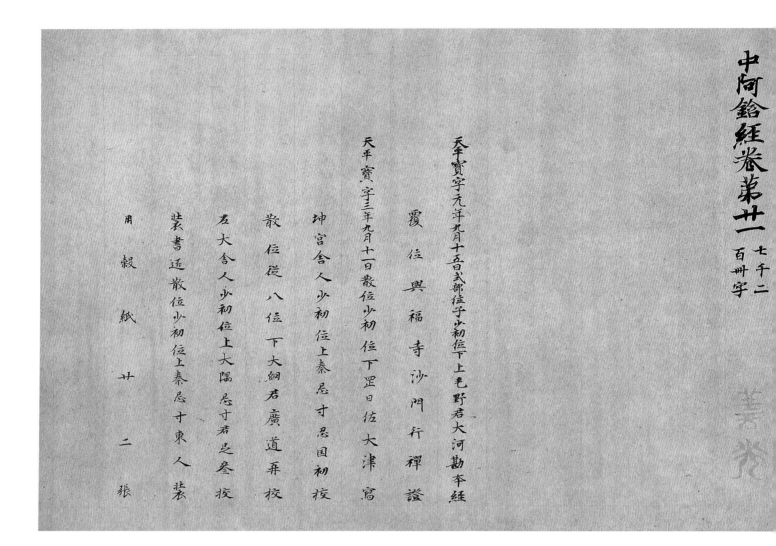

Perused by the monk Gyōzen of Kōfukuji temple.

Copied by Okahisa no Ōtsu on the eleventh day of the ninth month of the third year of the Tenpyō Hōji era [759].

First proofreading by Hata no Imiki Oshikuni.
Second proofreading by Ōami no Kimi Hiromichi.
Third proofreading by Ōsumi no Imiki Kimitari.
Mounted by Hata no Imiki Tōjin.
Twenty-eight sheets of mulberry paper.

The same individuals, in the same year, also produced chapter 29, the last section of which is owned by Chionin in Kyoto.[5] The copyist Okahisa no Ōtsu is a transitional figure. His thick, strong brushwork, less weighty than earlier calligraphy, is typical of the tight character structure of mid-Nara period style. At the same time, his calligraphy also serves as a forerunner of late Nara-period calligraphy in sutra-copying. The distinctions can be seen especially in the tails of strokes and at the angles of characters where a horizontal stroke becomes vertical.

The name "Zenkō" is shrouded in mystery. The nun Zenkō, the head of Hokkeji temple, has been suggested as the initiator of this sutra project because she was such a faithful devotee, donating one of a pair of the flanking attendant statues for the Vairochana Buddha in the Great Hall of Tōdaiji and offering a set of sutras, known as *Issaikyō,* to Tōdaiji. Nonetheless, the sutra scholar Tanaka

追阿難此頂法及頂法退汝當為諸年少比
丘說以教彼若為諸年少比丘說教此頂法
及頂法退者彼便得安隱得力得樂身心不
煩熱終身行梵行阿難我為汝等說憂及教
憂頂法及頂法退如尊師所為弟子起大慈
哀憐念愍傷求義及饒益求安隱快樂者我
今已作汝等當復自作至无事處山林樹下
空安靖處宴坐思惟勿得放逸勤加精進莫
令後悔此是我之訓誨佛所說如
是尊者阿難及諸年少比丘聞佛所說歡喜
奉行
陰內水識更　覺想思愛界　因緣念正斷　如意禪諦想
无量无色種　沙門果解脫　憂根力出要　財力覺道頂
說憂經第十五竟　五千二百十字
長壽王品第二竟　四万五千二字　第二小土城誦

Kaidō has suggested that "Zenkō" might be the owner's seal.[6]　　　　　MW

1. The Agon sutra group consists of the four sutras that more or less correspond to the Nikaya sutras of the Pali canon in the Theravada, or Hinayana, Buddhist tradition. The four sutras are *Jōagongyō* (S: *Dīrghagama*, P: *Dīgha Nikaya*), *Chūagongyō* (S: *Madhyamagama*, P: *Majjhimanikaya*), *Zōagongyō* (S: *Samyuktagama*, P: *Samyuttanikaya*), and *Zōichiagongyō* (S: *Ekottarikagama*, P: *Anguttarikaya*).
2. The *Chūagongyō* is a compilation of 222 medium-length sutras in 60 chapters. *Daizōkyō* 1924–34, vol. 1, pp. 565–66. The first half section of the 86th sutra in the Chinese version corresponds to the 148th sutra of the *Majjhimanikaya* in the Pali canon. Bhikkhu and Bhikkhu 1995, pp. 1129–36.
3. The wealthy merchant Anathapindika donated his estate to establish this monastery, where the historical Buddha stayed during the rainy season.
4. About nine fragments of the *Chūagongyō* from this group that include the inscription are extant, including examples in Daigoji temple, the Gotoh Museum of Art, and Chioin temple. Four other fragments of the Agon sutra, the *Zōichiagongyō*, also have a Zenkō seal.
5. Kyoto National Museum 1990, p. 38.
6. *Shodō zenshū* 1954–68, vol. 9, p. 171.

4.
Section of "Former Affairs of King Wonderful Adornment," Chapter 27 of the Lotus Sutra

Nara period (710–794), late
eighth century
Handscroll mounted as a hanging scroll, gold on purple-dyed
paper with silver ruling, 10 ×
20¼ in. (25.4 × 51.4 cm)

This fragment belongs to a set of the Lotus Sutra in
gold on purple paper which includes four scrolls at
the Nara temple of Tōmyōji and fragments in other
collections.[1] The gold characters against the dark
purple ground give the work a gloriously somber
quality. In the mid-eighth century sutras began to
be copied in gold and silver on purple or blue paper,
rather than in black ink on white paper. Among the
finest sutra copies in gold on purple paper are the
ten-scroll sets of the Sutra of the Sovereign Kings of
the Golden Light (*Konkōmyō Saishōōkyō*), a most
important early Mahayana sutra whose recitation
and duplication would guarantee the nation's safety

and prosperity.[2] Emperor Shōmu commissioned
many sets of this sutra to be installed at the state-
maintained temple (*kokubunji*) of each province.
This enormous project was undertaken by the
Bureau of Gold-Character Sutras, whose copyists
received twice the usual wage because of the difficulty of writing in gold on purple or blue paper.[3]

The brushwork of the Tōmyōji group is more
relaxed and softer than that of the *kokubunji* copies.
Interpreting this gentleness as a feminine quality,
Tanaka Kaidō suggests that the Tōmyōji copies
may have been ordered for the state-maintained
nunneries (*kokubunniji*) after the completion of the

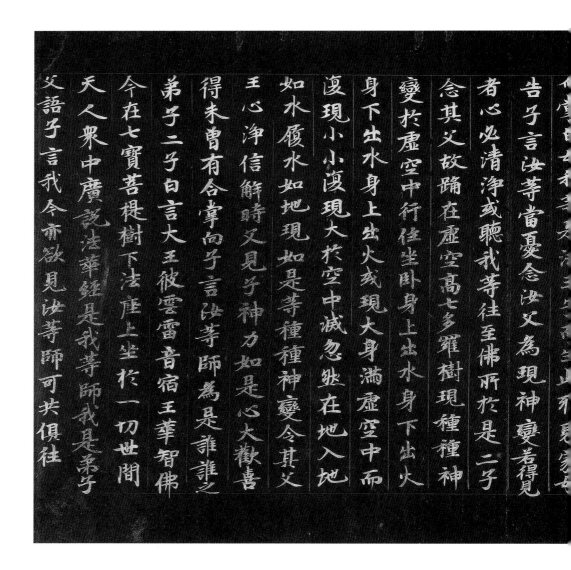

kokubunji project in the mid-eighth century. There is, however, no evidence to support this hypothesis. Most scholars regard the Tōmyōji calligraphy as a precursor of the Heian style with its characteristically calm brushwork and loosely structured characters.[4]

The present text is from chapter 27 of the Lotus Sutra, "Former Affairs of King Wonderful Adornment [Myōshōgon'ō Honji hon]." It tells of the two sons of King Wonderful Adornment who wanted to convert their father to Buddhism. Their mother suggested that they display their supernatural powers to their father, so they leapt into the air and performed "wonders: walking, standing, sitting, and lying down in midair; . . . manifesting huge bodies that filled the sky and then making themselves small again; . . . sinking into the ground as though it was water; walking on water as though it was land."[5] Impressed, their father devoted himself to the Buddha.

M W

1. Two other fragments are in the United States. See Rosenfield et al. 1973, pp. 48–49; Rosenfield and Shimada 1970–71, pp. 22–23.
2. Cunningham et al. 1998, pp. 60–61.
3. Komatsu 1997, p. 77.
4. Tanaka K. 1963, p. 210.
5. Watson 1993, pp. 313–14.

是二子有大神力福德智慧久脩菩薩所行之道所謂檀波羅蜜尸羅波羅蜜羼提波羅蜜毗梨耶波羅蜜禪波羅蜜般若波羅蜜方便波羅蜜慈悲喜捨乃至三十七品助道法皆悉明了通達又得菩薩淨三昧日星宿三昧淨光三昧淨色三昧淨照明三昧長莊嚴三昧大威德藏三昧於此三昧亦悉通達介時彼佛欲引導妙莊嚴王及愍念衆生故說是法華經時淨藏淨眼二子到其母所合十指爪掌白言願母往詣雲雷音宿王華智佛所我等亦當侍從親近供養礼拜所以者何此佛於一切天人衆中說法華經宜應聽受母告子言汝父信受外道深著婆羅門法汝等應往白父與共俱去爭藏淨眼合十指

Section of "The Emergence of the Treasure Tower," with Pagoda Decoration, Chapter 11 of the Lotus Sutra

Late Heian period (ca. 900–1185), twelfth century
Handscroll mounted as a hanging scroll, ink on paper with thin mica coating and mica-stamped decoration, 11⅛ × 13¾ in. (29.2 × 34.8 cm)
Literature: Morse and Morse 1996, no. 47; London Gallery, Tokyo 2000, no. 127

This fragment is part of a ten-scroll set of the Lotus Sutra decorated with jeweled pagodas, known in Sanskrit as three–four storeyed towers containing Buddha's relics. Togakushi shrine in northwest Nagano prefecture, which once owned the set, today preserves parts of four scrolls; the dispersed fragments, known as *Togakushigire* (pieces from Togakushi shrine), have been pasted in *tekagami* albums or mounted as hanging scrolls.[1]

The Lotus Sutra was by far the most popular and influential of the many Buddhist scriptures copied in Japan. It is conventionally copied in eight scrolls, which are often flanked by scrolls from other sutras. The ten-scroll Togakushi set originally took this form, with eight scrolls of the Lotus Sutra preceded by one scroll of the Sutra of Innumerable Meanings (*Muryōgikyō*) and followed by one scroll of the Sutra of Meditation on Samantabhadra Bodhisattva (*Kanfugenkyō*).

The present text is from chapter 11, "The Emergence of the Treasure Tower [*Ken hōtō hon*]," in scroll 4 of the Lotus Sutra. In this chapter the Buddha asks: "After I have passed into extinction, who can guard and uphold, read and recite this sutra?"[2] He repeatedly tells of the great difficulties that confront men who devote themselves to the Lotus Sutra but promises that good men who embrace it will attain the unsurpassed Buddha way.

The mica-stamped decoration of pagodas distinguishes Togakushi's copies of the Lotus Sutra. Eight pagodas in each column, thirty columns per sheet, were printed in mica on coated paper.[3] Each character is enshrined in a pagoda. Known as *ichiji hōtō hokekyō* (one character per jeweled pagoda), this format was popular for copies of the Lotus Sutra in the late Heian and early Kamakura periods. The Tendai school, rooted in the Lotus Sutra, built and venerated pagodas. In the opening passage of this chapter, the buddha Tahōbutsu (S: Prabhūtaratna; Abundant Treasure), who preceded Shakyamuni Buddha in an earlier world cycle, sits in a jeweled pagoda and invites Shakyamuni to enter. The Lotus Sutra proclaims the efficacy of offerings to pagodas, and many pagodas were built to enshrine sutra texts.[4]

The shape of the pagodas here echoes that of miniature bronze or iron pagoda reliquaries.[5] The circular body is covered with a roof and a ringed finial. Jeweled ropes are suspended from the top of the finial to the corners of the roof. Each pagoda in the Togakushi copy contains a character from the sutra, enshrining it like a Buddha in a pagoda. The characters fill only the center of the pagodas, the roof and finial stand out against the background, and their vertical and horizontal alignment is rhythmic rather than rigid.

The calligraphy of the Togakushi sutra has a distinctive energy. The right part of each character tends to be larger than the left, and horizontal strokes stretch upward toward the right. In *tekagami* albums the calligrapher was identified as Prince Shōtoku (574–622), an enlightened statesman and advocate of Buddhism. Scholars, however, usually attribute the calligraphy to Fujiwara Sadanobu (1088–1156?), the fifth-generation head of the Sesonji calligraphy school founded by Fujiwara Yukinari (972–1027), one of the greatest Japanese calligraphers.[6] Until the eighth-generation head Fujiwara Yukiyoshi formally established the Sesonji school, its style was not stable; instead, each master established his own individual style. Sadanobu's distinctive style is characterized by spontaneous, flowing brushstrokes in cursive script and oblique brushlines created by the side of the brush. These characteristics are evident in the present example (see also cat. no. 6).

MW

1. Four scrolls of the Lotus Sutra owned by the Togakushi shrine remain incomplete: two scrolls from Fascicle One, one from Fascicle Two, and one from Fascicle Four. The text of the Lotus Sutra most widely used in Japan was translated by Kumarajiva in 406 in China. When Kumarajiva introduced the Lotus Sutra to China, it consisted of twenty-seven chapters. The chapter "Devadatta" was added in the early sixth century, yielding a twenty-eight-chapter Lotus Sutra. The twenty-eight

chapters are grouped into eight fascicles or eight scrolls (J: *hachi kan*). For the structure of the Lotus Sutra, see Tanabe and Tanabe, eds. 1989, p. 28. The Lotus Sutra was particularly fundamental to the Tendai sect which was established by the monk Saichō at Mount Hiei in the ninth century.

2. Watson 1993, p. 180.

3. Since the paper is light gray, some believe that paper sheets of personal writings and letters which belonged to the dead were soaked in water and remade into paper for copying sutras as offerings for the dead, known as *tsuizen kuyō*. No document accompanies the set, so its patron is not known.

4. Ruppert 2000, p. 67.

5. A similar pagoda reliquary is found in Cunningham et al. 1998, no. 79.

6. Sadanobu's calligraphy seems to be closer to that of his grandfather Fujiwara Korefusa than to that of his father, Fujiwara Sadazane. Shimatani 1985; Shimizu and Rosenfield 1984–85, p. 48; Komatsu 1960; Carpenter 1997.

6.
Section of "Simile and Parable," with Pagoda Decoration, Chapter 3 of the Lotus Sutra

Late Heian period (ca. 900–1185), twelfth century
Handscroll mounted as a hanging scroll, gold on indigo-dyed paper, with silver-ruled lines and mica-stamped decoration, 11¼ × 5⅝ in (29.9 × 14.3 cm)
Literature: Nihon Bijutsu Kurabu 1925, no. 45; Gotoh Museum 1962, no. 19; Iijima, ed. 1975, p. 680

In contrast to the Togakushi copy (cat. no. 5), here gold characters within silver-ruled columns stand out beautifully against the indigo paper. This seven-line section was a part of a set of the Lotus Sutra from Kōryūji temple (Uzumasadera) in Kyoto.[1] Fragments of the sutra are called *Uzumasagire* (pieces from Uzumasa temple). Probably once part of a *tekagami* album, this segment was mounted as a hanging scroll. As in the *Togakushigire*, each character is enshrined in a pagoda stamped in mica. Since the mica has flaked away almost completely, it is nearly impossible to discern the nine pagodas that form each column.

These seven lines are identified as a text from chapter 3 (*Hiyuhon*) of the Lotus Sutra, in which Shakyamuni Buddha tells of a rich father who saves his sons from a burning house and comments that he is like the Thus Come One (Tathāgata Buddha, "the thus perfected one"), who saves all living beings.

The calligraphy of the *Uzumasagire,* like that of the *Togakushigire* has traditionally been attributed to the same person, Prince Shōtoku (574–622), but in fact both are very close to that of Fujiwara Sadanobu (see cat. no. 5). The calligraphy of the two seems at times almost identical. For instance both display a strikingly similar proportion of thick and thin for the character *ichi,* and the character *waka,* or *moshi,* is represented by a long, sharp diagonal stroke. However, there are subtle differences; for instance, the character *dai* in the *Uzumasagire* is less oblique in the final stroke.

Biographical information about Sadanobu is relatively abundant. One of his earliest calligraphies was *Sanjūrokuninshū* (Collection of the Thirty-six Immortal Poets) produced in 1112 when he was twenty-three years old. In 1118 he inscribed the square (*shikishi*) for the door of the Amida Hall in Saishōji temple. After his father retired from official duties in 1119, Sadanobu became the fifth-generation head of the Sesonji school. In 1123 and 1142 he inscribed folding screens for two *Daijōe*, the great thanksgiving ceremonies after the enthronements of

Emperors Sutoku and Konoe. Sadanobu was often asked to write official documents and petitions for emperors, ministers, regents, and high-ranking priests. He was renowned for copying the entire Buddhist canon, called the *Tripitaka* (J: *Issaikyō*), a compendium of more than five thousands scrolls, a feat that took twenty-three years. He dedicated the *Tripitaka* to the Kasuga shrine in 1151, and three days later he took the tonsure in Tōnomine, south of Nara, and received his priest name of Shōkō. The *Tripitaka* set was lost when Kōfukuji temple, to which the Kasuga shrine belonged, was destroyed by fire in 1180.

An appropriate comparison for the calligraphy of this fragment as well as for cat. no. 5 is provided by two scrolls. One is the *Hannya Rishukyō,* an Esoteric sutra copied by Sadanobu and dated 1150,[2] and the other is chapter 3, "Simile and Parable," from the so-called *Kunōjikyō,* a copy of the Lotus Sutra dated 1141 and attributed to Sadanobu.[3] The scrolls and the fragments are in two different hands, but the two fragments are stylistically close to the two scrolls. The two scrolls exhibit kinetic brush movements and abbreviated strokes, resulting in a loosely structured characters. The long strokes of the two fragments are more oblique, and their characters have more precise endings, perhaps in response to their pagoda surrounds. The two Barnet and Burto fragments may, therefore, be examples of the Sadanobu style rather than the work of Sadanobu himself.

The Sadanobu style was not known for elegance or solid character structure but for energy and loose forms, qualities that became more valued in the mid-twelfth century. Yamagishi Tokubei suggests that Sadanobu may have studied the work of such Chinese Northern Song calligraphers as Su Shi (1037–1101) and Huang Tingqian (1045–1105), whose work is marked by powerful angled strokes and free asymmetric brush movements.[4] Komatsu Shigemi points out that the shift in calligraphic taste may be an expression of the transition from the

Heian to the Kamakura period, when sociopolitical and cultural values were also changing.[5]

M W

1. Kōryūji was founded in 603 by Hata no Kawakatsu at the request of Prince Shōtoku.
2. See Komatsu, ed. 1978–80, vol. 2, pl. 47. Other major extant works by Sadanobu are *Sanjūrokuninkashū,* the Kanazawa version of *Manyōshu, Wakan Rōeishō,* colophons for Ono Michikaze's screens, and the *Po Jui Handscroll* by Fujiwara Yukinari. See *Shodō zenshū* 1954–68, vols. 12 and 14; Hasegawa 2000, p. 87; Murase 2000, pp. 62–63.
3. See Gotoh Museum 1991, pp. 26–29. The thirty scrolls of the Lotus Sutra set coordinated by Emperor Toba (1103–1156) and Empress Taikenmon'in (1101–1145) in 1141, known as *Kunōji-kyō,* were scattered to various collections including the Kunōji temple (presently Tesshōji) in Shizuoka, Tokyo National Museum, and Gotoh Museum in Tokyo.
4. Yamagishi 1965.
5. Komatsu 1953.

7.

Section of "The Bodhisattva Wonderful Sound," with Pagoda Decoration, Chapter 24 of the Lotus Sutra

Late Heian period (ca. 900–1185), twelfth century, dated 1163 Handscroll mounted as a hanging scroll, gold on indigo-dyed paper, with silver-ruled lines and gold painted decoration, 11¼ × 22⅛ in. (28.6 × 56.2 cm)

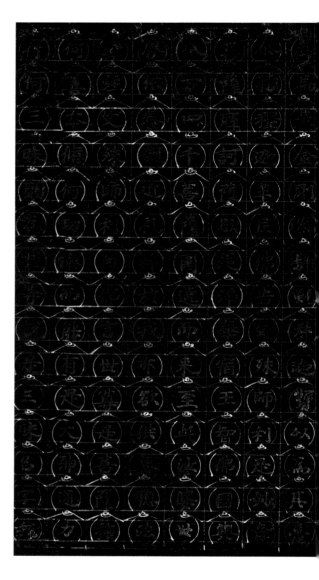

This fragment is another example of the format called *ichiji hōtō hokekyō* (one character per jeweled pagoda) (see cats. 5 and 6). The sutra fragment is a section from Chapter 24, "The Bodhisattva Wonderful Sound [Myōon Bosatsu hon]," of the Lotus Sutra.[1] Characters and pagodas were rendered in gold, while vertical and horizontal rules were painted in silver. The gold characters, enshrined in pagodas like relics of the Buddha, have greatly faded. Close examination, however, reveals powerful brushstrokes, each executed in a slow, smooth, yet forceful manner that embodies the strength of the Buddhist faith.

The pagoda form here is called *gorintō* in Japanese, literally "five-wheel pagoda." From top to bottom its five elements—jewel, semicircle, triangle, circle, and square—correspond in Shingon Buddhism to the five constituents of the universe: earth, water, fire, air, and ether.[2]

Chapter 24 portrays the Wonderful Sound Bodhisattva. The bodhisattva resides in the Land Adorned with Pure Light and has attained all the great samadhis (roughly, states of consciousness). The tale in the fragment describes the transcendental power of the Wonderful Sound Bodhisattva's samadhis. He came to the saha world (this world) with eighty-four thousand bodhisattvas to pay homage to Shakyamuni, to see his attendant bodhisattvas, and to hear the Lotus Sutra. Without rising from his seat, he entered into a samadhi to create a jeweled mass of eighty-four thousand lotus blossoms on Mount Gridhrakuta (Vulture Peak) where the Buddha preached the Lotus Sutra.

An inscription at the end of each scroll, with the date 1163, mentions a certain Shinsei (or Shinsai).[3] Some scholars believe this Shinsei to be Fujiwara Michinori, whose name as a monk was Shinzei and who first served as a noted scholar for the Emperors Toba, Sutoku, and Konoe. A clever advisor, he gained great power at the court of Emperor Goshirakawa because his wife, Kii no Nii, had been the emperor's wet nurse. This set of the Lotus Sutra was discov-ered in Jizōin, a subtemple of Hokkeji in Hyōgo prefecture. A document dated 1648 states that the set once belonged to Anrakujuin, a personal temple of Emperor Toba (Goshirakawa's father). Because of the close connection between the emperor and this temple, it is tempting to identify "Shinsei" with Fujiwara Michinori, but he was killed in the Heiji Rebellion (1159), which was aimed largely at eliminating his political influence, thus before 1163.

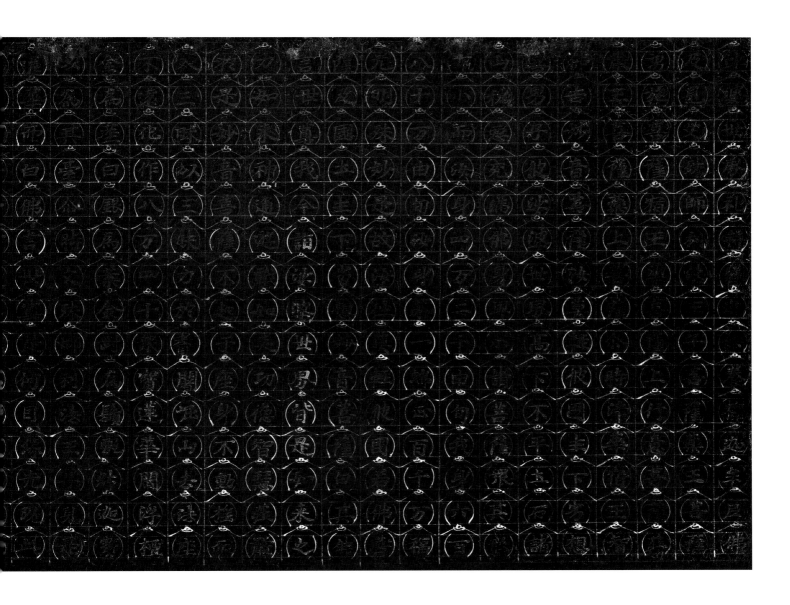

The present example is a recent addition to the Barnet and Burto collection; previously the collection had included a two-line fragment from this set.

M W

1. The translation of the text in the fragment is found in Burton Watson's translation of The Lotus Sutra, Watson 1993, pp. 291–92. Two scrolls (Scrolls 3 and 5) of the original Lotus Sutra set were owned by Sorimachi and the closing scroll (*Kanfugenkyō*) by Hattori Shōji. See *Jūyō bunkazai* 1972–78, vol. 20, pls. 8, 243–44. Each of these scrolls retains its frontispiece with an illustration that was copied from the Chinese prototype. See Miya 1983; Tanabe, W., 1988, p. 95 and pl. 107.

Fragments are widely dispersed: Kitamura Museum, Kyoto, and Nezu Institute of Fine Arts, Tokyo, among others. See Nezu Institute of Fine Arts 1994, no. 73; Gotoh Museum 1991, p. 112.

According to Kawase Kazuma, gilt-bronze rollers were decorated with a lotus-bud design. He also mentions that the set was once owned by Onsendera in Arima, Hyōgo. Gotoh Museum 1971, text, p. 24.

2. See Morse and Morse 1996, pp. 74–75 and 125.

3. See *Jūyō bunkazai* 1972–78, vol. 20, pl. 243–44. The inscription is most likely in the same hand as the main text, although the writing of the sutra is more square than that of the inscription, perhaps to make the characters better fit the shape of the pagodas.

8.

Section of "The Wonderful Adornments of the Leaders of the World," Chapter 1 of the Flower Ornament Sutra

Late Heian period (ca. 900–1185), ca. 1100
Handscroll mounted as a hanging scroll, ink on light indigo-dyed paper, with gold-ruled lines and gold-leaf foil flakes, 9¾ × 20 in. (24.8 × 50.8 cm)

This scorched fragment is part of the Flower Ornament Sutra (*Daihōkōbutsu Keyongyō* or *Kegongyō*) from Senpukuji, a temple in Osaka. It is not known when the sutra scrolls were damaged. Pieces from the sutra, mounted as hanging scrolls, were sold after World War II, as were sections of the so-called Burned Sutra from the Nigatsudō of Tōdaiji temple.[1] The Senpukuji sutra is copied on splendid paper, dyed with indigo (*aigami*), and decorated with gold-leaf flakes. Although *aigami* was used in the Nara period, it became more common in the late eleventh century, exemplified by the Lotus Sutra owned by Ryūhonji in Kyoto[2] and the *Manyōshū* (Ten Thousand Leaves) poetry anthology inscribed by Fujiwara Korefusa (1030–1096).[3]

The calligraphy of the Senpukuji pieces demonstrates typical Late Heian style. The brushwork is elegant and neat; the strokes are meticulously rendered and characters are carefully placed.

The fragment was originally part of "The Wonderful Adornments of the Leaders of the World [*Sekai Jōgan-hon*]," chapter 1 of the Flower Ornament Sutra. This fundamental sutra of the Kegon sect records the sermons delivered by Shakyamuni Buddha immediately after his enlightenment.[4] It was the essential text of national Buddhism in the Nara period, and the important Nara temple of

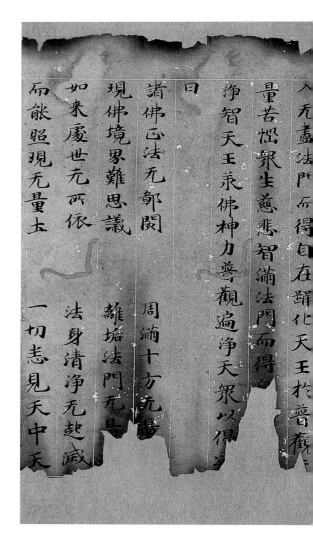

Tōdaiji was dedicated to the Vairochana Buddha of the Kegon cosmos. Kegon teaching stresses the unity of the universe, the belief that the entire universe is reflected in a single speck of dust and that every moment embraces eternity.

M W

1. On the Burned Sutra from Tōdaiji, see Murase 2000, pp. 24–25. Senpukuji fragments are also in the Nezu Institute of Fine Arts in Tokyo, the Century Museum in Tokyo, and a private collection in Tokyo (Iijima 1975, pl. 19). A rectangular red seal of Senpukuji appears below the sutra title at the beginning of the Nezu piece. See Nezu Institute of Fine Arts 1994, pp. 13 and 80–81.

2. A reproduction of the Ryūhonji Lotus Sutra is found in Nara National Museum 1988, pl. 31. The Ryūhonji example is datable to the mid-eleventh century. See Kyoto National Museum 1992, pl. 34.

3. This copy of the *Manyōshū* was formerly attributed to Fujiwara Kintō (966–1041) but has been reattributed to Korefusa. Korefusa was the grandfather of Fujiwara Sadanobu (1088–1156?). A discussion of Sadanobu and his calligraphy is found in cat. nos. 5 and 6 (*Togakushigire* and *Uzamasagire*).

4. The *Kegongyō* was translated from Sanskrit into Chinese in the early fifth century by Buddhabhadra (359–429). *Daizōkyō* 1924–34, vol. 9, no. 278. The translation of the text in the fragment is found in Cleary 1993, pp. 67–68.

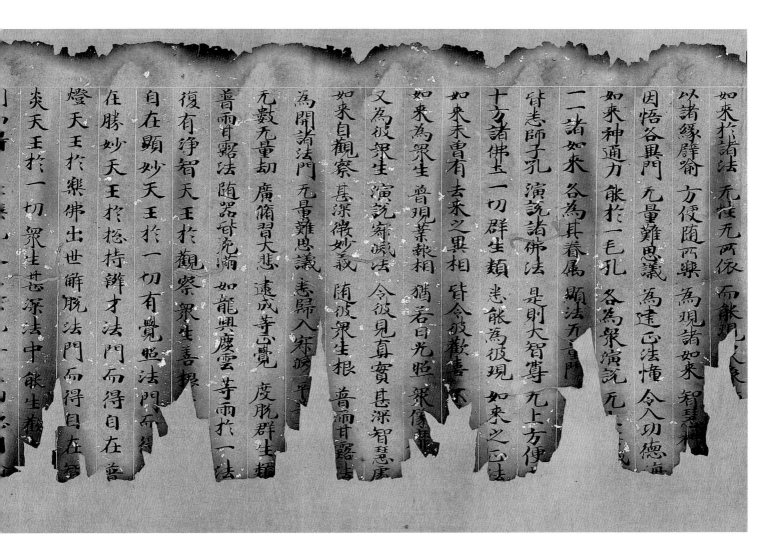

9.
Section of the Sutra of Contemplation on the Buddha of Immeasurable Life

Late Heian period (ca. 900–1185), 12th century
Handscroll mounted as a hanging scroll, malachite on paper, with gold-ruled lines and painted decoration in gold and silver, 9⅞ × 5¼ in. (25.1 × 13.3 cm)
Ex coll.: Maeda family, Kaga province
Literature: *Bessatsu Taiyō* 1999, no. 25

This fragment from the Sutra of Contemplation on the Buddha of Immeasurable Life (*Kanmuryōjukyō*) is from the *Karioshijō,* a *tekagami* album once owned by the Maeda family of Kaga province (Ishikawa prefecture), one of the most powerful daimyo. It is commonly referred to as a *Rengeōingire* ("fragment from Rengeōin temple") and was among the rarest and most sought after calligraphic specimens in the Momoyama and Edo periods. Such fragments have been highly admired by collectors for their beautiful decoration (here delicately painted butterflies and birds are shown in flight at the top and bottom). The text segments were also valued because of their attribution to the Cloistered Emperor Shirakawa (r. 1072–86), who played an energetic and powerful role in the court's cultural and religious activities when the imperial family regained power in the late eleventh and early twelfth century. The faintness of the text was appreciated by masters of the tea ceremony in the Momoyama period, when a sensibility of imperfection was cultivated.

Rengeōingire fragments, found in such famous *tekagami* albums as the Moshiogusa, Getsudai, Murasaki no mizu, and Somegamijō, usually consist of only one or two lines of text.[1] The present fragment, with five lines of text, is the longest known example. It may have been acquired by Maeda Toshiie (1538–1599), the most influential and cultivated daimyo in the Momoyama period, when the creation of *tekagami* albums became fashionable.[2] An identification slip, which was originally pasted next to the fragment, is inscribed "Shirakawa'in" (written by the Cloistered Emperor Shirakawa), followed by the fragment's first three characters. It also bears the seal of a calligraphy connoisseur certifying that the fragment text was inscribed by the Cloistered Emperor Shirakawa. The seal, which reads "kinzan" (Zither Mountain), is that of the connoisseur family established by Kohitsu Ryōsa (1572–1662) under the patronage of Toyotomi Hidetsugu (1568–1595), a nephew and adopted son of Toyotomi Hideyoshi (1536–1598), the all-powerful feudal lord and chief imperial minister. The seal's pictographic design was used by the branch of the Kohitsu family founded by Kohitsu Kanbei (d. 1650), Kohitsu Ryōsa's third son.[3] Kanbei moved to Edo and his descendants settled there under the patronage of the Tokugawa shogun. Later generations of the Kanbei branch used the same seal or seals with the same design.

This is a rare example of the use of *byakuroku* (powdery malachite) to inscribe characters.[4] The pigment has over time flaked off or faded, making the text difficult to read. Distinct edges contrast with flaked-off hollows in the center of strokes, inadvertently enhancing the overall impression.

Each well-balanced character displays careful unexaggerated brushwork. Roundness prevails, both at the beginning of the strokes, where the use of the tip is not evident, and at the corners, where the strokes are gently curved. This graceful round calligraphic style is typical of Japanese sutra copies of the Heian period. The present fragment includes marks of both numbers and Japanese syllables for Japanese reading of Chinese, probably added later.

For Japanese devotees the Sutra of Contemplation on the Buddha of Immeasurable Life is the most significant of the three major sutras of the Pure Land Buddhist sect.[5] It tells of Queen Vaidehi who was imprisoned by her evil son Ajatashatru. She worships Shakyamuni Buddha who appears and shows her visions of various Pure Lands. He explains the sixteen types of contemplation that help the devotee visualize the Buddha Amida's Pure Land and attain rebirth there. The practice of *shōmyō* (saying the name) is strongly encouraged and it became very popular among Pure Land followers. The sutra states that if at the moment of death a person invokes the name of Amida, saying "Namu Amida Butsu"—Hail to Amida Buddha—the Buddha will come with a host of bodhisattvas and lead the devotee to the Pure Land. This simple practice appealed to lay people who could not participate in monastic practices.

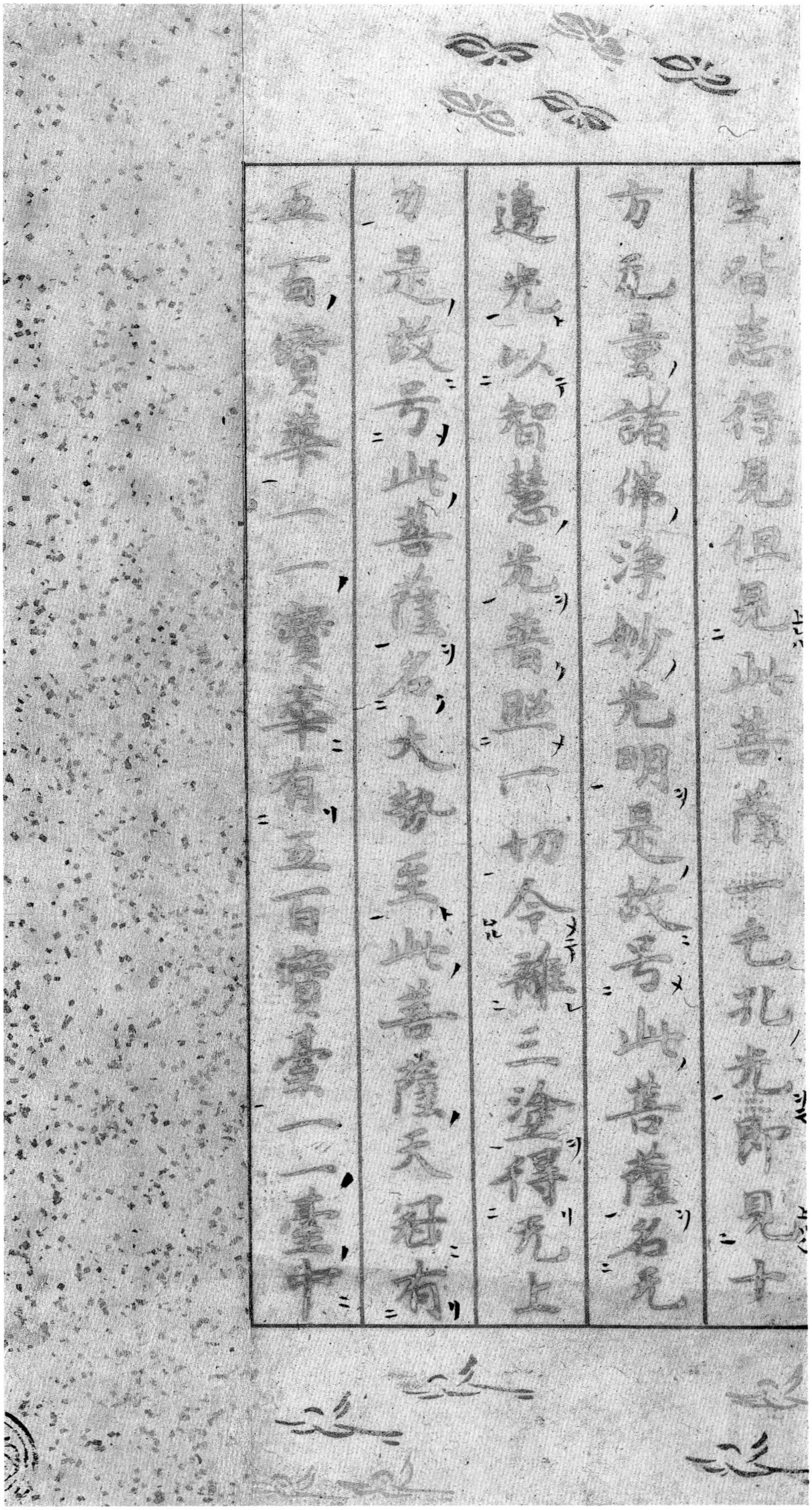

生ずるが故に惡道を見るも、但し見るこの菩薩を。一に先の北の光、即ち見るに十

方の無量の諸佛の淨妙なる光明を。是の故に號く此の菩薩を名づく

邊光、以ての智慧の光、善く照して一切を令す離れ三塗を得る光上

是の故に此の菩薩を名づく大勢至。此の菩薩の天冠に有り

五百の寶華、一一の寶華に有り五百の寶臺、一一の臺に十

The present text introduces the great bodhisattva Seishi, one of the two principal bodhisattvas (the other is Kannon) flanking the Buddha Amida.[6]

M W

1. Moshiogusa is in the collection of the Kyōto National Museum; Getsudai in the Tokyo National Museum; Murasaki no mizu, in a private collection in Tokyo (see Iijima 1975, pl. 24); and Somegamijō, in the Gotoh Art Museum. The Kyoto National Museum owns a handscroll from the same set as this as well as other Rengeōingire fragments; see Tokyo National Museum 1985, pl. 39.

2. The present fragment has an attachment of a small sheet from the back paper of the original scroll. An unidentified seal is cropped at the left bottom corner of the back paper.

3. Kinoshita 1973, no. 84.

4. Various writings about the *Rengeōingire* fragments mention gold characters. However, the pigment seems to be malachite, not gold. Malachite was traditionally used for green, and the finer it is ground, the lighter the green. The pigment's flaking and the chemical reaction evident on the hanging scroll's reverse are characteristic of malachite. I owe thanks to Takemitsu Oba, Asian Conservator in the Metropolitan Museum, for his observations.

5. The other major sutras are *Muryōjukyō* (Larger Sukhavativyuha), and *Amidakyō* (Smaller Suhavativyūha). See *Daizōkyō* 1924–34, vol. 12.

6. Inagaki, H., 1994, p. 336.

10.

Section of "The Former Affairs of the Bodhisattva Medicine King," Chapter 23 of the Lotus Sutra

Late Heian period (ca. 900–1185), mid-twelfth century
Handscroll mounted as a hanging scroll, ink on paper, with gold-leaf ruled lines, gold-leaf and silver-leaf decoration and painted decoration in margins, 9¼ × 16 in. (24.8 × 40.6 cm)
Literature: London Gallery, Tokyo 2000, no. 128; Nara National Museum 1988, pl. 46

Sumptuously embellished sutra copies (*sōshokukyō*) were among the most glorious offerings to Buddhist deities in twelfth-century Japan. This fragment exemplifies the aesthetic of *sōshokukyō*. Gold and silver dust and varied pieces of gold and silver foil embellish the dyed paper, and lotuses are lavishly painted in color at the top and bottom of the scroll. The rich ornamentation represents the magnificent sacred world of the Buddha who illuminates with his merciful radiance.

Two types of distinctive ornamentation help date this fragment to the mid-twelfth century. The first is the large scale of the torn pieces of gold foil scattered over the scroll. This is an expression of an aesthetic of irregularity evident in the early twelfth

century, when aristocratic patrons found irregular shapes graphically appealing.[1] The second feature is the clusters of silver dust in cloudlike shapes with a single straight edge (one of these forms cuts diagonally across six columns on the right). The earliest example of this stencil technique is in the *Kun ōjikyō*, a copy of the Lotus Sutra dated 1141.[2]

The calligraphy of this fragment also exhibits characteristic twelfth-century traits. The brushwork is regular and stately in its strokes and smooth and slow in movement. At the same time,

while there is enough space between characters in the upper sections, farther down the columns space becomes so tight that the characters are compressed or cross over the gold bottom line. The inscriber's hand is most distinctively revealed in diagonal strokes. In such characters as *ten* (heaven), *hito* or *nin* (a person), and *dai* (large), the last brushstroke with its rightward diagonal is much more elongated than the corresponding leftward stroke.

The sutra text is from chapter 23, "The Former

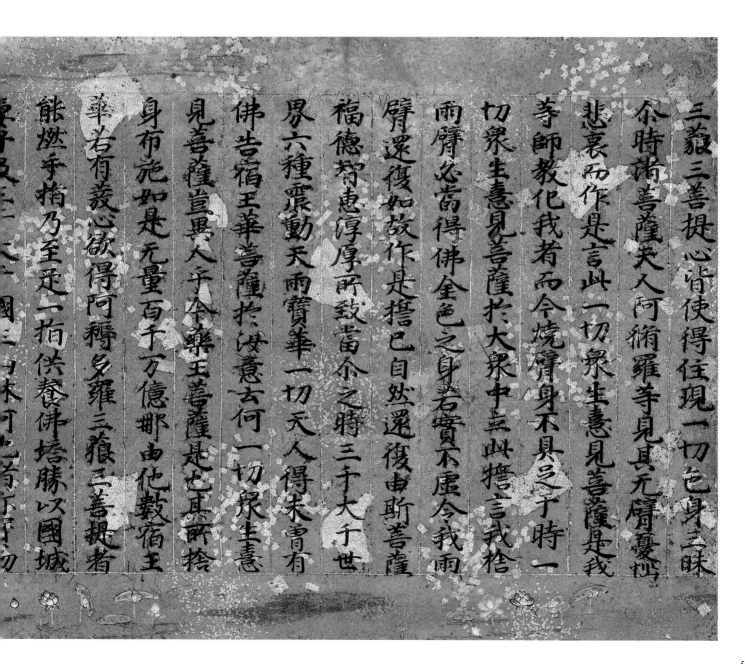

Affairs of the Bodhisattva Medicine King [*Yakuō Bosatsu Honji hon*]." It tells two stories of the bodhisattva's practice of self-sacrifice that led him to attain perfect universal enlightenment. In the first episode the bodhisattva Medicine King, in his former life as the bodhisattva Gladly Seen by All Living Beings (Issai-Shujō Kiken Bosatsu), offered his body to the Buddha Sun Moon Pure Bright Virtue. He wrapped himself in jeweled robes, poured fragrant oil over his head, and set fire to his body. This sacrifice caused him to be reborn in the land of the Buddha Sun Moon Pure Bright Virtue. In the second episode, after the Buddha Sun Moon Pure Bright Virtue entered nirvana, the bodhisattva burned his arms as an offering to the death of the Buddha. The inscription of the present fragment comments on this event as follows: "At that time, in the midst of the great assembly, the bodhisattva Gladly Seen by All Living Beings made this vow, saying: 'I have cast away both my arms. I am certain to attain the golden body of a Buddha. If this is true and not false, then may my two arms become as they were before!' When he had finished pronouncing this vow, his arms reappeared of themselves as they had been before."[3]

The sutra fragment breaks off in the middle of a passage extolling the benefits of accepting and upholding the Lotus Sutra. Two other fragments from the same scroll are housed at Kitamura Museum in Kyoto and the Sackler Gallery at Harvard University. The former preserves the text immediately preceding the present passage, and the Sackler fragment is from the final section of the scroll.[4]

MW

1. See, for instance, the irregular joined-paper designs in books of *Sanjūrokuninshū* (Collection of the Thirty-six Immortal Poets). Other early applications of large irregular foil shapes are seen in the Lotus Sutra in Fan-shaped Books (*Senmen Hokekyō*) datable to 1152 and the *Heike Nōkyō* (sutras donated to Itsukushima shrine by the warrior Taira Kiyomori [1118–1181] and his clan in 1164). See Akiyama et al. 1972; Kyoto National Museum 1974.
2. See Gotoh Museum 1991. Decoration on the reverse of the scroll of Chapter 19, "Benefits of the Teacher of the Law [Hōshi Kudokubon]," shows a similar decorative technique of a metallic dust cluster with a straight edge. Egami 1989, p. 36; a text section of the chapter "Suzumushi" (Bell Crickets) in *Genji Monogatari Emaki* from the mid-twelfth century was also decorated boldly with silver clusters having a single straight edge. See Komatsu, ed. 1977a, pp. 59–60.
3. Watson 1993, pp. 284–86.
4. See Gotoh Museum 1991, p. 121, for the Kitamura Museum version, and for the Sackler fragment see Cuno et al. 1996, pp. 74–75, and Shimizu and Rosenfield 1984–85, no. 6.

11.
Section of "Sermon," Chapter 2 of the Sutra of Innumerable Meanings

Late Heian period (ca. 900–1185), twelfth century
Handscroll mounted as a hanging scroll, ink on purple-dyed mica-coated paper, malachite-green ruled lines, and sprinkles of gold and silver foil, 10⅛ × 5⅛ in. (25.7 × 13 cm)

This seven-line text was inscribed on marvelously crafted paper. The paper was first coated with mica; purple dye was then used to create cloud shapes in some areas. After fine pieces of gold and silver foil were scattered over the surface, the columns were ruled in malachite green (*rokushō*). The exquisite result testifies to the sophisticated taste of the Heian aristocracy.

The elegant calligraphy is a match for the paper. Each character is well balanced in structure, and

each stroke is decisive but deliberate, almost meditative. The calligraphy bears some similarity to that of the Sutra of Innumerable Meanings of the Lotus Sutra from Kunōji temple.[1] They share a controlled handling of the brush, particularly noticeable in horizontal strokes where there is an increased pressure toward the right and a full thick ending. Both also feature abbreviated or linked brushstrokes as seen in the third column in the characters of *bosatsu*. The calligrapher of the *Kunōjikyō* is known

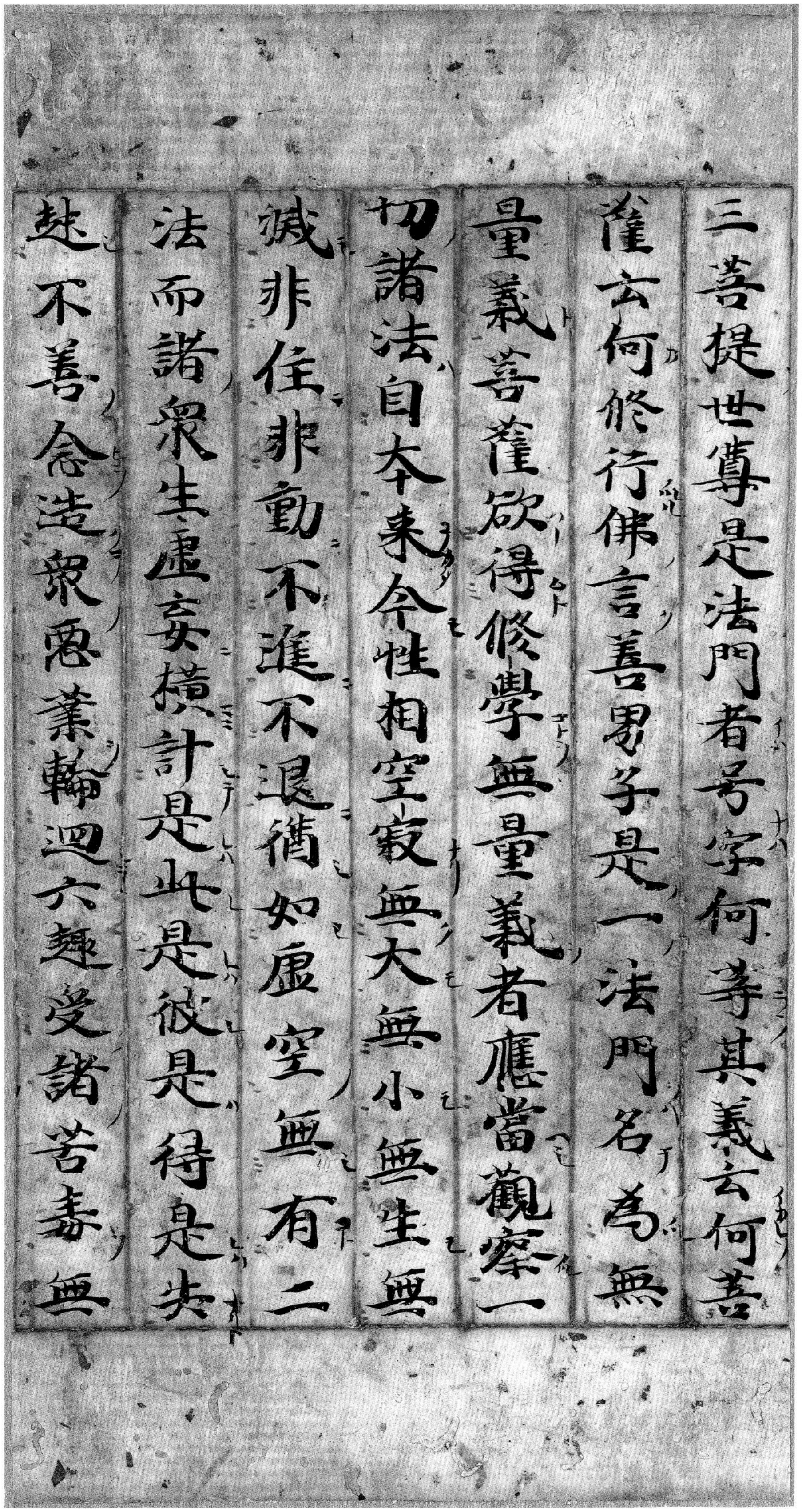

三菩提世尊是法門者号字何等其義云何菩
薩云何於行佛言善男子是一法門名為無
量義菩薩欲得修學無量義者應當觀察一
切諸法自本來今性相空寂無大無小無生無
滅非住非動不進不退猶如虛空無有二
法而諸衆生虛妄横計是此是彼是得是失
起不善念造衆惡業輪迴六趣受諸苦毒無

to be the aristocrat Taira Sanechika (1087–1148). He was close to the Empress Taikenmon'in who commissioned the Lotus Sutra set for Kunōji temple. The text of the present fragment may have been inscribed by Sanechika himself or by a calligrapher closely associated with Sanechika and the circle of Taikenmon'in in the mid-twelfth century.

The inscribed text is from chapter 2, "Sermon [*Seppōhon*]" of the Sutra of Innumerable Meanings (*Murōgikyō*).[2] This sutra was the opening scroll of a ten-scroll set; the text of the Lotus Sutra appeared in the next eight scrolls; one scroll of the Sutra of Meditation on the Samantabhadra Bodhisattva (*Kanfugenkyō*) ended the set. The Sutra of Innumerable Meanings seems to have been transitional. It has been said that Buddha preached this sutra more than forty years after he attained enlightenment but before the Lotus Sutra, which he taught in the last eight years of his life.[3]

The text includes numbers added in red that indicate the sequence of the Japanese reading of Chinese and also Japanese syllables (kana) in ink that were added to Chinese characters to show Japanese grammatical markers.   M W

1. See Gotoh Museum 1991, pp. 14–17. See also cat. nos. 6 and 10.
2. Ono and Maruyama 1978, vol. 10, pp. 424–25.
3. This sutra consists of three chapters: "Virtuous Practice [*Tokugyōhon*]," "Sermon [*Seppōhon*]," "Ten Virtues [*Jūkudokuhon*]." *Daizōkyō* 1924–34, vol. 9, no. 276.

12.
Section of "Peaceful Practices," with Canopy and Pedestal Decoration, Chapter 14 of the Lotus Sutra

Kamakura period (1185–1333), thirteenth century
Handscroll mounted as a hanging scroll, ink on paper, silver-ruled lines, one gold line, and silver-stamped decoration, 8¾ × 2¼ in. (22.2 × 5.7 cm)

This small fragment was probably from a *tekagami* album, a collection of ancient calligraphic samples. It shows three columns, each of which has four lines from the verse section of "Peaceful Practices [*Anrakugyōhon*]," chapter 14 of the Lotus Sutra . Each four-character line is enshrined between a canopy and lotus pedestal, deftly stamped in silver, rather like an image of Buddha seated on a lotus pedestal beneath a canopy in a Buddhist hall. (See the appendix for a discussion of this scroll's mounting.) Fragments with this particular decoration, among the favorite *tekagami* specimens, were known as *Kiyomizugire* (pieces from Kiyomizu temple).[1]

The calligraphy in the fragment displays sturdy brushwork, characteristic of the Kamakura period. These specimens were often attributed to Emperor Gotoba (1180–1239). A decorated sutra owned by Jikōji temple in Saitama prefecture is widely accepted as an example of the emperor's calligraphy.[2] However, comparison of the Jikōji sutra with the calligraphy of *Kiyomizugire* samples, including the present one, reveals different hands.

In chapter 14 dialogues between Manjushri and the Buddha show how the dharma (Buddha's law) should be taught. The text reads: "Manjushri, this Lotus Sutra is foremost among all that is preached by the Thus Come One [Tathāgata Buddha]. Among all that is preached it is the most profound. And it is given at the very last, the way that powerful ruler did when he took the bright jewel he had guarded for so long and finally gave it away."[3]

The Buddha then spoke in verse form, wishing to state his meaning once more: "[A powerful king rewards his soldiers with various articles, / elephants, horses, carriages, / adornments for their person, / fields and houses, / settlements and towns, / or] gives them clothing, / various kinds of precious objects, / men and women servants, wealth and goods, / delightedly bestowing all these. / But if there is someone brave and stalwart / who can carry out difficult deeds, / the king will remove the bright jewel from his topknot / and present it to the man. / The Thus Come One is like this. / He acts as king of the doctrines, / possessing the great power of perseverance / and the precious storehouse of wisdom. . . ."[4]

MW

1. Other *Kiyomizugire* fragments are housed in the Tokyo National Museum and the Gotoh Museum. For prose sections, only a canopy at top and a lotus pedestal at bottom are painted in each column.
2. Egami 1989, pl. 66.
3. Watson 1993, p. 207.
4. Watson 1993, pp. 207–8.

13.
Section of Chapter 3 of the Sutra of Cause and Effect

Kamakura period (1185–1333), late thirteenth century
Handscroll, mounted as a hanging scroll, ink and color on paper, 10¾ × 16½ in. (27.3 × 41.9 cm)
Ex coll.: Setsuda; Matsunaga Yasuzaemon, Tokyo
Literature: Kameda et al. 1959, p. 91

The Sutra of Cause and Effect (*Kako Genzai Ingakyō*) is a collection of stories about the incarnations of Shakyamuni Buddha, emphasizing that meritorious deeds in a previous life are always linked to positive qualities in the present life. The sutra, written in Sanskrit in the third century, was translated into Chinese by the Indian monk Gunabhadra in the fifth century and reached Japan in the seventh or eighth century. The Buddha himself narrates significant events from his earthly life including his birth, the renunciation of his princely life, his enlightenment and preaching, and the conversions of King Bimbisala and his disciples.

The *E-Ingakyō,* as the illustrated handscrolls of this sutra are called, is a set of eight scrolls; the sutra consists of four chapters, each of which is presented in two scrolls. The scrolls are divided into upper and lower registers, with illustrations at the top and the text below, written in eight-character columns.[1]

The earliest examples of *E-Ingakyō* are five versions from the eighth and ninth centuries.[2] In both calligraphy and painting these rely heavily on seventh-century Sui and Tang Chinese models. The calligraphic style reflects Chinese formal script in which characters are structured tightly and symmetrically. The painting also follows Chinese convention: a long continuous narrative scene is divided into small sections by groupings of hills, trees, and buildings.

In addition, four versions of *E-Ingakyō* are extant from the thirteenth and fourteenth centuries and are copies of the earlier models.[3] The present scroll belongs to the Matsunaga version, datable to the late thirteenth century. The episode here recounts that King Suddhodana had sent a minister and an army to report on his son Prince Siddhartha (future Shakyamuni Buddha), who had left the palace to become a wandering ascetic. After they saw him meditating under a tree, they returned and told the king how fully the prince embraced the austerities of his chosen life. At the right the minister and army have returned to the palace. The composition with

its diagonal placement of gate and fence was a typical means of depicting a visit to a palace in Japanese narrative handscrolls, and a procession to a palace is usually shown in a long sequence from right to left. The two figures who bow to the king at the left are probably announcing the minister's return.

The present scene is almost identical with that in the Shōriji version from slightly later in the Kamakura period. The same scene survives from the earlier Daigoji and Idemitsu versions, which date from the eighth and early ninth century, respectively. All four have the same compositional scheme. The Kamakura copies, however, reveal a somewhat more integrated space that creates a narrative flow, while the earlier illustrations separate one stage from the other with a gate, rocks, and trees. Tree trunks in the Kamakura pictures are delineated with thick and thin outlines, while there is a more schematic and abstract rendition of trees in the earlier versions. Following older models, the Kamakura works use bright colors such as red, blue, green, and yellow, but this coloration was less carefully applied (such freedom is common in Kamakura painting).

Both the ninth-century Idemitsu Museum sutra and the thirteenth-century Shōriji sutra were once part of the temple collections on Mount Koya, the center of Shingon Esoteric worship. It may be that the Idemitsu version served as the model for the Shōriji version. Perhaps the revival of *E-Ingakyō* is connected with the rise of the cult of Shakyamuni Buddha in the Kamakura period.

Unlike other Kamakura copyists of the sutra, the Matsunaga calligrapher, the author of the present example, did not use earlier versions as stylistic models. The powerful Kamakura style is evident in the diverse brushwork—thin and thick lines, short and long strokes, hooks and tapering at the ends of strokes, diagonal straight lines and undulating horizontals—and in the loose asymmetrical structure of the characters.   MW

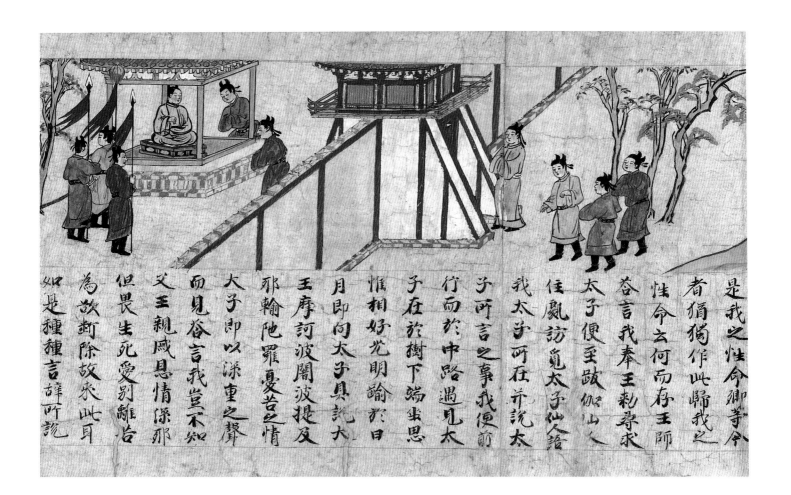

如是種種言辭所說
為欲斷除故來此耳
但畏生死受別離苦
父王親感恩情深重
而見谷言我豈不知
大子即以深重之聲
邪輸陀羅夏苦之情
王摩訶波闍波提及
月即向太子具說大
惟相好光明踰於日
子在於樹下端坐思
行而於中路遇見太
子所言之事我便前
我太子而在并說太
住亂訪覓太子仙人語
太子便至跋伽山人
荅言我奉王勅尋求
性命去何而存王師
者猶獨作此歸我之
是我之性命卿等今

1. This structure was not rare but is found in the materials from the Dunhuang cave in eighth- and ninth-century China.

2. Some are still in handscroll format, but most of the scrolls have been separated into fragments and dispersed into the collections of temples, museums, and individuals. The five versions are:

1. The *Jōbon Rendaiji* version (divided among Jōbon Rendaiji in Kyoto, Nara National Museum, and six other fragments), the first half of chapter 2 (scroll 3), 8th century. See Kameda et al. 1959, pp. 24–37 (illustrations).

2. The *Daigoji* version (known as the Hōon'in version, a subtemple of Daigoji temple); the first half of chapter 3 (scroll 5), 8th century. See Kameda et al. 1959, pp. 38–54 (illustrations).

3. The Tokyo University of Fine Arts version (Tokyo University of Fine Arts and eight other fragments); the second half of chapter 4 (scroll 8), 8th century. See Kameda et al. 1959, pp. 61–74 (illustrations).

4. The "Ten-sheet" version (formerly Masuda Collection, fragments in the Egawa Museum, the Gotoh Museum, MOA Museum, and Powers Collection); first half of chapter 4 (scroll 7), 8th century. See Kameda et al. 1959, pp. 54–61 (illustrations).

5. Idemitsu Museum version (formerly Masuda Collection, known as Masuda-ke bessatsu bon); the first half of chapter 3 (scroll 5), early 9th century. See Kameda et al. 1959, pp. 75–83 (illustrations).

3. The four versions are:

1. The Shōtokuji version (Shōtokuji and the Gotoh Museum), the first half of chapter 2 (scroll 3), late 12th century. See Kameda et al. 1959, pp. 97–98 (illustrations) and pp. 56–57 (text).

2. The Kenchōji version (Nezu Institute of Fine Arts and the Gotoh Museum), the second half of chapter 2 (scroll 4), dated 1254 (the sixth year of the Kenchō era). See Kameda et al. 1959, pp. 78–84 (illustrations) and pp. 64–65 (text). In the Kenchōji version inscriptions appear at the end of the scrolls, mentioning that the painters were Kennin and his son Shōjumaru in Sumiyoshi, that the copyists were Ryōkai and Ryōsei, and that Kushiro Koreyoshi had commissioned the copy and expressed his wish to be reborn in the Pure Land. There is a sixteenth-century copy of the Kenchōji version, known as the Nakazawa version. See Kameda et al. 1959, p. 96 (illustrations) and pp. 64–65 (text).

3. The Matsunaga version (six fragments outside Japan: the Mary Griggs Burke Collection [see Murase 2000, no. 24], two in the collection of Kimiko and John Powers [see Rosenfield and Shimada 1970–71, nos. 42 and 43], the Nelson-Atkins Museum of Art, and the Heinz Götze Collection, Heidelberg [see Komatsu et al. 1989, no. 27]), the first half of chapter 3 (scroll 5), late 13th century. See Kameda et al. 1959, pp. 86–95 (illustrations) and p. 62 (text). For the text of the present fragment, see *Daizōkyō* 1924–34, vol. 3, no. 189, p. 638.

4. The Shōriji version (Kubosō Museum, Izumi; Idemitsu Museum, and the Sackler Gallery, Washington, D.C.), the first half of chapter 3 (scroll 5), early 14th century. See Kameda et al. 1959, pp. 86–95 (illustrations) and pp. 62–63 (text).

SACRED IMAGES

Cat. no. 14: front

Cat. no. 14: back

14.
The Buddha at Birth

15.
The Buddha at Birth

Asuka period (538–710), seventh
century
Gilt bronze, h. 3⅜ in. (8.5 cm)
Literature: Uehara 1971a;
Kurata et al. 1980, pl. 42; Morse
and Morse 1996, no. 29

Asuka period (538-710), seventh
century
Bronze, h. 6¾ in. (17 cm)
Literature: Kuno 1965, p. 32

Images of a childlike Buddha standing with his right
hand raised to the sky and his left lowered toward
the earth are known in Japanese as Tanjō Butsu,
that is, the Buddha at birth. Sculptures of this type
illustrate the moments immediately following the
birth of the historical buddha Shakyamuni. He was
born Siddhartha Gautama in the town of Lumbini
near present-day Kapilavastu on the Indo-Nepali
border, most likely in the fifth century B.C.[1] According
to several texts, immediately after a miraculous birth
from his mother's side, the Buddha Shakyamuni
took seven steps, spoke his first words, and pro-
claimed himself both the lord of the cosmos and
the savior of all sentient beings. The poignant juxtaposition of an immature physique and traditional
emblems of enlightenment, such as the ushnisha
(J: *nikkei*) or cranial protuberance, elongated ear-
lobes, and long arms with overlarge hands, fore-
shadows the newborn's eventful life.

Such representations have a long history. Infant
Buddhas appear in narrative cycles of Shakyamuni's
life in the Gandharan art of northwest India from
the second and third century A.D. An image from
Loriyan Tangai of a newborn Buddha with his right
arm raised at the elbow and his left lowered to the
ground, identified as the moment when the Buddha
took his first seven steps, is one example preserved
in the Calcutta Museum.[2] Later works from Kashmir
and Tibet suggest that representations of this
momentous event continued to play an important
role in South Asia.[3] Representations of the Buddha
as a young boy with his arms at his sides are also
known.[4] They illustrate his lustration (purification
with water and flowers) by two nagas (serpent
kings), an event that occurred after his first steps.

Depictions of both these episodes are found in
Chinese Buddhist art in the late fifth century.[5] For
example, the lustration of the Buddha is one of the
scenes from his life depicted at the base of Cave 6 at

Cat. no. 15

Yungang in Shanxi province. In addition, both this scene and that of the seven steps, indicated by the raised right hand of the Buddha, are found on the back of a well-known stone stela dated 472 in the Shirakawa collection in Tokyo. Early Japanese sculptures, used in lustration rituals, conflate these images. The raised and lowered hands of the Japanese images refer to the Buddha's seven steps, while the ceremonies (J: *kanbutsu*), in which perfumed or colored water or sweet tea is poured over the sculpture, reenact the ablution of the infant Buddha by the serpent kings.

The use of sculptures in ceremonies celebrating the birth of the Buddha can also be traced to Indian traditions. The intrepid Chinese pilgrim Faxian (ca. 399–414), who traveled in India in the early fifth century, cites such practices in both the oasis city of Khotan in Central Asia and at Pataliputra (present-day Patna), a major Buddhist center in eastern India. He relates that at Pataliputra a statue of the Buddha was paraded in a carriage adorned with gold, silver, and lapis lazuli as part of an annual celebration of the Buddha's birth, traditionally held on the eighth day of the fourth month. In the record of his travels throughout India and Southeast Asia written in 691, the monk Yixing (682–727) describes ceremonies similar to the Japanese *kanbutsu* in various locations in South and Southeast Asia.[6]

Ceremonies marking the birth of the Buddha, often called *yu fo* (bathing the Buddha), are included in some of the earliest Chinese references to Buddhism dating to the second and third century A.D.[7] These celebrations involved religious observances as well as great feasts served to visitors on mats spread along roadways.

According to the Book of Wei (Wei Shu), Emperor Taiwu (r. 424–452) of the Northern Wei dynasty celebrated the Buddha's birth by scattering flowers onto images as they were paraded before him. One of his successors, Emperor Xiaowen (r. 471–499), assembled sculptures in the capital at Luoyang as part of his observance of the Buddha's birth.[8] In the eighth century two versions of a sutra describing the lustration of images

on the Buddha's birthday were translated into Chinese, attesting to the importance of the practice at that time.[9]

According to the Chronicles of Japan (Nihon Shoki), ceremonies celebrating the birth of the historical Buddha were first held in Japan in 606 when a vegetarian feast was served in honor of this event at every major temple in the country. Eighth-century Japanese temple records suggest that sculptures representing the new-born Shakyamuni were used in *kanbutsu* ceremonies during this period.[10] A more detailed description, found in the late-eighth-century Records of Possession of Saidai-ji Temple (Saidaiji-shizairukichō), indicates that the statue sprinkled with water was part of an assemblage of images illustrating the birth of the Buddha and subsequent events. A famous eighth-century Tanjō Butsu image preserved in the Tōdaiji temple in Nara[11] has a basin for catching the water that was poured over the sculpture, and it seems likely that other sculptures also had such receptacles. In 840 the *kanbutsu* ceremony was performed at the imperial palace in Kyoto for the first time. Still an important holiday, it is celebrated on April 8.

Tanjō Butsu are among the most numerous early Japanese Buddhist icons. Most are small, ranging in height from 2¼ to 8 inches (6 to 20 centimeters). Both gilded and blackened examples, such as the two discussed here, are extant. It seems likely that such blackened surfaces resulted from the fires that were a constant threat to wooden temples. The garment's length is used to date images of the Buddha at birth: those with shorter skirts date to the seventh-century; those with longer ones were produced during the eighth century and later.

The thin unarticulated physiques of the two Buddhas seen here also indicate a seventh-century date. Both Buddhas wear full skirts, based on the Indian dhoti, that are wrapped at the waist and fall into multiple folds. The garments are slightly longer at the sides than at the front and back, and both have a large pleated area at the center back. Although the digits are missing, the hands of the Buddhas display a distinctive gesture in which the index and middle fingers are raised. While there seems to be no textual source for this position, it does accord well with the iconography inherent in the seven steps during which the Buddha proclaims his dominion over heaven and earth.

The smaller gilded image (cat. no. 14) is more carefully crafted. The hair, the numerous pleats of the garment, and the two long belts looped at the waist are nicely detailed. A gentle fullness enlivens the young Buddha's chest, and the expressive face radiates an inner serenity. The almond-shaped eyes and slight smile show interesting parallels to the treatment of facial features in works associated with the renowned Tori school of early Japanese Buddhist art, and one scholar has attributed this piece to an atelier working in that tradition.[12] Often compared to a well-published example in the Shōgenji temple in Aizuchi prefecture,[13] this elegant sculpture ranks among the finest examples of early Japanese Tanjō Butsu images. DPL

1. Traditional dates for the life of the Buddha (ca. 566–ca. 483) are based on ancient chronicles preserved in Sri Lanka. Indian and Chinese sources, however, suggest that he may have been born later, sometime around 485 or 450 B.C. For discussion, see Bechert 1991–97.
2. Foucher 1905–8, vol. 1, fig. 154.
3. Pal 1988, figs. 4, 5, 6.
4. Kurita 1988–90, vol. 1, pp. 39–40.
5. See Lee 1955 and Asuka Historical Museum and Nara National Museum 1978 for illustrations of the Chinese examples. For a rare Central Asian example, see Härtel et al. 1982, fig. 3.
6. Asuka Historical Museum and Nara National Museum 1978 provides a good overview of this material, much of which is also discussed in de Visser 1935, vol. 1.
7. Tsukamoto 1979, vol. 1, pp. 73, 117.
8. These and other records are compiled in de Visser 1935, vol. 1, pp. 45–57.
9. These are preserved as the *Yukuzō Kudokukyō, Daizōkyō* 1924–34, vol. 16, no. 697, and the *Shinshū Yokuzō Giki, Daizōkyō* 1924–34, vol. 21, no. 1322.
10. Asuka Historical Museum and Nara National Museum 1978, p. 77.
11. Tanaka Yoshiyasu 1979, fig. 11.
12. Uehara 1971a, p. 96.
13. Tanaka Yoshiyasu 1979, fig. 1.

16.
Bodhisattva of Wisdom with Five Tufts of Hair

Kamakura period (1185–1333), second half of the thirteenth century
Gilt bronze, h. 5½ in. (14 cm)
Literature: Uehara 1971b

The large tufts of hair identify this sculpture as Monju with Five Tufts of Hair (J: Gokei Monju; S: Pancashikha Manjushri). The Bodhisattva of Wisdom, Monju, plays a preeminent role in early Mahayana sutras where he transmits wisdom, remembers past deeds, and counsels others in their spiritual quests. Despite his importance in texts, however, Monju does not appear in Indian art until the sixth century when he is shown both as an individual deity and as a participant in representations of the Mandala of the Eight Great Bodhisattvas.

Images of Monju debating the eloquent and learned layman Yuima (S: Vimalakirti; C: Weimo) became popular in sixth-century China.[1] Worship of the bodhisattva as an independent deity, however, flourished during the eighth century under the influence of the great Indian master Amoghavajra

(705–774) who stressed Monju's role as a personal savior and national protector.[2]

The present depiction of Monju as a young prince, holding a sword (the hilt remains) in his right hand and a text, the Perfection of Wisdom Sutra (S: *Prajna paramita sutra*; J: *Hannya haramittakyō*) (now missing) in his left, follows traditional iconography. His standard epithet in Sanskrit is *kumara-bhuta*, which can be translated "in the form of a youth [or a crown prince]." Due to his youthfulness, Monju is often shown in South Asia with three tufts of hair, a style that is usual for children.

Two sutras by Amoghavajra which were translated into Chinese suggest a connection between the five tufts of hair and the *gandharva* or youthful celestial being named Five Crests (Pancashikha) listed in early Indian sutras written in Pali.[3] They symbolize both the five realms of knowledge and the five-syllable prayer formula (or mantra) associated with this form of the bodhisattva.[4] Worship of Manjushri with Five Tufts of Hair spread to Japan in the ninth century. The characteristic hairstyle of this form of the bodhisattva appears to have become a standard for his imagery during the thirteenth century when devotion to Monju became widespread.[5] This growth is often credited to the monks Eizon (1201–1290) and Ninshō (1217–1303), who were the founders of the Shingon-Ritsu lineage. Active at the Saidaiji temple in Nara, they amalgamated devotion to the Lotus Sutra with belief in Monju's compassion for those in dire straits, using this hybrid dogma to justify preaching to all segments of society and undertaking social works such as the establishment of hostels for the sick and homeless.

The back of the figure and pedestal are incomplete, indicating that this small figure was once part of a *kakebotoke*, a decorative disk suspended from beams or rafters in Kamakura-period temples. *Kakebotoke* are thought to derive their shapes from mirrors, which were regarded as magical, able to reflect images even in the dark, and were associated with Amaterasu, the sun goddess. In Buddhist contexts, *kakebotoke* have been used as ritual burial objects (*chindangu*) as well as decoration for canopies and columns. It should be noted, however, that decorative disks embellished with figures in high relief are also depicted in late Tang caves in the renowned Mogao cave-temples near Dunhuang in Gansu province, which suggests a continental prototype for this type of Japanese decoration.[6]

Monju sits in a yogic posture on a lotus pedestal. He wears a skirtlike garment derived from the Indian dhoti, and a long thin scarf crosses his chest from his left shoulder. A fragment of a diadem is found at his left temple; and the pin that held it in place remains at the right. His broad features and flattened physique and the manner in which his garment hugs his lower legs parallel the form and drapery of images on late-thirteenth-century *kakebotoke* such as an example dated 1275 in the Tokyo National Museum that has Kannon (S: Avalokiteshvara) as its primary icon.[7] Monju may once have worn a necklace and other jewelry. Beads or dangles probably hung from small holes in the lotus petals of his pedestal, and a lion, his traditional mount, may have been attached to a hole in its base. Icons adorning *kakebotoke* are often elaborately presented with canopies above their heads, openwork mandorlas at their backs, and vases or other implements at their sides. It seems likely that this sculpture of the bodhisattva was once similarly enhanced with such individually cast elements.   DPL

1. This iconography is based on the *Yuimagyō* (S: *Vimalakirti-nirdesa sutra*) or Sutra of the Teachings of Vimalakirti, composed between the first century B.C. and first century A.D., and translated into Chinese seven times beginning in the third century A.D.

2. See Birnbaum 1983 for a discussion of Amoghavajra and his relationship to Manjushri.

3. *Gojidaraniju* and *Kongōchōkyō yuga Monjushiribosatsu Kuyō giki,* respectively nos. 1174 and 1175 in *Daizōkyō* 1924–34, vol. 20. The Sanskrit originals of these texts are no longer extant. Images of this form of the bodhisattva, while popular in China and Japan are rare in South Asian Buddhist traditions.

4. The five tufts of hair are also often interpreted as a reference to the five terraces on Mount Wutai in Shanxi province in China, which has been understood as Monju's abode since at least the seventh century. The five Sanskrit syllables are a-ra-pa-ca-na.

5. Many of the paintings and sculptures discussed in Kaneko 1992 show the bodhisattva with five tufts of hair (in these examples some seated Buddhas inhabit the five tufts, most symbolizing the five Buddha families). The present sculpture, which is incomplete, may have been part of a more detailed iconographic scene.

6. *Chūgoku Sekkutsu* 1980–82, vol. 4, fig. 33.

7. Naniwada 1990, fig. 62.

17.
Chakra (Wheel of the Law)

Kamakura period (1185–1333),
early fourteenth century
Gilt bronze, diam. 5⅛ in. (13 cm)

A number of ritual objects connected with Esoteric Buddhism such as the chakra (J: *rinpō*), or wheel, have a long history in Buddhist iconography, dating to the era before anthropomorphic depictions of the Buddha were established and standardized. In Buddhist texts and ritual, the phrase "Turning of the Wheel of the Law" refers to the act of teaching by the Buddha Shakyamuni, and in India the wheel was used in early Buddhist imagery to represent the historical Buddha himself. According to the Jōagongyō (S: Dirghagama), a chakra once preceded a military ruler into battle and miraculously vanquished his enemies.[1] Thus chakras were believed to be endowed with the power to overcome delusion. In Japan the image of a chakra hurtling through the air as it precedes a deity on his way to cure an ailing emperor was represented in one of the memorable scenes in the twelfth-century illustrated handscroll *Shigisan engi emaki* (Legends of Mount Shigi) in the Chōgosonshiji, Nara.[2] Appropriated as a ritual object by Esoteric Buddhism (Mikkyō), the chakra continued to symbolize the teachings of the Buddha and the ability to conquer delusion.

The chakra was introduced from China to Japan as an important ritual object during the earliest period in the history of Japanese Esoteric Buddhism. Its form was based on that of a wheel with a hub, spokes, and a felly. The eight spokes in this Kamakura-period wheel, which correspond to the eight points on the outer rim, are shaped like short, stout vajras. Two narrow rings and the wider inner ring are without decoration, while the outer ring is ornamented with chrysanthemum petals. The hub resembles a many-petaled chrysanthemum flower, indicating that this chakra is meant to be used in conjunction with the Diamond Mandala. Chakras with hubs shaped like lotus petals are used in ceremonies involving the Womb Mandala.　MM

1. *Daizōkyō* 1924–34, vol. 1, no. 151.
2. Komatsu, ed. 1977b, pp. 64–65.

18.
Temple Roof Tile

Kamakura period (1185–1333),
second half of the thirteenth
century
Earthenware, diam. 6¼ in.
(15.9 cm)

In 588, fifty years after Buddhism was first introduced to Japan from Korea, the aristocratic Soga family commissioned the building of Japan's first Chinese-style Buddhist temple in Asuka, southwest of Nara. The new architectural technology required for the temple came from the kingdom of Paekche (Korea) with the immigration of artisans including ceramic tile makers.[1]

Decorated circular tiles like this one were used to ornament temple eaves. Until the eleventh century most such roof tiles were decorated exclusively with lotuses, with a mold used to impress lotuses of ten or eleven petals, but the tiles became more elaborate and sculptural in time.[2] Toward the end of the Heian period the designs began to conform to indigenous Japanese sensibilities, with varied decorative motifs that included scrolling floral designs, pagodas, Buddhist figures, three commas in a circular whirling

arrangement (*tomoe-mon*), Buddhist implements, and Sanskrit characters.

In the present tile the Sanskrit letter *Hrih*, which stands for Amida Buddha, is surrounded by a lotus with eight double petals that is likewise encircled by a pearl border. Tiles with Sanskrit letters are rare, though another example with *Hrih* has been excavated from Ōjōin, a temple site in Osaka dated to the first half of the thirteenth century. The present tile is more elaborate,[3] which suggests a later date, perhaps the second half of the thirteenth century. It has a modern ink inscription—"excavated in 1939 from the north side of the valley of Tokujuji"—an otherwise unknown location.   M W

1. Inagaki Susumu 1971.
2. Cunningham et al. 1998, pp. 36–37, 39.
3. Yamazaki 2000, p. 272.

19.
Womb World Mandala

Kamakura period (1185–1333),
thirteenth century
Hanging scroll, gold and color
on indigo-dyed silk, 35½ × 31⅛ in.
(90.3 × 79 cm)
Literature: Rosenfield and ten
Grotenhuis 1979, no. 14; Sudō
1982, figs. 13–16; Morse and
Morse 1996, no. 37; ten
Grotenhuis 1999, pls. 10–12;
London Gallery, Tokyo 2000,
no. 99.

This deeply spiritual painting of the Womb World
mandala, a rare example of painting in gold on
indigo-dyed paper, is extremely important as a manifestation of distinctive Buddhist iconography.[1] The
liberal use of gold to illuminate Buddha's world,
in combination with the dark indigo background,
amplifies the majestic nature of that world.

The mandala,[2] a schematic vision of the cosmos,
represents the elaborate and profound Buddhist
iconography that developed with the rise of Esoteric
Buddhism known in Japanese as *Mikkyō* (secret
teachings).[3] As Elizabeth ten Grotenhuis points
out, although painted mandalas are presented as
"two-dimensional configurations like architectural
ground plans seen from an aerial perspective, they
are meant to be envisioned as three-dimensional
constructions." They are, after all, designed "for

mental journeys, for interior pilgrimages. In the case
of the Esoteric mandalas, pilgrims leave behind their
ordinary structures and journey into circular and
square cosmic realms. The outer halls or courts of
these Esoteric mandalas often house figures and
portals that bridge the everyday world of humans
and the sacred world of deities. In the Womb World
mandala gates at all four directions offer access to
the sacred world."[4]

In early Esoteric Buddhism the fundamental object
of worship was a new deity, the cosmic Buddha
Mahavairochana (J: Dainichi Nyorai). Originating in
India, Esoteric Buddhism made its way to Japan by
way of China. It was introduced to eighth-century
China by two Indian monks: Shubhakarasimha
(J: Zenmui, 637–735) and Vajrabodhi (J: Kongōchi,
671–741).[5] Shubhakarasimha reached China by land

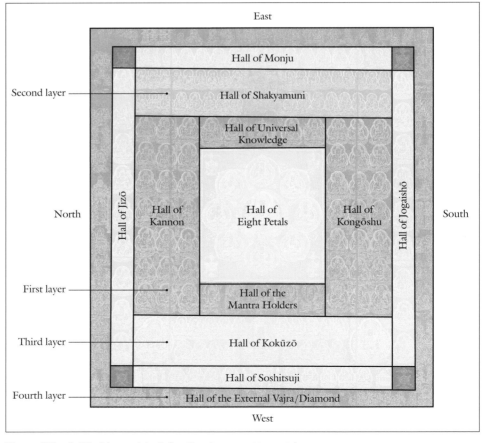

Fig. 15. Womb World mandala (after Snodgrass 1988, p. 185)

across Central Asia, while Vajrabodhi sailed to China through the seas of Southeast Asia. Both monks were welcomed by the Tang court.

Two monks were also instrumental in introducing Esoteric Buddhism to Japan. One was Saichō (posthumous title Dengyō Daishi, 767–822), who studied in China in 804–5 at the monastery of Tientai (J: Tendai). He concentrated on the Lotus Sutra and returned to Japan to institute the teachings of the Tendai sect, which integrate Esoteric Buddhism into the framework of the Lotus Sutra.[6] Saichō established the headquarters of the Tendai sect on Mount Hiei, located northeast of Kyoto and west of Lake Biwa. His great disciples Ennin (794–864) and Enchin (814–891) amplified Tendai Esoteric teachings and obtained significant patronage from the imperial court and powerful aristocrats.

The second Esoteric sect to gain significant prestige in Japan was instituted by the monk Kūkai (posthumous title Kōbō Daishi, 774–835), who, starting in 804, studied Esoteric Buddhism with Huiguo (J: Keika, 746–805), the seventh patriarch of the Shingon (True Word) sect in Tang China. Kūkai was officially designated by his master as the eighth patriarch and carried Shingon teachings and teaching materials, including mandala paintings, back to Japan in 806. The focus of Shingon worship was the Mahavairochana Sutra and the Vajrashekhara Sutra. The bases for Kūkai's activities were the monastery compound on Mount Koya, south of the ancient capital of Nara, and Kyōōgokokuji, also known as Tōji (Eastern Temple), in the Heian capital, present-day Kyoto.

The Mahavairochana, or Great Sun, Sutra[7] and the Vajrasekhara, or Diamond, Sutra[8] place Mahavairochana Buddha at the center of the Buddhist universe. The Great Sun Sutra explains the Three Mysteries (J: *sanmitsu*)—Speech, Body, and Mind. Kūkai emphasized the mystical and ritualistic practices of the Three Mysteries that lead one to "become a buddha in this body" (J: *sokushin jōbutsu*).[9] "Speech" refers to the recitation of various mantras (true words) and dharanis (mystic syllables). "Body" refers to the hand positions, or mudras, characteristic of the deities evoked. "Mind"

refers to meditation through focusing on mandalas in order to foster spiritual union with a particular deity.

The mandala, with its schematic representation of the Buddhist pantheon in the form of a painting or three-dimensional sculpture, is central to monks' initiation rites (*kanjō*). The initiate tosses a flower onto the mandala, and the deity the flower lands on becomes the monk's personal deity. During the practice of meditation, the monk visualizes the deity and unites his speech, body, and mind with the deity's. Legend has it that when Kūkai performed his initiation ceremony under the guidance of his master Huiguo, his flower landed on Mahavairochana Buddha at the very center of the mandala.

A set of one Womb World (J: Taizōkai; S: Garbhadhatu) and one Diamond World (J: Kongōkai; S: Vajradhatu) mandala was the most basic expression of the philosophical basis of Esoteric Buddhism.[10] The two mandalas contain in their realms different but complementary aspects of existence: reason and compassion, masculine and feminine, spiritual and material, the absolute and the relative, and so on. Though two "worlds," the mandalas represent aspects of a single, encompassing truth.[11] The pair of mandalas flanks the main ritual hall during public ceremonies, with the Diamond World mandala on the west side (left) and the Womb World mandala on the east side (right). The practitioner sits facing the altar, which is on the north side. The Diamond World mandala that originally accompanied the present Womb World mandala is missing.[12]

An early extant pair of mandalas of the Womb and Diamond Worlds, based upon the mandalas Kūkai brought back from China, is owned by Tōji and is datable between 859 and 880. Since the pairing was most likely formulated by Huiguo, the Shingon master, it became standard.[13] The present mandala displays some variations from the standard Womb World mandala (discussed below), but it does not differ in its fundamental structure. It comprises twelve halls or courts in a concentric formation (fig. 15). The central hall, the primary and essential sanctuary, is the Hall of Eight Petals (J: *chūdai hachiyōin*). In the center of the lotus flower sits the cosmic Buddha, Mahavairochana, who, through his great compassion, guides sentient beings to the attainment of buddhahood.[14] He holds a wheel in his open hands. This gesture—"turning the wheel of Buddhist law"—expresses the determination of the historical Buddha, Shakyamuni, to disseminate his buddhahood.

Surrounding the cosmic Buddha are the buddhas of the four directions and the four great bodhisattvas, who sit on eight lotus petals. The five buddhas represent knowledge and the five-stage progression toward attainment of perfect buddhahood. In a standard mandala, at the top (east) the Jewel Pennant (S: Ratnaketu; J: Hōdō) Buddha designates the quickening of mind, the first step in attaining buddhahood. To the right (south) the Opening Flower King (S: Samkusumitaraja; J: Kaifukeō) Buddha stands for the accumulation of practices to attain buddhahood. To the bottom (west), the Immeasurable Life (S: Amitayus; J: Muryōju) Buddha signifies the awakening of buddhahood (bodai). To the left (north) the Thunderous Sound of the Celestial Drum (S: Divyadundubhimeghanirghosha; J: Tenkuraion) Buddha stands for the final buddhahood, nirvana.

The present mandala shows an uncommon arrangement of two buddhas in the central hall. Hōdō, usually seated in the top petal, is here seen in the left petal, and the buddha Tenkuraion, usually seated in the left petal, is seen here in the top petal. As will be discussed below, other examples of this exceptional arrangement have been found in temples associated with the Tendai sect.[15]

Also in the central court are the four great bodhisattvas: Fugen (S: Samantabhadra) at the southeast (upper right), Monju (S: Manjushri) to the southwest (lower right), Kannon (S: Avalokiteshvara) to the northwest (lower left), and Miroku (S: Maitreya) to the northeast (upper left). The bodhisattvas represent preliminary stages in the attainment of buddhahood. Fugen opens the gate of the quickening mind, Monju opens the gate of practice, Kannon opens the gate of awakening, and Miroku opens the gate of nirvana.[16]

Above the central hall is the Hall of Universal Knowledge (henchiin), standing for the ability to differentiate the real from the illusory. At its center is a flaming triangle called the Universal Knowledge Seal (issai henchiin), flanked on either side by two deities.[17]

The section below the central hall, known as the Hall of the Mantra Holders (jimyōin), houses five deities. The bodhisattva of Perfect Wisdom (S: Hannyaharramitta; J: Hannya Butsumo) sits at the center. At each side are two mantra kings, or kings of wisdom,[18] who represent the subjugation of evil by the cosmic Buddha.

The Hall of Kannon or the Lotus Hall, to the left of the central hall, represents great compassion. Twenty-one deities with attendants are shown, including Kannon[19] who is the central figure in the hall's inner row.

The Hall of Kongōshu, to the right of the central hall, represents great wisdom, complementing the compassion embodied in the opposite hall. This hall too has twenty-one deities with attendants, here including Bodhisattva Diamond Being (J: Kongōshū)[20] as the central figure in the hall's innermost row. The pairing of the halls of Kannon and Kongōshu suggests the uniting of Buddha's compassion and wisdom.

The five halls just described, the first layer or center of the mandala, represent buddhahood in the world of Mahavairochana. The second layer, which lies above the first, is the Hall of Shakyamuni, an independent sphere which occupies an intermediate place between buddhahood (first layer) and the practices that lead one to buddhahood (third layer of outer halls). Reflecting the iconography pertaining to the life of the historical Buddha, thirty-nine figures reside in two registers of the Hall of Shakyamuni. As the central icon Shakyamuni Buddha sits within an archway attended by four deities. The remaining thirty-four deities include eight that personify Shakyamuni's forms of knowledge and virtue, Shakyamuni's disciples, and solitary awakened buddhas.

In the remaining halls in the mandala's third layer the practices that lead the adept to enlightenment are exemplified by specific bodhisattvas. The Hall of Monju at the top (east), above the

Hall of Shakyamuni, embodies wisdom. Monju sits inside an arch with four attendants, ten deities (five on each side), and a five-figure group at each end.[21] The bodhisattva is often represented as a youth whose five knots of hair symbolize his great knowledge. The lotus in his left hand stands for magnificent knowledge and the vajra on the lotus for his invincible power over earthly passions. The gesture of the right hand with palm outward indicates his offering of his wisdom for the salvation of sentient beings.[22]

Jogaishō (S: Sarva Nivarana Vishkambhi) presides with eight attendant deities at the center of the long vertical Hall of Jogaishō, located at the right (south). The bodhisattva, who embodies great knowledge for removing obstacles to the attainment of enlightenment, relays the knowledge from the Hall of Monju and vows to actualize the virtues of the deities who preside in the Hall of Kongōshu.

The Hall of Jizō, complementing the Hall of Jogaishō, is located to the left (north). It has a similar arrangement, with the nine deities in the long vertical hall absorbing the great compassion extended from the inner hall of Kannon to the right. At the center presides Jizō (S: Kshitigarbha), embodying the virtues of the earth that allow the removal of obstacles in the Hall of Jogaishō.

The Hall of Kokūzō (Void Storehouse), located below (west), represents the results of the bodhisattva practices initiated by the Monju, Jogaishō, and Jizō halls. The hall consists of three groups, each centered on a bodhisattva: Kokūzō (S: Akashagarbha [void storehouse]) at the center; Senju-sengen Kannon (S: Sahasrabhujarya Avalokiteshvara [Avalokiteshvara of a thousand hands and a thousand eyes]) at the left (north); and Ippyaku Hachi Kongōzōō (S: Ashtottarashatabhuja-vajragarbharaja [108–armed diamond storehouse king]) at the right (south).

In the upper row attending Kokūzō are the ten Bodhisattvas of Perfect Wisdom (S: Paramita; J: Jūharamitsu). They represent aspects of the bodhisattva of Perfect Wisdom, Hannya, who is the central figure in the Hall of the Mantra Holders, directly above, and who extends his influence directly to the Kokūzō Hall below through these

ten representatives. Kokūzō holds a sword in his right hand, symbolizing the embodiment of Hannya's keen wisdom, and in his left hand a lotus with a jewel, which represents the awakening to enlightenment of the Hall of Jogaishō.

Senju-sengen Kannon represents the fulfillment of the virtues contained in the mandala's Lotus section (on the left), and Ippyaku Hachi Kōngōzōō represents the attainment of the virtues of the mandala's Diamond section (on the right). Finally, at the center, Kokūzō represents the achievement of the virtues of the Buddha section at the center.

The lower row of the Kokūzō Hall usually has nine attendant figures (five on the right and four on the left), who are associated both with Kokūzō and with Ippyaku Hachi Kongōzōō.[23] The present mandala shows only eight. The missing deity is Mandara Bosatsu (S: Mahachakra Bodhisattva), who appears as the far rightmost figure in the Hall of Soshitsuji below, which otherwise has eight bodhisattvas who represent the complete attainment of Kokūzō's virtues. Moreover, the figures of Senju-sengen Kannon and Ippyaku Hachi Kongozōō, at the north and south ends of the Hall of Kokūzō, are usually depicted occupying both this hall and the Hall of Soshitsuji below it. In this mandala, however, there is a clear demarcation between the two halls so that the mandala's upper and lower halves are symmetrical.

The fourth and outermost layer of the mandala is the Hall of the External Vajra/Diamond (*saigein* or *gekongōbu*). About two hundred figures reside in this section, including guardian kings, the twelve devas, and the sun, the moon, planets, and constellations. The section also includes sentient beings whose souls have been reborn in the six realms of existence, including those reborn in hell. The figures in the outermost layer protect the inner sacred world and, by receiving Mahavairochana's virtue, which radiates from the mandala's center, attain virtue as pure as that of Mahavairochana.

Opposite: Fig. 16. Detail of Womb World mandala

Mention was made above concerning the unusual arrangement in the Hall of Eight Petals of the buddhas Hōdō and Tenkuraion. In the "standard" Womb World mandala, these deities reside in the east and north, respectively. Their position in the present mandala, however, is reversed and is the same as that found in mandalas of temples of the Tendai sect, e.g., those housed at Taisanji in Hyōgo prefecture, Shitennōji in Osaka, and Saimyōji and Ashiura Kannonji in Shiga prefecture, located at the foot of Mount Hiei.[24] The situation was, from an iconographic point of view, very fluid in the early stages of Esoteric Buddhism, particularly in the eighth–tenth centuries. By the beginning of the tenth century, differences in iconography in Shingon and Tendai Womb World mandalas already existed, as noted in the *Shosetsu Fudōki* (Iconographical Discrepancies in Various Womb World Mandalas) written by the Shingon monk Shinjaku (886–927).[25]

The difficulty in attributing an origin for the "nonstandard" arrangement in this mandala derives from the various Chinese models on which the Japanese might have drawn, many of which ultimately have their source in India. These include the *Taizō zuzō* (Iconographic Illustration of the Womb World), a drawing brought by the Tendai monk Enchin from China in the mid-ninth century that reflects the teachings of Shubhakarasimha, one of the Indian monks who introduced Esoteric Buddhism to China. This drawing shows the same arrangement of the two buddhas as in the present mandala.[26] Second, there are the carved wooden mandalas found at Mount Koya, which were probably imported from Tang China, perhaps as early as the eighth century.[27] Third, the *Soki Zōhen*, Enchin's miscellaneous writings,[28] attributes the iconography of the position of the two buddhas to a monk named Don-tai-tei. (This is the Japanese reading; the name seems to be Indian, beginning with Dharma).[29] Enchin suggests that the positions of the four buddhas in the Hall of Eight Petals were changed so that they were identical with their positions in the Diamond World mandala, with Ashuku (equivalent to Tenkuraion) in

the east and Fukujōju (equivalent to Hōdō) in the north. Finally, an example with a similar arrangement of the buddhas survives in one of the Yulin caves in China.[30] In this example, a different figure, the Immeasurable Life Buddha in the west, is at the top, and his counterpart in the east at the bottom seems to be Tenkuraion.

Adding further complexity to the discrepancy between "standard" and "nonstandard" mandalas is the offering table that appears below Kokuzō in the Hall of Kokuzō, a feature which is typical of "Tendai" mandalas. A few examples of standard mandalas, however, also include offering tables.[31]

1. Red was applied for the border of the central square, which symbolizes a boundary path defining the sacred center. In polychrome paintings of Womb World mandalas, the boundary path usually appears in five colors instead of only red.

2. The Sanskrit word *mandala*, which literally meant "circle, group, or collection," referred in Esoteric Buddhism to the combination of *manda* (essence) and *la* (possession or attainment) and denoted the state of inner enlightenment. The Chinese interpretation of mandala (translated as *wantuolo*; Japanese reading, *mandara*) is "an assembly of the divine" or "the place of an assembly of the divine" in contrast with the Indian meaning.

3. Buddhism in Japan is broadly divided into two types: Exoteric or revealed, and Esoteric or secret. While "Exoteric" teachings can be freely transmitted and understood by all, "Esoteric" teachings can only be verbally and secretly transmitted from master to disciple. Differences between the Exoteric and Esoteric types are summarized in Matsunaga and Matsunaga 1974–76, vol. 1, pp. 182–83.

4. Ten Grotenhuis 1999, pp. 78–80.

5. Shubhakarasimha had many disciples, including his great disciple Yixing (683–727), but had no established lineage of transmission. Vajrabodhi's teaching, however, was the basis of transmission of the Esoteric sect, the lineage of which was as follows: 1. Mahavairochana (J: Dainichi Nyorai), 2. Vajrasattva (Kongōsatta), 3. Nagarjuna (Ryūmō or Ryūju), 4. Nagabodhi (Ryūchi), 5. Vajrabodhi (Kongōchi), 6. Amoghavajra (Fukūkongō), 7. Huiguo (Keika) and 8. Kūkai.

6. Stone 1999, pp. 20–21.

7. This sutra is known as *Mahavairochana Sutra* in Sanskrit, and *Dainichikyō* in Japanese, shortened from *Daibirushana Jōbutsu jinben kajikyō*. It was translated into Chinese by Shubhakarasimha in 724. *Daizōkyō* 1924–34, vol. 17, no. 848.

8. This sutra is known as *Sarva-tathagata Tattva Samgraha Sutra* in Sanskrit, and *Kongōchōkyō* in Japanese, from *Kongochō issai nyorai shinjitsu shōdaijō genshō daikyōōkyō*. It was translated into Chinese by Amoghavajra, the Indian monk. *Daizōkyō* 1924–34, vol. 8, no. 865.

9. Ten Grotenhuis has pointed out, "mandalas are embodiments of the sacred, instruments of power that help practitioners] realize their essential buddha natures, each to become, as Kūkai said, a buddha in the very body." (Ten Grotenhuis 1999, p. 77).

10. Ten Grotenhuis 1999 includes stimulating discussions, especially of the formation in China of the Womb and Diamond World mandalas as a pair and also of the incorporation of indigenous cosmic structures.

11. For another interpretation, see ten Grotenhuis 1999, p. 37: "Broadly speaking, the Diamond World mandala represents reality in the buddha realm, the world of the unconditioned, the real, the universal, and the absolute. The Womb World mandala represents reality as it is revealed in the world of the conditioned, the individual, the particular, and the relative. Each mandala is fully meaningful, however, only when paired with the other."

12. This mandala probably belonged to one of two types. The first type features a composition typical of Diamond World mandalas of the Shingon sect, with nine assemblies in a three-by-three grid, such as the mandala owned by Shitennōji in Osaka. (Sawa and Hamada 1983, pl. 17. See also ten Grotenhuis 1999, p. 48.) The other type, which depicts only the central square from that grid (Perfected-Body Assembly, Jōjin-e), is known as the Diamond World mandala with Eighty-one Deities (Kongōkai hachijūisson mandara). It is exemplified by mandalas at the Nezu Institute of Fine Arts in Tokyo and Taisanji in Hyōgo prefecture. (Sawa and Hamada 1983, pls. 18 and 20. See also ten Grotenhuis 1999, p. 94.) Originally owned by Kongōrinji, a Tendai temple near Lake Biwa, the Nezu mandala has an inscription on the back relating that the founder of the Ogawa branch of the Tendai Esoteric sect, Chūkai (b. 1160), copied it from a Chinese model brought to Japan by the Tendai monk Ennin, who introduced the Diamond World Mandala with Eighty-one Deities from China in 847. See Morse and Morse 1996, p. 96.

13. See ten Grotenhuis 1999, pls. 6–8.

14. Yoritomi 1991, pp. 121–22. For other interpretations, see Ishida H. 1979, Snodgrass 1988, and ten Grotenhuis 1999.

15. The author plans an article on the irregular arrangement of the two buddhas in the Womb World mandalas and its relation to the Tendai sect.

16. Snodgrass 1988, pp. 219–20.

17. Snodgrass 1988, pp. 251–68.

18. Snodgrass 1988, pp. 269–83.

19. Another name of Kannon is Kanjizai, literally "Freely Contemplating" bodhisattva. The Sanskrit name is Avalokiteshvara.

20. Also called Kongōsatta in Japanese, and Vajrasattva in Sanskrit.

21. For the names of each deity, see Snodgrass 1988, pp. 378–91.

22. See Ishida H. 1979, p. 71.

23. Snodgrass 1988, pp. 417–44.

24. Sasaki 1985b and Sasaki 1985a. See also Matsuhara 1990; Matsuhara 1993; Matsuhara 1999.

25. The full name of *Shosetsu fudōki* is *Daihi taizō futsū daimandara chū shoson shūji hyōshi gyōsō shōi shosetsu fudōki. Daizōkyō* 1924–34, *zuzō* section vol. 1, pp. 17–134.

26. Even though only the twelfth-century copy of the *Taizō zuzō* is extant, the iconographical content reflects the original brought by Enchin.

27. Izutsu 1992.

28. *Soki Zōhen* were compilations of Enchin's writings that were selected by the Tendai monks Gyōjun (1265–1333) and Saichin (1143–1219). See Onjōji, ed. 1978, vol. 3, pp. 1122–23 and Matsuhara 1999.

29. The author plans further study of this document.

30. Dunhuang Academy 1990, pl. 154.

31. A Womb World mandala with offering table as a standard type is housed at the Brooklyn Museum of Art. See Poster 1989, pls. 4 and 5.

20.
One Hundred Images of Amida Buddha

Late Heian period (ca. 900–1185), eleventh–twelfth century
Woodblock print, ink on paper, 18 × 14⅛ in. (45.5 × 35.6 cm)
Ex coll.: Jōruriji, Kyoto

Buddhist printmaking spread from India through China and Korea to Japan.[1] The existence of printed or stamped images (*shūbutsu* or *inbutsu*) of Buddhist icons is recorded in documents preserved in the eighth-century Shōshōin imperial repository in Nara.[2] The practice of making a great number of images, by which the believer accumulated great merit and thus affected his future lives, was based on the Buddhist doctrine of cause and effect (S: *karma*). Stamping or printing images every day (nikka kuyō) was a particularly common practice.[3] Small sheets stamped with Buddhist deities, used to solicit contributions to temples, generally displayed small single images with inscriptions. In contrast, large printed images of Buddhist deities, often hand colored, began to be made as objects of worship in the Nanbokuchō and Muromachi periods (1333–1573).[4]

Printed images were also commonly placed inside the hollow wooden Buddhist statues, often representing the same icon as the sculpture and linking the donor of the printed image and the deity. The present sheet with one hundred images of Amida, the central deity of Pure Land Buddhism, is one of the earliest surviving Buddhist prints.[5] It was discovered with many similar sheets inside the central Amida sculpture in the Main Hall at the Jōruriji temple. This statue is flanked by eight slightly smaller sculptures of Amida. There is a question concerning the exact dating of the central sculpture—and the present sheet—and the eight flanking sculptures.[6] The original hall for the Amida Buddha, built in 1047, was destroyed for unknown reasons and rebuilt in 1107. Scholars tend to agree that the central statue of Amida and the eight flanking sculptures differ stylistically and that the central image should be dated earlier than the others, which could have been made in 1107.[7]

Some hints as to dating are suggested by the two types of prints found inside the central statue. One type, which includes the present page, has a hundred printed Amidas per sheet: a single woodblock of ten rows of ten images, each about 1⅛ inches in height. The block was a little too large for the paper it was printed on, and a narrow vertical strip was added to each side of the paper to accommodate the block. The other type, on sheets that are dated to 1105, has seventy-two images (each 1⅞ inches in height): a woodblock carved with four rows of three Amidas was stamped six times on a sheet.[8] On both types the figures are seated and exhibit the hand gesture for meditation, but the lotus pedestal for the sheet of one hundred Amidas is a single-layered lotus, while the lotus pedestal for the sheet of seventy-two is double-layered. The hundred images also appear to be simpler and more elegant than the seventy-two, which suggests to most scholars an earlier date for these sheets, the second half of the eleventh century, when the central Amida statue was made. The sheets of seventy-two Amidas were then added later, when the hall was rebuilt in 1107.[9]   MW

1. Publications in English on Buddhist printmaking include Baskett 1980 and Ichida, M., et al. 1964, pl. 39.
2. Kikutake 1984, p. 18; Kikutake et al. 1984, pp. 7–8 (text vol.).
3. Kikutake 1984, pp. 26–27.
4. Among the popular subjects in collections of these hand-colored prints are Fudō Myōō and his two attendants, the Taima mandalas, the Twelve Devas, and pairs of the Womb World and Diamond World mandalas.
5. Pages from the same group of one hundred Amidas are found in other Western collections. See, for example, Baskett 1980, no. 2; Rosenfield and Shimada 1970–71, no. 28.
6. Tanaka Yoshichika 1976–78.
7. Nishikawa et al. 1984, pp. 154–55; Kurata 1973, pp. 73–74.
8. See Baskett 1980, nos. 3, 4.
9. See Machida City Museum of Graphic Arts 1994, pp. 100–101.

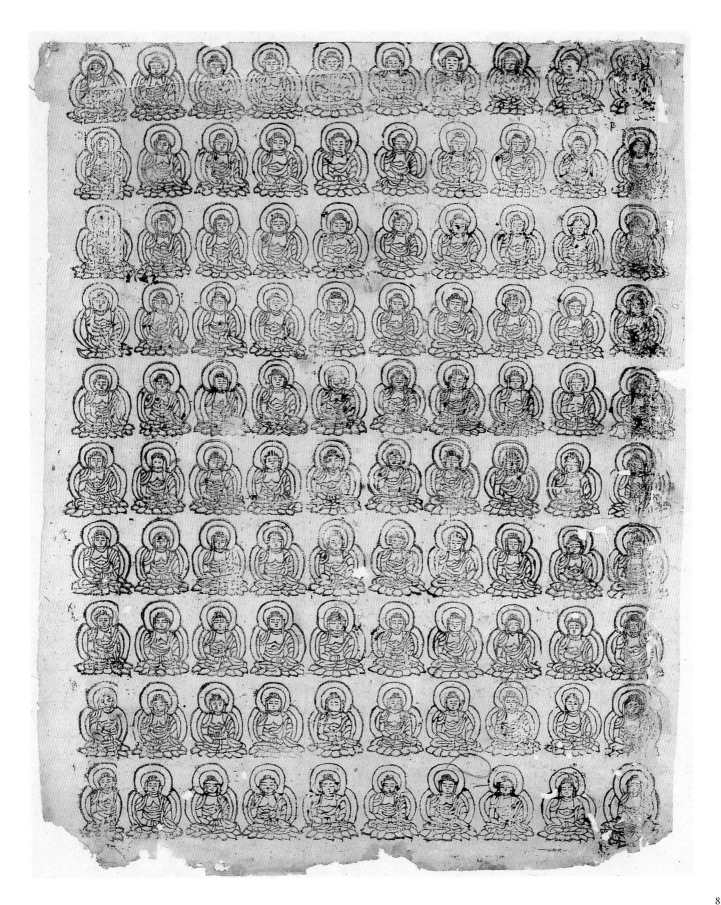

21.
One Hundred Images of Fudō Myōō

Nanbokuchō (1336–1392)–
Muromachi (1392–1573) period,
fourteenth–fifteenth century
Woodblock print, ink on paper,
18¾ × 12¼ in. (47.3 × 30.8 cm)
Ex coll.: Kyōōgokokuji (Tōji),
Kyoto

This print was recently discovered with hundreds of other sheets of Fudō images inside a seated statue of Fudō Myōō in Kyōōgokokuji, a temple also known as Tōji, the center of Shingon Esoteric Buddhism, founded by the monk Kūkai in the ninth century.[1] A woodblock carved with ten images (each 1¾ × 1⅛ in.) in a row was stamped ten times from top to bottom to create the sheet of one hundred Fudō figures. The stamping slants slightly upward toward the right. This group of prints, including this example, can be dated from around the fourteenth to the fifteenth century.[2]

Fudō Myōō, originally a Hindu god, Acala, who was adopted into the Buddhist pantheon, became the protector of the Buddhist law and in Esoteric Buddhism eventually became the supreme guardian king, a manifestation of Dainichi Nyorai (S: Mahavairochana). Known as the Immovable One, Fudō is seated on a cubic rock formation holding a sword in his right hand and a rope in his left, symbols of his power to repel evil, which is also suggested by his ferocious appearance. The tight arrangement of one hundred images in a vertical and horizontal grid creates an energetic field that probably enforced the practitioner's belief in Fudō Myōō's power to ward off evil.   M W

1. For other examples of sheets with this image see Rosenfield and Shimada 1970–71, no. 45; Baskett 1980, no. 6.
2. Mitsui 1986, pp. 38–40.

22.
Amulet with Buddhist Icons

Edo period (1615–1868)
Handscroll, woodblock print,
ink on paper, 3 × 420 in. (7.6 ×
1067 cm)
Literature: Perkins et al.
2000–2001, fig. 39

Such narrow but extremely long handscrolls, veritable encyclopedias of Buddhist iconography, received the name *kokonoe no mamori* (amulet in nine layers) during the Edo period, because they begin with a red seal in the shape of a cauldron containing characters that can be read *kokonoe no mamori*.[1] All the scrolls start with an image of Ususama Myōō (S: Ucchushma), the king who has the power to burn away impurity and evil, and is followed by powerful magical syllables (J: *shingon*, S: *mantra*), various "seed" mandalas in Sanskrit, and sutras in Chinese. Next, Buddhist deities, including Esoteric icons, are depicted along the length of the handscroll: buddhas, bodhisattvas, the four guardian kings, the five great kings of light, Yakushi Buddha with sixteen protectors, and a thousand-armed Kannon (S: Sahasrabhuja) with twenty-eight attendants.[2] Many cosmological deities are included: the nine luminaries and Taizanfusei (related to the Big Dipper).[3] Such popularized Esoteric icons as Shōten (S: Nandikeshvara), Dakiniten (S: Dakini), Idaten (S: Skanda), Gozu Tenno, and Tawara Daikokuten (S: Mahakala) are also shown. The last section of the scroll contains a series of dharani sutras in Sanskrit, magical formulas of knowledge that are composed of syllables with symbolic content.

Two types of *kokonoe no mamori* became popular in the Edo period as talismans for journeys and pilgrimages and as a part of the wedding trousseau.[4] One type has at the end of the scroll a portrait of Kūkai, the founder of Shingon Esoteric Buddhism, while the other portrays Saichō, the founder of Tendai Esoteric Buddhism. The present scroll belongs to the latter type and also includes a number of popular icons, such as Uhō Dōji and Shōmen (Seimen) Kongō, gods that protected the faithful from calamities.

The section of the scroll illustrated here includes, from right to left, five deities whose intercession serves to protect believers: Daizuigu Bosatsu

(S: Mahapratisara), Daishōten (S: Nandikeshvara), Marishiten (S: Marici), Kishibojin (S: Hariti), and Gozu Tennō. Many-armed Daizuigu Bosatsu, an Esoteric icon, protects the devout from calamities with the power of magic syllables (dharani), while Daishōten, or Kankiten, originally a Hindu icon whose popular form is that of an elephant-headed couple embracing, symbolizes the power of ecstasy to repel evil. Marishiten, with three faces and eight arms, symbolizes the illumination of the sun and moon. Kishibojin, or Kariteibo, was originally a female demon who devoured infants, but redeemed from her sin after her own child was kidnapped, she became a Buddhist deity who protects Buddha's law. Finally, Gozu Tennō, originally a protector of Gion Shōja (Jetavana monastery in Shravasti in India), became the popular deity of Gion Shrine in Kyoto, protecting the faithful from illness.   MW

1. Two pre-Edo examples of this type of amulet scroll without the seal, both dated 1285, have been discovered: one was inside the Kamakura-period statue of Monju Bosatsu (S: Manjushri Bodhisattva) from Saidaiji in Nara, and the other was inside the statue of Daimyō (Daimei) Kokushi, also known as Mukan Shinmon (1212–1291), the third abbot of Tōfukuji in Kyoto. Machida City Museum of Graphic Arts 1994, pp. 38–39; Uchida 2000, pp. 1–19; Brinker and Kanazawa 1996, pp. 95–97; Mitsui 1986, pl. 139.
2. Another handscroll, datable to the sixteenth century, was found in a statue of Miroku Bosatsu at Shōmyōji in Kanagawa. It depicts more icons than the handscrolls dated 1285. See Ishida, M., et al. 1964, pl. 157; Uchida, M., et al. 2000, pp. 12–13.
3. Uchida 2000, p. 6.
4. A handscroll with encyclopedic iconographies, datable to the Genna era (1615–24), was published by Shūson, a monk in Jōmyōji, Ise province; Mitsui 1986, pl. 140.

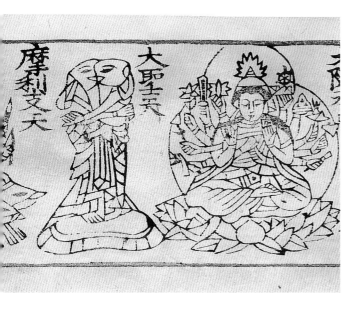

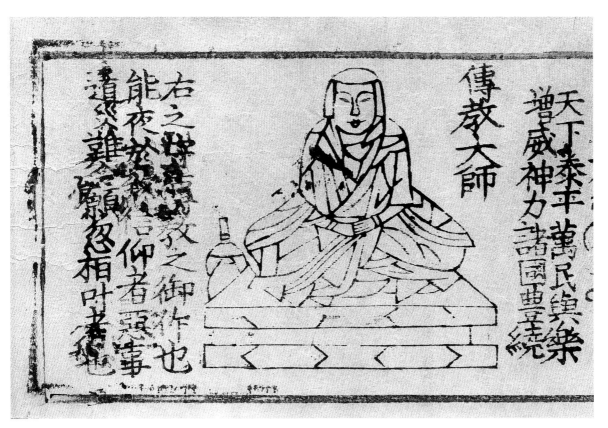

Fig. 17. Detail of cat. no. 22

23.
Kasuga Shrine Mandala

Kamakura period (1185–1333),
ca. 1300
Hanging scroll, ink, color, and
gold on silk, 31 × 11 in. (78.7 ×
27.9 cm)
Literature: Leidy and Thurman
1997–98, no. 44; ten Grotenhuis
1999, pls. 13–17; London
Gallery, Tokyo 2000, no. 111

Here a large luminous disk enclosing five Buddhist deities casts a serene light over the site of the Kasuga Shinto Shrine in Nara. One of the most ancient and beloved Shinto structures in Japan, the Kasuga Shrine complex is depicted in a half-idealized, half-realistic manner at the foot of Mount Mikasa (center) and Mount Kasuga (left) with the Kasuga mountain range in the background. Pines and cypresses interspersed with blossoming cherry and plum trees, a group of deer—sacred intermediaries between the Kasuga gods and humans—crimson torii gates, paths, and hillocks washed with gold mist are partly hidden behind dark clouds, once painted a brilliant green.

The Kasuga area of Nara, extolled since ancient times for its natural beauty, is the site of two of the most important religious institutions built by order of the aristocratic Fujiwara clan: the Buddhist temple of Kōfukuji, constructed around 720, and the Kasuga Shrine, founded in 768. The Kasuga Shrine was dedicated to the clan's guardian deity, Ame no

Koyane no mikoto (God of Heavenly Roof; enshrined in the third shrine building), and his consort Himegami (Princess; in the fourth shrine). Two additional gods, Futsunushi no mikoto (God of Sword) and Takemikazuchi no mikoto (God of Relentless Thunder), protectors of eastern Japan, were later invoked to inhabit the first and second shrines, respectively. In 1135 a new structure was constructed to house the Wakamiya (Young Prince), the purported son of Ame no Koyane. Like the approximately one hundred similar paintings, the present hanging scroll depicts four structures within the main precinct of the Kasuga Shrine at the upper left and the Wakamiya at the upper right.

Kasuga Shrine mandalas follow a basic iconographic canon, firmly established by the close of the thirteenth century. A standard Kasuga mandala includes the first torii gate at the bottom of the composition; two pagodas, placed prominently in the lower left, represent edifices destroyed by fire in the fifteenth century and never reconstructed.

Fig. 18. Detail of cat. no. 23

Gold-colored paths, which lead to the innermost sanctuary, and surrounding vegetation are also arranged according to a set scheme. These paintings serve a twofold purpose: they adhere to a codified paradigm for landscape depiction while retaining a certain degree of verisimilitude.

Although known as mandalas, Shinto shrine paintings differ from the rigidly schematized mandalas of Esoteric Buddhism (see cat. no. 19). Kasuga Shrine mandalas represent a bird's-eye view of the sacred precinct, allowing more space for the natural environment than for the actual shrine structures. While the latter are not delineated in a strictly realistic manner, with every architectural detail reproduced, their general appearance corresponds to that of the actual buildings as they have existed since 1179. The nucleus of the compound faces south (to the right), while the Wakamiya in its own precinct faces west. Not surprisingly, mandalas often functioned as general guides to architects during the periodic reconstruction of shrine buildings.

A unique feature of this particular Kasuga mandala painting is the large luminous disk that hovers above the entire area, as if protecting the precinct below. Outlined in thin cut-gold leaf (*kirikane*) and filled with pale blue color over which gold pigment seems to have been applied, it supports five Buddhist deities, each in his own aureole. The five buddhas, regarded as the shrine's *honji* (original forms)—Buddhist equivalents of the Shinto gods— can be identified as Shaka (in the center) for the Shinto god at the first shrine, Yakushi (above Shaka) for the deity of the second shrine, Jizō (to the right) for the third shrine, and Monju (below) for the Wakamiya, with Jūichimen (to the left) for the fourth shrine. Two *hiten* (angel-like beings) fly toward the buddhas, one (on the right) holding a lotus throne, the other an unidentifiable object. The disk, reminiscent of the small golden moon that often graces Kasuga mandala paintings, can be equated with the lunar disk featured in the Diamond Mandala of Esoteric Buddhism.[1]

With its two pagodas, modeled after the pagodas of Buddhist temple compounds, the Kasuga Shrine gives the impression of having been absorbed within a Buddhist-like paradise, a reflection of the Fujiwara clan's increasing devotion to Pure Land Buddhism during the twelfth century. The Fujiwaras viewed the sacred mountains beyond the shrine and the Kasuga area as a Shinto paradise on earth, a parallel of the Pure Land of Amida Buddha.[2] Just as Buddhist Pure Land paintings displayed buddhas and bodhisattvas in their beautiful residences, Shinto mandalas depicted the earthly sites where native gods dwelled. At the same time the Fujiwara clan regarded Kasuga gods as potent protectors of nearby Kōfukuji and its Buddhist deities.

Kasuga Shrine mandalas testify to the popularity of *honji suijaku,* the syncretic concept which viewed Shinto gods as manifestations of Buddhist deities. The ideology of *honji suijaku* is indicative of the efforts made by both Buddhists and Shintoists to reconcile the two religions in order to ensure mutual survival and prosperity.

The earliest painting to hint at the beginnings of a Kasuga mandala format, a work depicting Mount Mikasa and the Nan'endō building of Kōfukuji, is mentioned in a record of 1181.[3] Only three years later, in 1184, a courtier's journal made note of a ritual involving Kasuga paintings, performed during the fifth month.[4] The worship of such paintings in aristocratic homes was apparently a substitute for actual visits to a site. An ostensibly realistic view of the shrine precinct, with vegetation, buildings, and sacred deer, was essential to this ritual. Paintings of this type were displayed in a special ceremony held at the shrine each year on the twenty-first day of the fifth month.

Attempts have been made recently to identify Kasuga mandalas as examples of a genre of secular painting known as *meisho-e* (pictures of famous places). The Kasuga area was known as a *meisho* (famous place) long before it became a sacred site,[5] it was represented in *meisho-e* as early as 905,[6] and the established rule was to depict it in the spring season. This traditional iconography underwent a major alteration during the late twelfth century, when faith in the Kasuga gods, in particular worship of the shrine's

sacred deer, became popular. Consequently paintings of the Kasuga area began to depict the site in autumn, an appropriate time for deer, together with spring season's cherry blossoms. The Kasuga mandala thus reflects the transformation of Shinto imagery by the ideology and pictorial traditions of Buddhism as well as the perpetuation of the time-honored traditions of secular painting, especially *meisho-e.*

Names of painters are seldom associated with Kasuga Shrine mandalas, though it is thought that the paintings were produced by artists employed at Buddhist workshops in Nara, especially those at Kōfukuji. Although these artists mainly created Buddhist icons for temples, they also made secular works such as pictorial histories of temples and illustrated biographies of famous monks. They may have also produced purely secular landscapes such as *meisho-e.*[7] Some of these *meisho-e* may have resembled the mandala seen here, with gentle landscapes whose low-lying hillocks are bathed in gold, flowering trees partly hidden by mist, and darkly silhouetted mountains in the distance.

This small elegant painting was most likely commissioned—as were most Kasuga Shrine mandalas—by an aristocrat from the capital city of Kyoto. Almost no secular landscape paintings of the Heian and Kamakura periods are extant, and Kasuga Shrine mandalas such as this serve as vivid reminders of the lost splendors of secular landscape imagery. The use of gold for the paths, hillocks, and mountains in Kasuga mandalas is thought to have begun in the fourteenth century,[8] with the present hanging scroll an early example of the practice.   MM

1. Ten Grotenhuis 1999, p. 154.
2. For a comparison between paintings of the Buddhist Pure Land and Shinto shrine mandalas, see Gyōtoku 1994, p. 244.
3. *Yuima-e narabini Tōji kanjōki* (Record of Rituals Dedicated to Yuima [S: Vimalakirti] and Ordination Rites Performed at Tōji). See Hirata 1994.
4. It is described in the *Gyokuyō,* a journal kept by the courtier Kujō Kanezane (1149–1207); see Kujō 1993. See also Kawamura 1981, pp. 92ff.
5. Chino 1991.
6. In the fifth year of the Engi era; Ienaga 1966.
7. Gyōtoku 1994.
8. Gyōtoku 1994, p. 243.

WRITINGS IN KANA SCRIPT; CORRESPONDENCE

24.
Kasuga Kaishi

Kamakura period (1185–1333),
ca. 1243
Section of a handscroll mounted
as a hanging scroll, ink on paper,
11⅝ × 16⅝ in. (29.5 × 42.2 cm)
Literature: Iijima 1977, no. 180;
Kyoto National Museum 1992,
no. 83

In the Heian period, by the second half of the tenth century, it became customary to keep pieces of unsized white paper—usually plain but sometimes decorated—handy in the bosom of one's robe. In a society where refined aristocrats expressed emotions and exchanged thoughts by means of extemporaneously composed waka (thirty-one-syllable poems), such papers were an indispensable item of daily life. Court ladies and gentlemen composed impromptu poems on every conceivable occasion, from chance meetings with friends to rests during trips. Poems were sent as messages between lovers or as remembrances between acquaintances. One of the most important functions of the slips of paper, known as *kaishi* or *futokoro-gami* (bosom paper), was their employment at popular poetry parties. Consequently both the blank "bosom-papers" and the papers inscribed with poems were referred to as *kaishi*.

One group of *kaishi*, inscribed with waka and called "*Kasuga kaishi*," comprises more than one hundred of these slips of paper.[1] The inscribed poems were composed and dedicated to gods of the Kasuga Shrine in Nara by a number of men serving the shrine in various capacities and by Buddhist priests from the nearby temples of Tōdaiji and Kōfukuji, both of which were closely connected with the shrine. The *Kasuga kaishi* may also contain poems created at poetry parties held in Kyoto for the benefit of the Kasuga deities. Most of the verses included in this group were composed between about 1241 and 1275 (poems composed after 1275 are not referred to as *Kasuga kaishi*).

At the outset of the Kamakura period, in the early years of the thirteenth century, the ancient aristocratic regime was replaced by a new government of military rulers. It was a time of frenetic activity in Nara—the old capital city of the Nara period—where the major Buddhist sanctuaries of Tōdaiji and Kōfukuji, destroyed by a military campaign of 1180, were being rebuilt. The project brought new life not only to the artists of Nara but also to its poets. The increase in literary activity was enhanced by the

renewed interest of the Fujiwara aristocrats in the Kasuga Shrine. Their frequent visits to the compound of their clan's titular shrine revitalized the poetry circles of Nara, and multitudes of poems were composed in literary gatherings. The *Kasuga kaishi* are important representative works from this era of artistic endeavor and stand as a monument to the literary fervor of the poets of thirteenth-century Nara.

The history of the *Kasuga kaishi* is complex. Originally part of the collection of the Chidori family, which provided head priests for the Kasuga Shrine, the *kaishi* were eventually acquired in the late Edo period by the Maeda family, the great art collectors of Kanazawa, before they were finally dispersed in modern times. In 1243 and 1244, while they were still in the possession of the Chidori family, one of the clan patriarchs, Nakatomi no Sukesada (1198–1269), copied the poems from the eighth-century *Man'yōshū* (Collection of Ten Thousand Leaves) anthology onto the back of the *kaishi*. This practice was not unusual: paper was a precious commodity and pieces were often reused in this manner. It is most likely that the individual *kaishi* were originally mounted in the handscroll format, but Sukesada, who was also head priest of the Wakamiya shrine at Kasuga and a poetry aficionado and leading literary figure of the Nara region, had the sheets separated and bound into books—a procedure that created holes and creases in a number of the *kaishi*.

Much later it became fashionable in tea circles to admire the beauty of unpretentious poetic jottings like the original verses on the *Kasuga kaishi*. In conformance with this new taste, most of the *Man'yōshū* poems written on the backs of the *Kasuga kaishi* were scraped off, and the *kaishi* were remounted as hanging scrolls to be displayed in tearooms. In the early twentieth century, however, it was discovered that the *Man'yōshū* poems formerly inscribed on the *Kasuga kaishi* were one of the earliest and rarest manuscripts of the ancient anthology. Thus

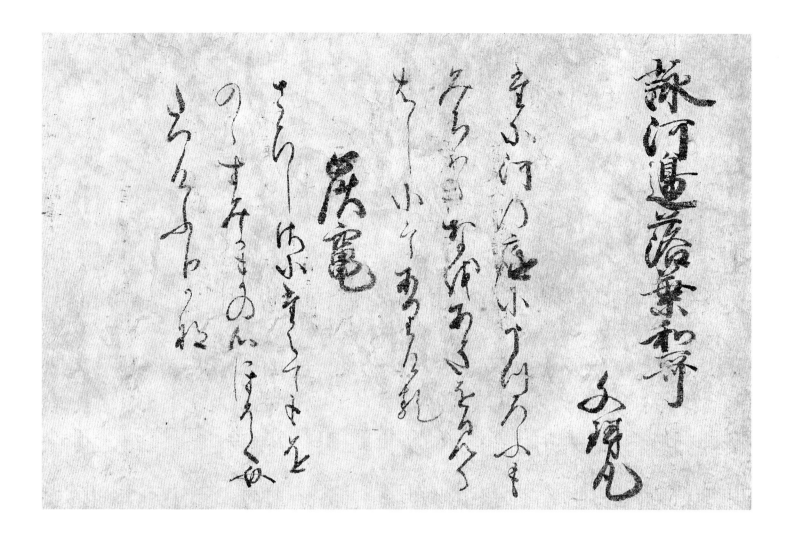

the *kaishi* that retained these poems on their reverse sides were even more highly regarded than before. Two dated inscriptions were found in association with the reverse-side *Man'yōshū* texts copied by Sukesada: Kangen 1 (1243) and Kangen 2 (1244). It can be surmised that the original *kaishi* poems were written prior to 1243.

This sheet exhibits the damage typical of attempts to remove *Man'yōshū* poems. The paper was washed, eliminating some of the contrasting gradations in the ink; most of the writing on the back was scraped off, but some is still visible to the naked eye. In spite of this surface damage the rhythmic flow of the brush, especially noticeable in the Chinese characters used for poem titles and poets' names, can still be appreciated. The poems are written in kana script and the tall elongated syllabic characters run together, revealing the speed of the brush and reflecting the casual nature of the occasion on which the impromptu verses were inscribed.

The two poems, one about fallen leaves on a riverbed and the other about a charcoal kiln, were composed and inscribed by a man whose signature contains only the youthful-sounding name of Monjumaru (Monju is a young bodhisattva; *maru* is used by a youth). The two poems read as follows:

Ei Kawabe (no) ochiba waka
Monjumaru

Tanigawa no soko ni utsurou
momijiba wa nao aki o miru
hashi nizo arikeru.

Composed on the sight of leaves fallen on
the riverbed by Monjumaru

Reflected on the bottom of the river
Are the fallen crimson leaves,
Like a sign that autumn can still be seen.

Sumigama

Sabishisa ni taetemo Ono no
sumigama no kokoro bosokumo
tatsu keburi kana.

Charcoal kiln

Loneliness is subdued,
Yet the thin smoke rising from
The charcoal kiln at Ono adds weariness.

In writing these poems on a *kaishi*, Monjumaru
followed a procedure that was beginning to be
codified in the Kamakura period. The rule was to
inscribe two or three poems per sheet, with the first
heading (at right) preceded by the word "ei"—
meaning to compose or recite a poem—and followed
by the poem's title, ending with the word "waka."
The poet's name was placed beside this, and the
poem was written in three lines. The text, as here, is
concluded by the second poem, preceded by its title.

As very few early specimens of Japanese calligraphy are signed and dated, works like the *Kasuga
kaishi* provide invaluable information for both historians and art historians.   M M

1. Furuya 1975, p. 187.

25.
The Poet Fujiwara Kiyotada from the Narikane Version of the Thirty-six Immortal Poets

Kamakura period (1185–1333),
second half of thirteenth century
Section of a handscroll mounted
as a hanging scroll, ink and light
colors on paper, 10⅜ × 10⅛ in.
(26.4 × 25.7 cm)
Ex coll.: Kohitsu Ryōetsu
Literature: Shimizu and
Rosenfield 1984–85, no. 37;
Akiyama et al. 1980, pl. 44;
Mori et al. 1979, pl. 64; Shinbo
1983, fig. 67

Refined aristocrats of Heian-period Japan exchanged
thoughts and expressed their views and emotions—
both public and private—through waka, short
verses consisting of thirty-one syllables. The ability
to compose waka extempore was an essential element of aristocratic deportment; for ambitious
courtiers of both sexes it was a prerequisite to
achieving recognition and promotion in the capital.

Courtly pastimes of the period included a variety
of contests or competitions in almost every field
of artistic endeavor. The custom can be traced to
the 880s and the games played among women of
the court.[1] Painting competitions (*e-awase*) and
perfume-blending contests (*kō-awase*) were popular,
but poetry competitions (*uta-awase*)—parties at
which aristocrats gathered to enjoy one another's
company and compare their versifying skills—were
a vital component of patrician life. The contestants
and judges at the earliest *uta-awase* were female;
gradually, however, men appropriated both roles.
The portrayal of *uta-awase* participants in painting
became a tradition, and the portraits came to be
known as *kasen-e* (pictures of the Immortal Poets).

The establishment of the Thirty-six Immortal
Poets (*Sanjūrokkasen*) is traditionally thought to
arise from a dispute between the renowned scholar,
critic, and poet Fujiwara Kintō (966–1041) and the
poet-critic Prince Rokujō Tomohira (964–1009).
The two differed in their choice of the greatest waka
poet.[2] Kintō nominated Ki no Tsurayuki (ca. 872–
945) for first place, whereas Tomohira preferred
Kakinomoto no Hitomaro (seventh to early eighth
century). To buttress his opinion, Kintō selected
thirty-six poets of the Nara and Heian periods and
requested other waka connoisseurs to evaluate and
rank them. But the majority rejected Kintō's favorite
and gave the highest honor to Hitomaro. Consequently it became popular to put together lists of
great poets, usually thirty-six in number, with
Hitomaro in the premier position. When Kintō
selected the thirty-six masters soon to be known as
kasen (Immortal Poets), he also chose representative
verses from each—a total of 150 poems.[3]

One literary record implies that *kasen-e* were
made as early as 1050;[4] however, the oldest firmly
documented work dates to the late 1170s.[5] It is likely

清正

ねのひこ志めつるのひの
まほらゝそてらのを沙よたさ春

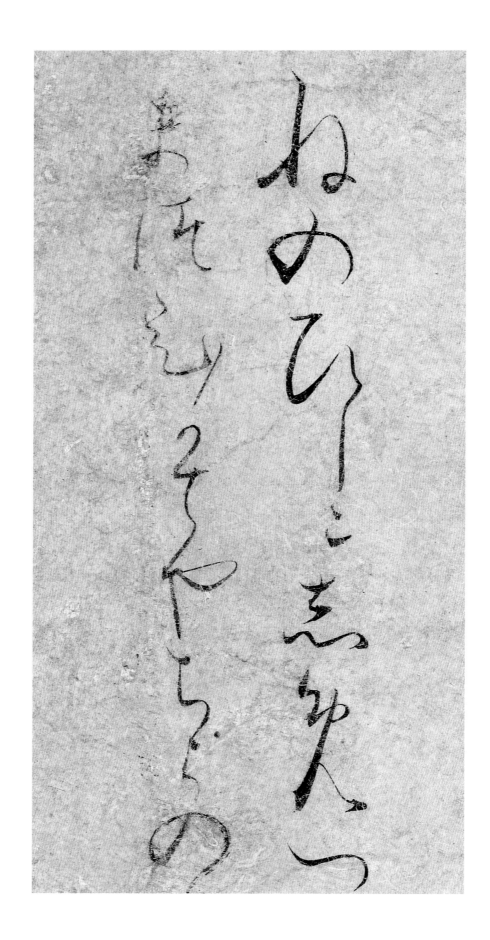

that an earlier custom of paying homage to the painted image of Hitomaro inspired artists to produce the first examples of *kasen-e*. Veneration of Hitomaro's portrait as an icon is traditionally said to have been initiated in 1118. The ceremony—which endured for centuries—was obviously based upon the Chinese custom of paying homage to portraits of Confucian sages, and on its first public viewing a newly made imaginary portrait of the genius of poetry was displayed with flowers and offerings before it.[6] Hitomaro was portrayed as an aged gentleman informally clad, with a sheaf of writing paper in his left hand and a writing brush in his right.

Hitomaro's appearance is traditionally thought to have been based on a vision of a certain Awata Sanuki no kami Kanefusa, an aficionado of waka.[7] Kanefusa, who aspired to poetic greatness, had prayed to the spirit of Hitomaro for divine assistance. One evening a pensive old gentleman in casual attire, a bundle of writing paper in his left hand and a writing brush in his right, appeared to Kanefusa in a dream and identified himself as Hitomaro. In the morning Kanefusa had his dream-figure rendered as a painting, intending to use the image as an icon for personal worship. Thereafter Kanefusa's poetry showed great improvement. The miraculous portrait was willed to the emperor Shirakawa (1053–1129), another aficionado of waka. Many copies of this painting were made, and they became indispensable in ceremonies dedicated to the "holy man" of waka.

The Kamakura period witnessed the peak of *kasen-e* production. Among the factors that contributed to the popularity of this genre was the fierce determination of the politically enfeebled Kyoto court to maintain its role as the guardian of aristocratic cultural traditions. A tendency toward realism in the arts of the period resulted in an appreciation for portrait paintings known as *nise-e* (likeness pictures), while a new awareness of history and a keen interest in historical personages resulted in a wealth of historical writings and paintings depicting important events of

the recent past. Although *kasen-e* were imaginary likenesses of men and women who lived long before the paintings were made, the desire to create individualized "portraits" of the Immortal Poets exemplified the spirit of the Kamakura era.

One of the oldest extant examples of *kasen-e* is a set of two handscrolls known as the Satake-bon (Satake family version), dated to the first half of the thirteenth century; originally part of the Satake collection, it was divided among various owners in 1919.[8] Nearly contemporary with the Satake scrolls is a similar set of handscrolls known as the Agedatami-bon (Poets-Seated-on-Mats version).[9] It is believed that both versions were modeled after earlier scrolls whose artists divided the poets into two competing groups in the tradition of *uta-awase-e* (pictures of poetry competitions). Although an atmosphere of competition is not apparent in these two works, many later paintings on the same subject depict the poets as opposed pairs. Some pictures also record the names of judges and their decisions. These later works, which emphasize interaction among the poets, are usually referred to as *uta-awase-e*, whereas paintings in which the poets are shown primarily as individuals are known simply as *kasen-e*. The distinction between the two genres is, however, never truly clear-cut.

The richness and diversity of Kamakura-period *kasen-e* are impressive. Variations on the *kasen-e* theme resulted in new types of poet pictures which deviated from the Kintō model in their choice of poets and sample verses. The *kasen-e* tradition endured into the Muromachi and later periods and continued to offer ever richer variations and innovations on the poet-portrait theme, all the while retaining its vigorous ancient roots.[10] For all of their deceptively simple content *kasen-e* express the quintessential Japanese reverence for the power of word and image, while uniting the three high arts of literature, calligraphy, and painting.[11]

The present fragment depicting Fujiwara Kiyotada was separated from the Narikane version, so named because its calligraphy was attributed by an Edo-period connoisseur to Narikane (d. ca. 1209) of the Taira family. Inscriptions in the Narikane

Fig. 19. Detail of cat. no. 25

scroll consist of each poet's personal name without titles or biographical data, and a single two-line poem for each. The oldest known *kasen-e* version after the Satake and Agedatami versions, this work, cut apart during the late Edo period, occupies a pivotal position in the history of *kasen-e*.[12] In the Narikane version the earlier format for *kasen-e* was drastically modified; the sequence of poets differs from that of the older Satake version; and only twenty-two of the thirty-six poems quoted are from the Kintō selection, the remainder having been chosen from other anthologies. The figures of the poets are close together, almost claustrophobically boxed in by rows of poetic text. Today only about fifteen pieces from this scroll are known; the present fragment is the only portion said to be in an American collection.[13]

In the original arrangement of the Narikane version, the two teams of poets occupied separate scrolls, but they were depicted as though they were facing each other. Most of the poets from the "left" team, like the example shown here, appeared in the first scroll, facing the viewer's left with their verses also inscribed to the left of the figures. In the second scroll members of the "right" team were depicted in reverse arrangement. A sense of competition was graphically rendered here for the first time. Two copies of the Narikane scrolls, made before the originals were cut apart, exist today. One, in the Tanaka Shinbi collection in Tokyo, was signed by Sumiyoshi Gukei (1631–1705);[14] it seems to have served as a model for Kano Osanobu (1796–1846), who produced a copy (now in the Tokyo National Museum) in 1837. In the Gukei copy, the poet Kiyotada was portrayed as the thirteenth contestant in the "left" group.

All inscriptions in the surviving fragments of the Narikane version were written by the same, as yet unidentified calligrapher. In the present work, as in the other fragments, the name of the poet is inscribed in Chinese characters, with the poem in kana. The poem itself appears in the anthology of Kiyotada's works, the *Kiyotadashū* (Collected Poems of Kiyotada), as poem no. 6, as well as in the *Shin Kokinwakashū* (New Collection of Poems Ancient and Modern), as poem no. 709. In both anthologies the poem is preceded by a headnote stating that it was composed upon the celebration of the First Day of the Rat in Kii province (modern Wakayama prefecture). It may be translated as follows:

Ne no hi shite[15]
Shimetsuru nobe no
Himekomatsu
Hikadeya chiyo no
Kage o matamashi.

On the First Day of the Rat
A tiny pine stands in a roped-off field;
Rather than plucking it
Why not wait a thousand years
Until they cast thick shade.[16]

The poet is portrayed as a rather youngish fellow, holding himself erect and apparently concentrating his energy on versifying. His robe is painted off-white, but no color was applied to his face, except for a hint of pale pink on the lips. Thin, even, sharply angled lines define the stiff costume with its severe folds. The poem was inscribed in small, evenly spaced letters which seldom flow into one another. Brush lines have little in the way of inflection. The traditional attribution of calligraphy to Narikane has no historical basis, and stylistic features of the calligraphy and painting help to date this work to the second half of the thirteenth century.[17]

In the fragments from the Narikane scrolls many of the poets, like Kiyotada, are informally dressed; the paper used for the handscrolls is unsized. By the time this work was produced, patronage of *kasen-e* seems to have widened to include persons from less aristocratic levels of society. In their departure from the idealizing tendency of earlier *kasen* paintings, the Narikane scrolls constitute a superb example of the move toward realism that dominated the aesthetic spirit of the Kamakura period. Many later versions created after the Muromachi period — especially works produced by members of the Kano and Tosa schools — reflect the influence of the Narikane version. MM

1. Minegishi 1954, p. 13.

2. For literary records on this dispute, see Hasegawa 1979.

3. The first four poets on Kintō's list (Hitomaro, Tsurayuki, Mitsune, and Ise) and the last two (Kanemori and Nakatsukasa) were represented by ten poems each, whereas the remainder were represented by three poems each.

4. See the section on the *uta-awase* of the fifth year of the Eishō era (1050), in Nagazumi and Shimada, eds. 1966, p. 313, and the entry for the fourth month, the twenty-sixth day of the same year in Hagitani, ed. 1959.

5. Our understanding of the history of *kasen-e* and *uta-awase-e* owes a great deal to Mori Tōru, whose various articles on this subject are published in his *Uta-awase-e no kenkyū* (Mori 1978). This portrait of poets is known as *Jishō Sanjūrokunin uta-awase-e,* after the Jishō era (1177–1180). It is known only from literary records and one small fragment of a mid-thirteenth-century copy in the Masaki Museum, Osaka. It apparently included a statement to the effect that it had been edited and its poets selected according to Kintō's model; see Mori 1978, pp. 77–80, fig. 17.

6. *Kakinomoto eigu ki* (Record of the Worship of Kakinomoto Portrait) was edited by Fujiwara Atsumitsu (1061–1144). See Kawamata, ed. 1928–38, vol. 13, p. 53.

7. For a record of this dream, see Izumi, ed. 1982, pp. 118–19.

8. Mori et al. 1979, pls. 7–47.

9. For sections from this scroll, see Mori et al. 1979, pls. 48–61; and Suntory Museum of Art 1986, nos. 22–26.

10. For some of the later variations, see Murase 1986, nos. 14 and 16. In most of these works from the Kamakura and later periods, poets were represented by one poem each.

11. Graybill 1984–85, p. 106.

12. Graybill 1984–85, p. 106.

13. Graybill 1984–85, p. 106. Many of the fragments are reproduced in the Suntory Museum of Art 1986, nos. 27–32; Mori 1978, pl. 6; Mori et al. 1979, pls. 63–70; and Shinbo 1983.

14. A faithful copy by Sumiyoshi Gukei in the Tanaka Shinbi collection preserves the original form of the complete work. See Mori et al. 1979, unnumbered plate, and Mori 1978, fig. 7. An 1837 copy by Kano Osanobu, now in the Tokyo National Museum, is reproduced in Shinbo 1983, pp. 90–92, fig. 1.

15. *Ne no hi,* the First Day of the Rat, is traditionally celebrated by collecting pine seedlings in a field.

16. For other translations, see Graybill 1984–85, p. 106 and Honda 1970.

17. See Shinbo 1986, p. 83.

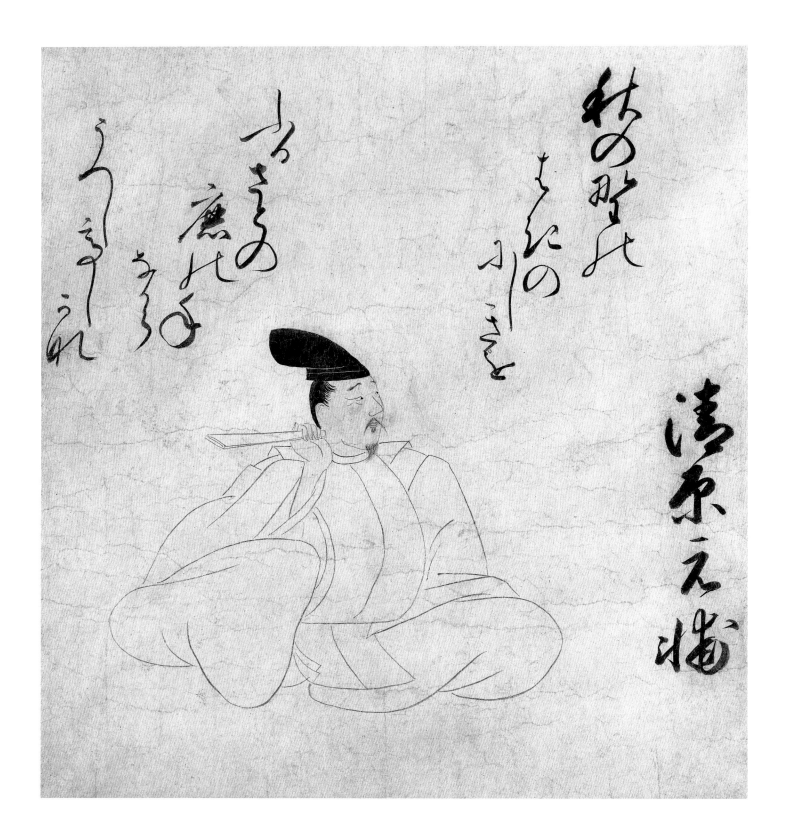

秋の野の
ぐさのいろ
このいきと

ちさき
鹿ぞ
なく

うゑ
やれ

清原元輔

26.
The Poet Kiyohara Motosuke from the Tameshige Version of the Thirty-six Immortal Poets

Muromachi period (1392–1573),
early fifteenth century
Section of a handscroll mounted
as a hanging scroll, ink and light
colors on paper, 11⅛ × 10 in.
(28.4 × 25.4 cm)
Literature: Kyoto National
Museum 1992, no. 71

The poet Kiyohara Motosuke (908–990) turns his head toward his name, boldly inscribed to the right in four large characters. The bearded Motosuke directs his gaze upward, as if he has just uttered the words of the poem above him:

Aki no no no
Hagi no nishiki o
Furusato ni
Shika no ne nagara
utsushi teshi kana.

I wish
I could bring home
the brocaded autumn field of *hagi,*
complete with
the baying of deer.

An important poet, Kiyohara Motosuke was the father of the celebrated woman writer Sei Shōnagon (late tenth century), author of *Makura no sōshi* (*The Pillow Book*). Motosuke himself was one of the five compilers of the second imperially sponsored anthology of classical poems, the *Gosen wakashū* (Later Collection of Japanese Poetry, edited 951; the first anthology was the *Kokin wakashū* [A Collection of Poems Ancient and Modern] of 905). The third imperial anthology, the *Shūi wakashū* (Collection of Gleanings, ca. 1005–11), includes almost fifty of his works.

At first glance the painting appears monochromatic, with dark ink defining the poet's cap, hair, beard, and whiskers. Closer inspection reveals the application of pale colors on the poet's body: ocher on the face and arm and a pinkish tint on the cheeks and lips. Face, hand, scepter, and court costume are delineated by thin, even brushstrokes with little

inflection. Tiny black dots for the eyes and a triangle indicating wrinkles under the poet's right eye contribute to the strong sense of realism. In sharp contrast to the simply rendered figure, the calligraphy filling the space above is bold and assertive. The largest, most heavily inked characters, written with a slow-moving brush, give the poet's name, while the verse is in abbreviated *gyōsho* (semicursive script). The poem is divided into two groups of twelve and nineteen syllables each with a space between them; although the letters are smaller, they are as clearly written as the poet's name.

This fragment was once part of a handscroll depicting the Thirty-six Immortal Poets (*Sanjūrokka-sen*). Only one other poet's portrait from this work has been identified: a fragment[1] depicting the royal woman poet Saigū no Nyōgo with calligraphy attributed to Nijō Tameshige (1334–1385), an influential poet and calligrapher who is also thought to have painted *kasen-e* in the *hakubyō* technique ("white drawing" which uses only ink or ink with slight color). The two fragments from the Tameshige version resemble each other in several respects: the poets' names are written in large script; poems are inscribed in two blocks of text—twelve and nineteen syllables respectively, with a considerable space between them; a fluid *gyōsho* is used for the poems; and figures are rendered in *hakubyō*-like ink drawing. The calligraphy has been traditionally attributed to Tameshige, but the relaxed, large-scale letters in *gyōsho* reflect stylistic features of Muromachi-period kana writing of the early fifteenth century. The rather stiff ink drawing of the figure is characteristic of the same period.   MM

1. This fragment is reproduced in Suntory Museum of Art 1986, no. 62.

Myōe Kōben (1173–1232)

27.
Dream Record with Painting of Mountains

Kamakura period (1185–1333),
ca. 1203–10
Hanging scroll, ink on paper,
12 × 19 in. (30.5 × 48.3 cm)
Ex coll.: Chōkai Seiji; Shirasu
Masako
Literature: Shirasu 1967, fig. 29;
Shirasu 1974, p. 189; Shimizu
and Rosenfield 1984–85, pp. 61–
63; Girard 1990, p. 168

Kōben is better known by his monastic nickname Myōe(bō), often followed by the honorific Shōnin (saint).[1] Today he is celebrated for his role in reviving the older teachings of the Flower Garland Sutra (*Kegongyō*), which had flourished at Tōdaiji in Nara from the middle of the eighth century. He also excelled at Esoteric Shingon practices, especially those of healing. Myōe stressed the importance of vow taking by the laity, and he gained notoriety for his criticism of Hōnen (1133–1212), later revered as the founder of Pure Land teachings in Japan.

Myōe's extraordinary talents, especially his remarkable predilection for dreaming or seeing visions, were well recognized during his lifetime. From the 1190s to his death in 1232, Myōe kept records of his dreams, collectively titled *Yumenoki* (Dream Record). After the saint's death his many followers recorded every detail of his life, his sayings and lectures, his poems, and the history of his temple, Kōzanji, which he founded in 1206. Over the last thirty years, as these eyewitness hagiographies and Kōzanji's voluminous collection of primary documents and early manuscripts have been catalogued, annotated, interpreted, and published, the life of Myōe has come into ever sharper focus.[2]

The most fateful event of Myōe's career took place in the winter of 1203, when the saint was thirty-one.[3] Trained by prominent teachers at Jingoji and Ninnaji in Kyoto and at Tōdaiji in Nara, Myōe had spent the previous eight years of his life trying to establish himself. As a member of the Yuasa family, a powerful warrior clan in Kii province (Wakayama prefecture), Myōe could hardly be unaffected by the military conflicts and shifting political alliances of his era. After the death in 1199 of Japan's first shogun, Minamoto Yoritomo, Jingoji and Myōe's family suffered the loss of income and property rights, a situation that persisted for several years.[4] Nonetheless, members of Myōe's family provided him with a succession of retreats in the mountains along the Arida River, where he immersed himself in scholarship.

For Myōe it was a time of hopelessness, fueled by an intense regret that he had been born too late, in a far distant land, to meet his beloved spiritual father Shakyamuni, the Historical Buddha. Seeing no future in Japan, Myōe made plans to travel to India in order to visit sacred sites. One day the young wife of his maternal uncle, Yuasa Munemitsu (before 1175–after 1238), became possessed by the Great-Illuminating Deity (Daimyōjin) of the Kasuga Shrine. The oracles she delivered to Myōe caused him to abandon his travel plans and to decide to establish a temple near the capital. During the next three years Myōe spread the word of this miraculous oracle and eventually gained imperial support for the founding of Kōzanji as a Kegon subtemple of Jingoji.

Myōe's devotion to the Kasuga deity is the focus of this fragment of the Dream Record. The text, written in five lines of mixed Chinese characters and katakana, should not be mistaken for an inscription on the painting of mountains that otherwise occupies so much space since this single sheet of paper might, in fact, originally have been part of a longer handscroll recording many more dreams. The text reads as follows:

Same month, twenty-first day. I went from the capital to the mountain. That night I had the following dream: the Itono Guards Captain invited Gedatsubō for a visit. He arrived on the night of the fifth, and wanted to leave after one day. I, Jōben, thought he must be the Great Deity. But my heart tells me, if he is the Great Deity he should be bigger. Then I took Gedatsu's long cane and measured him as two feet, one inch. His human form is so marvelous it penetrates my heart. I said to myself, without a doubt he is the Great Deity.[5]

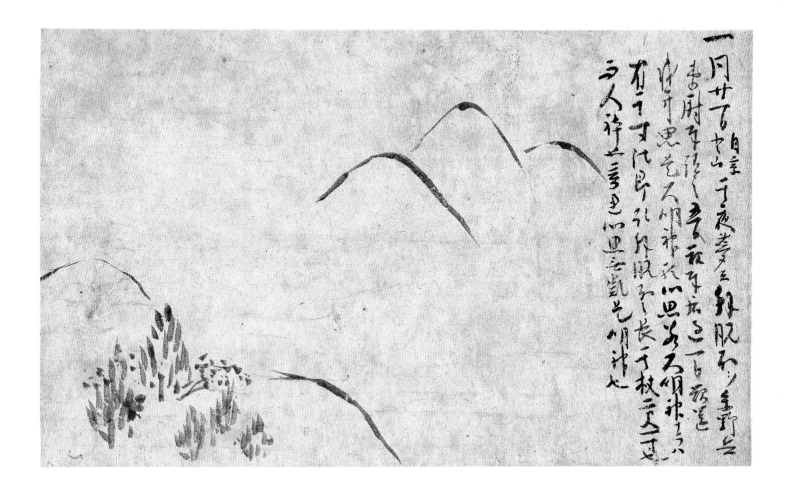

In this fragment Myōe calls himself Jōben ("becoming articulate"), a name he used until the seventh month of 1210 when he changed his name to Kōben. Thus this name change narrows the dating of this fragment to the period 1203–10.

The two people named in the dream were both important to Myōe during this period. "Itono Guards Captain" refers to Yuasa Munemitsu, who had acquired his military rank serving the powerful Minamoto family in the 1180s. A year after Munemitsu's wife delivered the Kasuga deity's oracles (in 1204) Myōe held a lecture-ceremony in honor of the deity at Itono, site of Munemitsu's primary residence and one of Myōe's retreats.[6] The second name, Gedatsubō, refers to the prominent cleric

Jōkei (1155–1213), a member of the Fujiwara clan who was then living in reclusion on Mount Kasagi on the Kizu River southeast of Kyoto. According to records of Myōe's encounters with the Kasuga deity, after receiving the oracles Myōe paid visits to the Kasuga Shrine in Nara and then to Gedatsu on Mount Kasagi. Myōe and Gedatsu had much in common besides their desire for reclusion, as both were devoted to Shakyamuni. They regarded the Kasuga deity as a "manifest trace" (*suijaku*) of Shakyamuni, and both invited the deity to guardian shrines within their temple grounds.[7] Myōe and Gedatsu corresponded, but there is no record of Gedatsu actually visiting either Myōe or Yuasa Munemitsu.

Several scholars have identified the mountains

in the drawing as Mount Kasagi, site of Gedatsu's mountain retreat.[8] But since Kasagi is not mentioned in the dream, and since it is Gedatsu who left Kasagi to visit Itono, we should consider two other possibilities. The phrase "went to the mountain" alludes to the Takao-Toganoo mountain ridges northwest of the capital where Jingoji and Kōzanji are located. The second "mountain" implied by the dream could be the natural embodiment of the Kasuga deity located behind the Kasuga Shrine. The drawing sketches two groups of mountains, with the foreground hills aligned diagonally toward the three peaks in the distance. At the place where the two forested slopes come together, a few lines and clusters of triangular-shaped dots stand out among the surrounding trees. Perhaps this detail represents a clearing at Takao or Toganoo where Myōe placed paper offerings (*gohei*) of worship to the distant Kasuga deity, represented by the three peaks in the background.

Myōe wrote his Dream Record in a variety of formats: books, scrolls, scraps of paper, even in inscriptions on manuscripts. The primarily Chinese text is brushed in an angular, left-leaning running script (*gyōsho*). He consistently used a firm touch, loading his brush with ink and then letting it thin out to pale gray strokes. After having learned to write under his family's tutelage in Kii province and at Jingoji, Myōe developed an abbreviated utilitarian script that suited his prodigious sutra-copying efforts. While Myōe's idiosyncratic hand would never be mistaken for the elegant writing of an aristocratic calligrapher of the capital, its power and austerity reward prolonged viewing. Because he kept the Dream Record for his own use, lines of text frequently run close together, as if he wished to save paper. He occasionally made corrections and sometimes wrote variant versions of his dreams.   KLB

1. Bō is an honorific for monks and nuns that literally refers to their living quarters and is a component of their monastic names. Myōebō means "room of bright wisdom." The term Shōnin was reserved for monks of extraordinary wisdom or charismatic powers or who were perceived as being exceptionally like the Historical Buddha.
2. *Kōzanji shiryō* 1968– ; Okuda 1978; Girard 1990; Tanabe, G. 1992.
3. Brock 2001.
4. Matsumoto 1979.
5. Girard 1990, p. 168.
6. A chronology of Myōe's activities appears in Okuda 1978, pp. 305–16.
7. Morrell 1987, pp. 44–88; Tyler 1990, pp. 258–84; Grapard 1992.
8. Shimizu and Rosenfield 1984–85, pp. 61–63.

Myōe Kōben (1173–1232)

28.
Dream Record

Kamakura period (1185–1333), dated 1225
Hanging scroll, ink on paper, 13¼ × 21⅝ in. (33.7 × 54.9 cm)
Seals: Kōzanji; Hōbenchiin; two unidentified seals
Ex coll.: Kōzanji; Yamanaka collection
Literature: Shimizu and Rosenfield 1984–85

This lengthy fragment of Myōe's Dream Record bears an uncharacteristically complete date: the sixteenth day of the eighth month of 1225. On this day three tutelary shrines were to be dedicated at Kōzanji, but the ceremonies were held up by a typhoon. The first ten lines describe the actual events, while the remaining eleven lines record Myōe's two dreams on that night. A fragment of the Dream Record still extant at Kōzanji contains nearly identical wording, although it lacks the final six lines. Both versions have been translated into French by Frédéric Girard, who regards this as the earlier and more complete version.[1]

The installation of deities (kami) in the three shrines was an occasion of considerable importance for the Kōzanji community, and at least two other accounts of the ceremony survive. One of these, by Myōe's closest follower and biographer, Kikai (1178–1250), who participated in the ceremonies, is a detailed and vivid record that includes the debate questions (*mondō*), descriptions of the weather, and explanations of Myōe's two dreams.[2] The second account appears in the official temple history, Origin Tales of Kōzanji, written by Kōshin (1191–ca. 1263).[3]

According to all of these records, the three east-facing tutelary shrines and their worship hall were still under construction in 1225. Myōe decided to invite deities from three countries to reside there, ranking them according to the dreams recorded here. Byakkō (White Light), a deity of the Himalayan

snows, occupied the most important central shrine. The prominence of this otherwise unknown deity stems from Myōe's meditative practices focused on Shakyamuni's radiance.[4] The second-rank shrine, on the south, was for the Great-Illuminating Deity of the Kasuga Shrine, who had protected Myōe throughout his life and delivered the fateful oracles that led to the founding of Kōzanji (see cat. no. 27). To the north Myōe invited the female deity Zenmyō of Silla (Korea), who "vowed to protect Kegon" through her transformations into a dragon and a rock.[5] Zenmyō was the namesake of Kōzanji's affiliated nunnery, Zenmyōji, established in the wake of the Shōkyū War of 1221, where her carved embodiment (*shintai*) had been installed in 1224. Embodiments of Byakkō and Zenmyō, three pairs of Chinese lions and Korean dogs, and a complete transcription of the Flower Garland Sutra (*Kegongyō*) were all dedicated and placed in the Byakkō shrine by Gyōkan (1169–after 1225), a high-ranking cleric of Ninnaji. On the day of the ceremony the assembled monks huddled in the worship hall as rain poured outside. As the ceremony progressed, the clouds suddenly parted and a ray of bright sunlight shone down. All who witnessed the event interpreted the rain and the sun as auspicious signs of Zenmyō's and Byakkō's protection of the temple. Although the shrine precinct has since disappeared, the sculptures of the two kami and six animals, the sutra volumes, and Gyōkan's handwritten dedicatory vow all survive to the present day.

Myōe's two dreams determined his ranking of Byakkō, the Kasuga deity, and Zenmyō; both involve his interpretations of people in his dreams as incarnations of these deities. In the first dream he sees a pavilion in one room of which sits his recently deceased follower Dōchū (1178–1223), and in the adjoining room the nun Maya gozen. Myōe writes that Dōchū and Maya live in separate places, but they have come together so that Dōchū can instruct her in proper vow-taking practice. In the second dream Myōe sees an aristocratic acquaintance, the lay monk Fujiwara Chikayasu. He regrets that he cannot visit him, because he is engaged with another matter at the residence of Lady Sanmi.

There he sees a portrait painting on the wall that does not look like Chikayasu.

In their accounts Kikai and Kōshin explain the rather complicated connections between these two dreams and the installation of Kōzanji's tutelary deities. Myōe is said to have viewed Dōchū as Byakkō. Kikai goes on to identify Maya gozen as a daughter of Yuasa Munemitsu, hence Myōe's cousin, whom Myōe recognizes as Zenmyō. As for Chikayasu, Kikai records a lengthier version of the dream wherein Chikayasu claims to be the brother of the Ichijō Prime Minister (Konoe Iezane, 1179–1242). Myōe then paints Chikayasu's portrait, but discovers that he has actually drawn his own face. Myōe ponders the implication of the "brother" relationship and states that a Fujiwara-born prime minister must take precedence over a woman of his own family, hence the Kasuga deity ranks higher than Zenmyō.

The fourth person mentioned in these dreams, Lady Sanmi (Jishi, ca. 1170s–after 1244), was one of Myōe's first benefactors. She contributed to the building of Kōzanji and fostered Myōe's growing reputation among the Konoe branch of the Fujiwara family. A member of the imperial wet nurse family, she was raised together with Emperor Gotoba (1180–1239). Her older sister became Gotoba's empress, and Lady Sanmi served at court as wetnurse of her own nephew (Tsuchimikado, 1195–1231). She had become Myōe's patron by 1216, contributing the main icon of Shakyamuni to Kōzanji's Golden Hall in 1219. Following Gotoba's failed rebellion in 1221, Lady Sanmi retired from court and largely withdrew from Kōzanji's affairs. Myōe's dream of being at her residence, however, suggests they were in contact as late as 1225.   K L B

1. Girard 1990, pp. 194–95, and Girard 1999.
2. Known either as "Kikai's Debate" or "Kikai at Age 48"; see Koizumi 1987. Curiously, Kikai completely omits the event in his official Life of Myōe, written seven or eight years later. *Kōzanji shiryō* 1968– , vol. 1, pp. 9–80; the event should appear on pp. 58–59.
3. *Kōzanji shiryō* 1968– , vol. 1, pp. 642–43.
4. Tanabe, G. 1992, pp. 137–52.
5. Brock 1990.

Myōe Kōben (1173–1232)

29.
Letter to Jōjūbō

Kamakura period (1185–1333),
ca. 1221
Hanging scroll, ink on paper,
8¼ × 17 in. (21 × 43.2 cm)
Signed: Kōben

Throughout his life Myōe (see nos. 27 and 28) maintained an active correspondence of which more than twenty letters survive.[1] Some, quite lengthy, provide intimate glimpses into his thoughts, relationships, and circumstances. Other brief notes, such as this one written in response to a query by one Jōjūbō, are difficult to interpret. Since this letter has not previously been published or scrutinized by Myōe scholars, the following discussion remains tentative pending a definitive transcription of its text. The letter reads: "I am completely involved with a commentary on the Manifestation Chapter. As for whether to [live at, construct] the buddha-place (*bussho*) by yourself, I really do not know. Regretfully, fifth day. Kōben. To Jōjūbō."

Despite its brevity the letter suggests a date, recipient, and context. The first sentence provides a significant clue to the letter's date. Manifestation Chapter (*Shutsugen-bon*) denotes chapter 37 of the Flower Garland Sutra.[2] According to Kikai's official Life of Myōe, Myōe carried out discussions on a commentary to this chapter with his followers during the seventh and eighth months of 1221.[3] Kikai generally kept a careful record of his teacher's scholarly activities, and since this reference appears to be the only specific mention of the Manifestation Chapter in Kikai's text or elsewhere, the letter may be tentatively dated to autumn 1221. Due to disruptions at Jingoji and Kōzanji during the Shōkyū War that summer, Myōe and his followers had moved to a retreat behind the Kamo Shrine in north-central Kyoto. There they copied sutras, engaged in scholarly discussions, and interacted with a variety of patrons.

Comparison of this letter with examples of Myōe's calligraphy from 1220–22 supports this dating and also aid in its transcription. (See the appendix for a discussion of the mounting.) Not long after the Shōkyū War Myōe also wrote a long letter to a nun named Inouedono.[4] In both letters, Myōe's cursive Chinese characters form heavy accents within his otherwise fluid and connected hiragana script, a

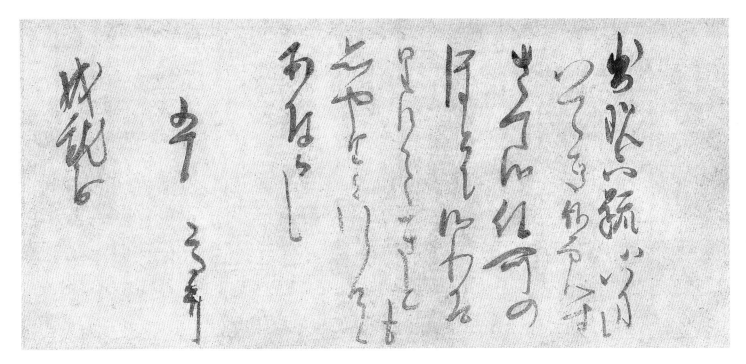

combination he may have used exclusively in correspondence with women. His spacing between lines and characters and the fluctuations from wet to dry ink also link the two letters. In addition the Chinese characters in both most resemble Myōe's calligraphy in volume 10 of the Dream Record, which records dreams from 1220 through 1222.[5]

The monastic nickname Jōjūbō ("complete attainment") appears in a few revealing inscriptions on manuscripts in the Kōzanji storehouse, all referring to a nun (*bikuni*). The earliest inscription, dated the ninth month of 1210, was written by Myōe on an Esoteric practice manual. In it he says that he wrote the text for teaching a secret dharani (a mystic spell) while instructing Jōjūbō in this practice.[6] Myōe was then living at Sakiyama in Kii province under the protection of his maternal aunt and foster mother, known as "the Sakiyama nun." Jōjūbō must have been a member of the Sakiyama or Yuasa families, many of whom became nuns after their husbands died. Since Myōe taught Jōjūbō a secret chanting practice, we should assume he held her in high regard.

A second reference to Jōjūbō appears much later, after Myōe's death, in an inscription on a copy of the Flower Garland Sutra written by Kikai in 1236. In his inscription Kikai reports that Jōjūbō of Zenmyōji died on the twenty-third day of the seventh month. These two inscriptions document a twenty-six-year relationship between Jōjūbō and Myōe's circle. Assuming she was an adult of Myōe's age or older in 1210, she would have been at least in her sixties at her death.

Kikai's description of Jōjūbō as a Zenmyōji nun also hints at her importance to Myōe and Kikai. Might the cryptic reference to a "buddha-place" in the second sentence of this letter refer to plans for the building of Zenmyōji, in which Jōjūbō played a role? Given the closeness to Myōe, the teacher-student relationship, and her age, perhaps Myōe even invited her to Zenmyōji to serve in a position of responsibility. Indeed Myōe mentions several Sakiyama and Yuasa nuns in volume 10 of the Dream Record mentioned above. While the name Jōjūbō does not appear in the diary, "the Sakiyama nun," "the Minami nun," or "the Miyahara nun" may refer to Jōjūbō. Myōe's maternal uncle Jōkakubō, the senior monk at Jingoji, had ultimate authority over both Kōzanji and Zenmyōji. Thus if Jōjūbō was a sister, niece, or cousin of both Jōkaku and Myōe, this brief letter may open a new window into the identities of the Zenmyōji nuns.   K L B

1. Girard 1990, pp. 12–32.
2. *Daihōkōbutsu Kengongyō,* in eighty scrolls, translated by a Khotanese monk into Chinese between 695 and 699; *Daizōkyō* 1924–34, vol. 10, p. 279.
3. *Kōzanji shiryō* 1968– , vol. 1, no. 56.
4. Girard 1990, p. 418; illustrated in *Nihon kōsō iboku* 1970–71, no. 46.
5. Tanabe, G. 1992, pp. 174–87 (dreams 66–139); Girard 1990, pp. 139–60, dreams 64–134. Photographs of the Kōzanji fragments of the Dream Record appear in *Kōzanji shiryō* 1968– , vol. 7, pp. 7–101, with vol. 10 appearing on pp. 53–89. According to Okuda 1980, pp. 171–79, the sheets of paper in this booklet are out of order.
6. *Kōzanji shiryō* 1968– , vol. 10, p. 139.

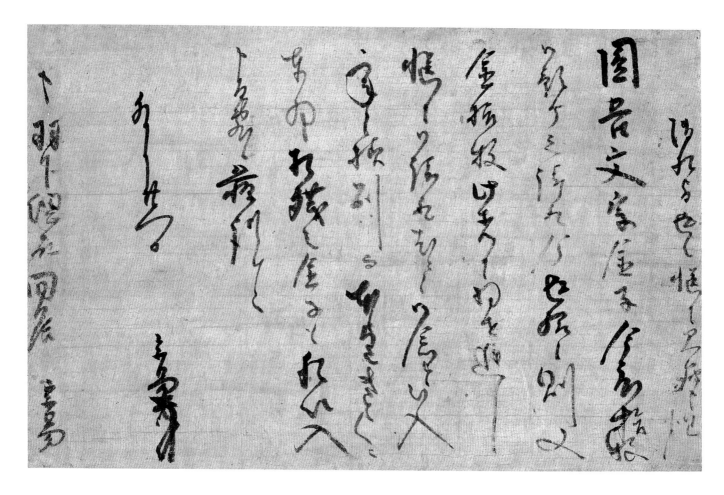

Sen no Rikyū (1522–1591)

30.
Letter to Takigawa Katsutoshi

Momoyama period (1573–1615),
dated April 21
Hanging scroll, ink on paper,
10⅞ × 15⅞ in. (27.6 × 40.3 cm)
Signed: Sōeki, with a cipher
Ex coll.: Takigawa Katsutoshi;
Murakami Kōsuke
Literature: Komatsu 1985,
no. 222; Komatsu 1996, no. 226;
Komatsu 1999, no. 226

A seminal figure in the history of the chanoyu (tea ceremony), Sen no Rikyū played a pivotal role in elevating the choreographed preparation and serving of the beverage to the level of a revered art form, complete with an aesthetic canon. As legitimate heir to the ideology of *wabi cha* (rustic tea; *wabi* roughly means "simplicity" and "absence of ornament"), formulated by Murata Jukō (1423–1502) and further developed by Takeno Jōō (1504–1555), Rikyū established and codified the highest standards for tea-ceremony taste. He was born in 1522 in the port city of Sakai, south of modern Osaka, which in his time was an autonomous, prosperous urban port, likened to Venice by visiting Europeans. His youthful name of Yoshirō appears in

tea-ceremony records of an event that took place in the ninth month, thirteenth day, of the sixth year of the Tenmon era (1537)[1] when the teenage practitioner invited to his tea gathering Matsuya Hisamasa of Nara, a well-known and wealthy tea master many years his senior. This action indicates that the young man had already attained a high level of proficiency in the chanoyu.

Yoshirō received Zen training at Daitokuji, a major Zen temple in Kyoto, where he was given the Buddhist name Sōeki in 1540. This name, which he used throughout his life, appears frequently in tea-ceremony records, and the detailed descriptions of the utensils he used suggest that he was deeply committed to the austere aesthetic of *wabi cha*. His fame as a tea master brought him into the circles of the most influential political figures of the time. In 1575 he was appointed tea master to Oda Nobunaga (1534–1582), the unifier of a war-torn Japan. After Nobunaga's assassination in 1582, Sōeki served his successor, Toyotomi Hideyoshi (1536–1598), in the same capacity under the Buddhist name Rikyū, which he adopted around 1585 (this is the name by which he came to be known). He prospered under Hideyoshi's patronage, becoming not only his aesthetic adviser but also his political confidant.

Rikyū's sudden falling out with Hideyoshi has never been satisfactorily explained. In a series of incomprehensible acts Hideyoshi placed Rikyū under house arrest in Sakai and then ordered him to commit seppuku (ritual suicide) in Kyoto. Speculations regarding this reversal of fortune were widespread among his contemporaries, and modern scholars have not presented a convincing account. The most often cited cause of his downfall is the so-called arrogance he displayed when he helped finance the building of the main gate at Daitokuji. Rikyū had a statue of himself placed in the second story of the gate as a disciple of Shaka Buddha; consequently Hideyoshi and others—including emperors—had to pass under Rikyū's portrait when entering the temple through this gate. It has also been suggested that Rikyū's refusal to offer his daughter to Hideyoshi provoked the warlord's rancor. Some historians cite contemporaneous comments that he had made inappropriate profits from appraising and selling tea utensils.

None of these explanations seems to justify such an extreme act by Hideyoshi. It may be that a profound clash of aesthetic standards may have contributed to the great warlord's displeasure with his tea master. Hideyoshi's predilection for lavish ostentation in matters of tea are well known, particularly in connection with his gold-lined tearoom and the mass outdoor tea ceremony which he officiated over in 1587. This taste was diametrically opposed to Rikyū's preference for utter simplicity and the use of extraordinarily small tearooms, large enough for only one and a half floor mats (a mat is about 6 feet by 3 feet [2 meters by 1 meter]). Whatever the reason for his

forced suicide, Rikyū is still regarded as the master who fused various tea traditions and codified the *wabi cha* aesthetic, thus inaugurating the golden age of tea.

This letter by Rikyū is addressed to Hashimo Osanosuke and dated the twenty-first day of uzuki (April). "Hashimo" is not the recipient's real name, which was Takigawa Katsutoshi (1543–1610). Katsutoshi, a vassal of Oda Nobunaga, later served Toyotomi Hideyoshi who gave him his own earlier family name of Hashiba with the title Shimofusa no kami (lord of Shimofusa). A warrior and tea master himself, Katsutoshi befriended Rikyū.

The letter reads:

> I shall personally keep an eye on the payment for this work.
>
> > Respectfully yours.

Please return your receipt of the deposit of ten gold pieces that I had entrusted you with as a payment for Engo calligraphy. I shall entrust this messenger with another ten pieces of gold as the next down payment. Please be absolutely sure to receive it and let me know when you do. Also, your wishes are especially praiseworthy. The balance of the payment is supposed to come in soon.

> Respectfully yours
> twenty-first day, the fourth month   Sōeki
> > [*kaō*]
> Ha Shimofusa no kami   as reply   Sōeki

The letter is one of about thirty that seem to confirm that Rikyū acted as a middleman in the selling and appraising of art objects.[2] The object referred to in this letter was a treasured piece of Chinese calligraphy by the Southern Song Chan (Zen) monk Yuanwu (J: Engo; 1063–1135), which Rikyū was helping Katsutoshi to sell. In the late sixteenth century Yuanwu's works were regarded as among the finest known examples of calligraphy. These examples were owned by connoisseurs in the city of Sakai, and Iseya Dōwa, one of these owners, may have been the purchaser of the piece belonging to Katsutoshi. Prior to Katsutoshi, the piece had been owned by the great tea master Murata Jukō, who had in turn received it from the famous Muromachi-period Zen master Ikkyū (1394–1481) as a certificate of Zen training.[3]

The missive ends with the signature *Sōeki*, with a handwritten cipher beneath. The cipher, a tall, lean combination of brushstrokes shaped roughly like a table, is one of the three ciphers (*kaō*) used by Rikyū. Known as *keraban* because of its resemblance to the cricketlike insect known as a *kera*, it appears in almost all of Rikyū's correspondence. The first line (at right) in this letter is a postscript for which Rikyū did not have space at the end of the page (left). It assures the addressee that he will make every effort to guarantee payment.

It is possible to date the letter from a stylistic point of view to 1584/85.[4] The highly idiosyncratic writing style reflects the sensibilities of the master and has no characteristics in common with any established school of calligraphy.[5] Casual-looking yet powerful characters of thickening and thinning strokes, produced with the blunt tip of the brush loaded with ink, create a natural rhythm. The spontaneous quality of the brushwork, suggestive of a powerful personality, was attractive to many tea cognoscenti. As early as 1601, only ten years after his death, a record of a tea gathering chronicles the first known use of one of Rikyū's letters as a work of art. According to this document, the letter was mounted as a hanging scroll and displayed in a tearoom on the twentieth day of the leap-eleventh month in the sixth year of the Keichō era.[6] (See the appendix for a discussion of this scroll's mountings.) Rikyū's letters were preserved in great numbers as remembrances of the revered master, and they became enormously popular as objects to be displayed in tearooms. The demand for his letters was so strong that missives written by Rikyū's surrogates were treasured as much as his own work. Several of Rikyū's surrogates, the best known of whom was a certain Narumi, were mentioned in documents shortly after Rikyū's death, complicating the issue of authenticity of the letters believed to be from his hand.[7] From the enormous number of Rikyū-attributed letters, Komatsu Shigemi has selected a total of 265 examples as works of the master's own hand.[8]   MM

1. Matsuya 1967.
2. Haga 1963, p. 277.
3. Komatsu also believes in Rikyū's ownership of this Chinese calligraphy at one point. See Komatsu 1996, p. 316.
4. Komatsu 1996, no. 226.
5. Komatsu 1996, no. 264.
6. Matsuya 1967.
7. Some seventeenth-century connoisseurs took an extreme position that most of the so-called Rikyū letters were actually written by Narumi. For the problem of surrogates, see Komatsu 1999, pp. 574ff.
8. Komatsu 1996; Kuwata on the other hand included 263 examples in his book. See Kuwata 1971.

Hon'ami Kōetsu (1558–1637)

31.
Poem from "Senzai wakashū" with Design of Butterflies

Underpainting: Tawaraya Sōtatsu (died ca. 1640)
Momoyama period (1573–1615)
Segment from a handscroll mounted as a hanging scroll, ink and mica on paper, 11⅜ × 16 in. (28.9 × 40.5 cm)
Seal: Kōetsu
Literature: Fischer et al. 2000, no. 47

A protean figure in Japanese art, Hon'ami Kōetsu was a master calligrapher who is also admired for his contributions to lacquerware design, metalworking, pottery making, and the Noh theater. The tea ceremony was among his principal interests, and he was a great disciple of the tea master Furuta Oribe (1544–1615). Kōetsu's aesthetic vision, his involvement with various aspects of the visual and performing arts, and his personal and professional life have been the subject of recent studies.[1] He was born to a family whose trade—the cleaning, polishing, and appraising of swords—placed them in the upper class of Kyoto merchant society. He therefore had access to aristocratic circles of courtiers and warriors and enjoyed the privileged life of a wealthy and cultivated man. Important information on Kōetsu's life and family is found in the *Hon'ami gyōjōki* (Annals of the Hon'ami Family), a biography that was begun by his adopted son Kōsa (1578–1637) and completed by his grandson Kōho (1601–1682).[2] A more objective account appeared in *Nigiwai gusa* (Flourishing Grasses) of 1682, an essay collection by the noted tea master Sano Jōeki (also known as Haiya Jōeki, 1610–1691).[3] Some three hundred of Kōetsu's personal letters to his friends and acquaintances have recently come to light.[4] This correspondence provides insights into his daily affairs, but little mention is made of his artistic activities, except for frequent references to the tea ceremony and an occasional mention of pottery making.

Kōetsu's creative energy was focused on calligraphy, examples of which have been preserved in great number. In the first years of the seventeenth century he and the painter Tawaraya Sōtatsu (active about 1600, died about 1640)[5] began to work together in the production of spectacularly beautiful handscrolls, *shikishi* (square poem cards), *tanzaku* (narrow poem cards), folding fans, and books. Sōtatsu decorated the text paper, using primarily gold and silver, upon which Kōetsu inscribed classical poems from anthologies of the late Heian and Kamakura periods. This superbly satisfying body of work brings together the three great arts of poetry, painting, and calligraphy. The two artists initiated a spectacular revival of Heian-period aesthetics, but Sōtatsu's designs were also strikingly innovative and bold.

The joint efforts of Kōetsu and Sōtatsu ended in 1615, when Kōetsu moved from the city of Kyoto to the northwest suburb of Takagamine, where he had received a land grant from Tokugawa Ieyasu (1542–1616).[6] His community of friends and colleagues there did not include Sōtatsu, who apparently decided to pursue an independent artistic career, starting around 1620 when he began to receive larger commissions for screens and wall paintings.

In their eagerness to see Kōetsu as a great artistic visionary, past art historians have formulated a highly romantic view of the man, claiming that he excelled in all forms of art and adding painting to the traditional list of calligraphy, pottery making, and metal and lacquerware design. Of painting Kōetsu himself commented that he "did not become proficient" in that area,[7] although some have attributed to him the simple but charming design of a hare among grasses that decorates a small *kōgō* (incense container) in the Idemitsu Museum, Tokyo.[8] His contributions to the field of lacquer and metalwork production may have

been limited to providing ideas and guiding craftsmen, a possibility that led to his modern reputation as an "art director." It is also known that Kōetsu's involvement with ceramics began only after his move in 1615 to Takagamine, where he produced tea bowls characterized by utter simplicity combined with highly dramatic effects of surface texture.

Recent studies by Japanese scholars have traced the source for Kōetsu's calligraphic style beyond the sphere of influence of traditional calligraphy masters. A large number of Noh libretti (*utaibon*) in the so-called Kōetsu style, emphasizing the contrast between thick and thin brushstrokes, were traditionally attributed to Kōetsu himself. The calligrapher lived near Kanze Tadachika (later known as Kokusetsu, 1566–1626), the leader of the Kanze group of Noh performers, and both were members of Kyoto's elite class of cultured connoisseurs. A large body of signed and dated *utaibon* that Kokusetsu produced for the Noh theater reveals that his calligraphy closely resembles "Kōetsu style" writing. Recent scholarship has reattributed them to Kokusetsu and other Kanze calligraphers.[9] The consensus today is that Kōetsu, deeply involved with Noh, studied with and was influenced by Kanze masters, not the other way around as was believed in the past.

Both Kōetsu and Sōtatsu were involved in the epoch-making project known as the Sagabon (Saga Books) publications, so-named because the books were published in Kyoto's northwestern suburb of Saga. Under the direction of the wealthy Kyoto merchant Suminokura Soan (1571–1632), the books were printed with movable type rather than with the traditional block-printing technique, which had been in use in Japan since the eighth century, mainly for Buddhist texts. Printing with movable type was a new technique, possibly introduced from Korea shortly before the Saga project. However, whereas Korean movable type employed only Chinese characters, the Sagabon versions of Japanese classics like the *Tale of Genji* and *Tales of Ise* were printed using movable type of kana script. In this their creators may have been influenced by contemporary Christian publications.[10] Only a few years earlier Christian missionaries based in Nagasaki had pub-

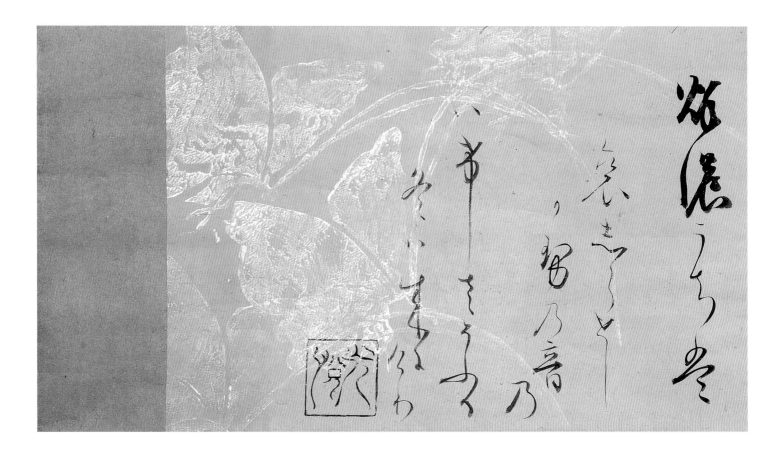

lished a series of books, both religious and secular, using movable type with kana letters, a revolutionary advance in Japanese printing. The text of the *Tales of Ise,* published at Saga in 1608, seems to have utilized Kōetsu's calligraphy as a model for the typeface, and other Saga books were decorated with designs which can be attributed to Sōtatsu.

Chinese paper decorated with printed patterns using mica or other pigments (known as *kara-kami,* or Tang paper) had been popular in Japan during the Heian era, and its use continued into later periods. Sōtatsu was probably influenced by these Chinese papers, but his own were startlingly new in their layout. Their fresh-looking printed designs offered close-up views of nature: dramatic shapes with a minimum of detail. His new approach had technical as well as stylistic elements: stamps, most likely made of wood (although some scholars have suggested copper), were inked only with gold or silver pigment, or with silver-white mica. Stamps were combined to create new shapes, and additional variation was provided by contrasting the forms made by using a whole stamp with those made by inking only a part of the stamp.

The design of butterflies that decorates this fragment made its first appearance in one of the earliest printed *utaibon*, dated about 1605 and entitled *Ōhara gokō* (Royal Visit to Ōhara). The design was repeated, not only in mica but also in gold and silver, on other books and scrolls in whose production Sōtatsu was involved.

The poem inscribed here by Kōetsu was taken from *Senzai wakashū* (Collection of Japanese Poems of a Thousand Years), the seventh imperial poetic anthology of 1188. The poem, number 393, was composed by Fujiwara Norinaga (1109–ca. 1180).

Aki no uchi wa
Aware shiraseshi
Kaze no oto no
Hageshisa souru
Fuyu wa kini keri.

Now the wind's moaning
That in autumn brought us knowledge
Of a gentle sorrow
Speaks in harsh voice that tells
Winter is here at last.[11]

Kōetsu transcribed poems from the anthologies of the Heian and Kamakura periods in a distinct calligraphic style—rich, fluid, sensuous, and spontaneous. The sense of vigor and liveliness in his works is due to the extreme contrast in character size—some large and darkly inked and others small and thin when the ink was running low. The characters tend to be round and tightly constructed but often lack a balance of scale among the individual strokes, and they may veer away from their central axes. Especially noticeable are the irregular spacing between characters and the slanting of the vertical lines.

Several features of the calligraphy in this piece make it rather unusual among Kōetsu's works, however. Here Kōetsu's characters are slightly elongated and each line of characters is rigidly straight. There is no strong contrast of ink tonality or brushstrokes, except for the first two letters "Aki no." Each character is written carefully with ample space within. As a result, this piece lacks the rhythmic movement, energy, and spontaneity of many of his other works.

Although similarities in brushstrokes and dimensions have been noted between this piece and a Kōetsu handscroll of the same anthology in the Tokyo National Museum, thought to have been produced around the same time,[12] visual evidence suggests that the pieces belong to different periods in Kōetsu's career. The present work may perhaps date from a later phase in Kōetsu's life than the Tokyo scroll. Unfortunately no other fragments of the handscroll from which this section was taken have been discovered.

Immediately following the poem is a square seal reading "Kōetsu" in dark ink. Both the writing and the seal have been partially obliterated by silver mica, as the ink was not easily absorbed by the mineral substance. A piece of dark brownish paper of coarse quality (width 2 7/8 in. [7.3 cm]) was added at the end of the fragment. Although faint traces of sprinkled gold are visible on this paper, it is unlikely that it was part of the scroll's backing since its dark color would have dimmed the pristine whiteness of the scroll paper. The addition of this paper of different quality and color has yet to be explained.

Many scholars have puzzled over the absence of any contextual relationship between Sōtatsu's decorations and the poems that Kōetsu inscribed over them.[13] It must be remembered, however, that Kōetsu inscribed poems upon commission, and it was most likely his clients who specified which poems were to be copied. The thematic disparity may have arisen if at the time of the commission clients provided Kōetsu with papers that were already decorated by Sōtatsu.   M M

1. For an English-speaking audience, two exhibitions and accompanying catalogues, one at the Honolulu Academy of Arts and Japan Society Gallery in New York of 1980–81, and another at the Philadelphia Museum of Art, held in 2000 (Link and Shimbo 1980–81; Fischer et al. 2000), helped clarify some aspects of Kōetsu's life and the circumstances that led to the extraordinary activity of the man. The catalogue of the Philadelphia Museum exhibition in particular contains an almost full rendering in English of the pertinent materials on Kōetsu's life, known in the past only to those capable of translating Japanese-language materials.
2. Masaki 1965.
3. Nakatsuka, ed. 1927–30, vol. 18, pp. 89–189.
4. Hayashiya et al. 1964, pp. 103–36, in which 138 of them are published.
5. Nothing is known about Sōtatsu's life before 1602, when he was commissioned to repair a group of scrolls from the famous Heike Nōkyō (sutras donated by the Heike family in 1167) at the Itsukushima Shrine. For Sōtatsu's life, see Link and Shimbō 1980–81, pp. 22–33.
6. See the map in Fischer et al. 2000, fig. 2.
7. *Hon'ami gyōjōki.*
8. Fischer et al. 2000, no. 102.
9. Itō 1978.
10. Akai Tatsurō in Hayashiya et al. 1964, pp. 82–96.
11. Translation by Edwin A. Cranston in Fischer et al. 2000, no. 47.
12. Fischer et al. 2000, nos. 46 and 47.
13. The last of whom was Edwin A. Cranston, in Fischer et al. 2000.

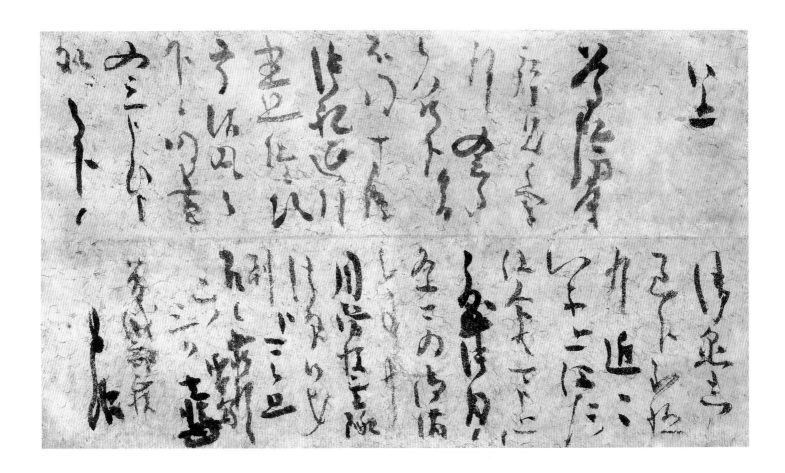

Hon'ami Kōetsu (1558–1637)

32.
Letter to Suganuma Sadayoshi

Edo period (1615–1868), 1625
Hanging scroll, ink on paper,
11⅛ × 18¼ in. (28.3 × 46.4 cm)
Signed: Tokuyūsai Kōetsu,
followed by a cipher (*kaō*)
Ex. coll.: Tabata Kihachi
Literature: Hayashiya et al. 1964,
p. 118, no. 67; Komatsu 1980,
no. 20

The calligraphy in Hon'ami Kōetsu's letters, all written in cursive *sōsho*, is markedly different from that of his poem scrolls and cards (cat. no. 31). The works inscribed with poetry were commissioned pieces, and the writing was carefully executed; in contrast the letters were apparently dashed off hastily and have far more spontaneous brushwork. Kōetsu's correspondence, numbering more than three hundred extant items, consists for the most part of invitations to tea, thank-you notes following tea gatherings, messages accompanying an exchange of gifts, references to Noh drama performances, or notes about Noh libretti and art objects such as Noh masks.[1] These letters cover a roughly fifty-year period and document a wide circle of friends and

acquaintances, including the highest class of court nobles, warrior rulers, tea masters, and Noh performers. The large number of letters that have been preserved indicates the reverence and affection with which Kōetsu was regarded, particularly in tea circles. The letters reveal the scope of Kōetsu's activities and his intimate thoughts and feelings, but their calligraphic style, with its casualness, immediacy, spontaneity, and warmth, was clearly reason for treasuring them as works of art. Although most of Kōetsu's correspondence was dated to the month and day, none of the inscriptions include the year, and only a small number of the letters can be dated precisely from evidence contained within the text.

Kōetsu's initial calligraphic endeavors were not

particularly auspicious. The earliest example of his correspondence is datable, from internal evidence, to about 1585; its writing style, like that of his early poetry inscriptions, lacks the beauty that characterizes his later works.[2] That letter, written when Kōetsu was about twenty-seven years old, is indistinguishable in its calligraphic style from the work of many other contemporary calligraphers. In about 1602, as demonstrated by a letter of that year,[3] Kōetsu's distinct personal style emerged, with its more pronounced contrast of thickening and thinning brushlines, rich plasticity of form, and rounded profile of characters.

The present letter,[4] dated the third day of the second month, was addressed to Suga Oribe no shō (Suganuma Sadayoshi, 1587–1643), lord of Zeze fief in Ōmi (modern Shiga prefecture), who served the second Tokugawa shogun Hidetada (1579–1632) and was awarded the title of Oribe no shō in 1614. This is one of the rare examples of a letter by Kōetsu that was folded in half, top to bottom. Originally, when the folded paper was opened, the writing on what is now the lower portion was literally upside down. When it was mounted as a hanging scroll, the letter was cut in half and rearranged so that the writing could be read without difficulty. The letter reads:

> As above
> Thank you for your esteemed letter, which I read with deference and pleasure. I do apologize for the delay in thanking you for your letter, as I was involved with the preparation for Matasaburō's travel to Edo. I understand Usamaru too is going to Edo, although I had invited Matasaburō to visit me tomorrow noon. I deeply appreciate your kindness. I shall visit you soon and report to you about my trip to Edo. I am glad to hear that you were able to meet him, and you must be quite happy about it. This is all thanks to the adroitness and good will of Suō no kami and Gentaku hōin and I would like to remind you of this.
> Respectfully yours,

> third day, the second month   Tokuyūsai
> Kōetsu [kaō]
> Kan Oribe no shō
> Respectfully reporting

Kōetsu acknowledges receipt of a letter from Suganuma, apologizes for his delay in responding, and refers to two individuals, Matasaburō and Usamaru, who are otherwise unidentified. He expresses gratitude to Lord Suō (most likely Itakura Shigemasa, 1587–1656), who was appointed to the all-powerful position of Kyoto Shoshidai (shogunal deputy) in 1620, and Noma Gentaku (1585–1646), the shogunal physician. Gentaku, a noted doctor, was named Hidetada's Edo-based personal physician in 1626, and thus the letter must be earlier than that date. Kōetsu mentions his own plans to travel to Edo. He is known to have taken such a trip in the early spring 1625, following the sudden death of Kōshitsu, the head of the Hon'ami family, in Edo. While in the city Kōetsu was given an audience by the third Tokugawa shogun, Iemitsu (r. 1623–1651).[5] On the basis of these facts, this letter may be dated to 1625.

As in all of Kōetsu's letters, the writing style of the present example is rather blunt yet supple. Thick strokes in dark ink alternate with small letters rendered in thin strokes with lighter ink tones and a drier brush, indicating where Kōetsu had to pause to replenish his brush. The rhythmic flow of brushstrokes, the contrast between large and small characters, thick and thin lines, and dark and light ink, and the slight leftward slant in the balancing of the text lines create a sense of spontaneity and a casual yet direct mastery of the brush.   MM

1. See Komatsu 1980 and Masuda 1980; see also Fischer et al. 2000, pl. 1.
2. Komatsu Shigemi in Hayashiya et al. 1964, p. 37.
3. Komatsu Shigemi in Hayashiya et al. 1964, p. 37, and Fischer et al. 2000, pl. 3.
4. This letter was transcribed by Komatsu; information on individuals mentioned in it is given in Komatsu 1980, no. 20.
5. See *Kōetsu nenpyō* (Kōetsu Chronology), in Hayashiya et al. 1964, n.p.

Ōtagaki Rengetsu (1791–1871)

33.
Hazy Evening Moon

Edo period (1615–1868), dated
1867
Hanging scroll, ink on paper,
38⅜ × 7⅞ in. (97.5 × 20 cm)
Signature: Rengetsu nanajū-
nana sai

Women artists, many of whom were also known
for their waka poetry, distinguished themselves in
nineteenth-century Japan.[1] In fact, women poets
and novelists are prominent throughout the annals
of Japanese literature. Women authors, most notably
the renowned Murasaki Shikibu, had flourished in
the Late Heian period (ca. 900–1185), only to see
their fortunes decline following the rise of the warrior class; male poets and painters dominated the
cultural arena in the war-ravaged days of the Muromachi and Momomaya periods. However, a modest
revival took place during the later years of the
Edo period with an increasing number of women
achieving artistic and literary fame.[2]

Ōtagaki Rengetsu, the creator of this ethereal and
charming work, was one of the women artists who
achieved success within the new social order of the
Edo period. Unlike their courtly Heian forebears,
these women were not necessarily from the upper
echelons of society but often belonged to the lower
or middle class. Their less exalted social status
allowed them a greater freedom than their aristocratic counterparts, whose actions were strictly limited by the rigidly patriarchal Confucian ideology
imposed by the shogunal government. Increased
educational opportunity for people of the lower
classes during the latter half of the Edo period also
contributed to this second flowering of literary and
artistic activity among women.

Rengetsu's life began inauspiciously;[3] her parentage
was uncertain and she was adopted by the Ōtagaki
family. A series of deaths in her family, including
those of her two husbands and infant children,
wreaked havoc with her life. Amazingly she survived
adversity and created a series of gentle, lyrical, and
highly sophisticated paintings, embellished with
refined verses inscribed in elegant calligraphy. In
1823 at the age of thirty-two she took the tonsure,
adopting the Buddhist name of Rengetsu (Lotus
Moon). After her stepfather's death in 1832 she
began a serious study of waka, progressing so

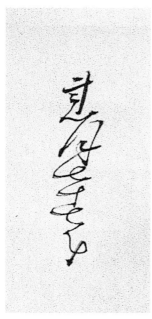

Fig. 20. Detail of cat. no. 33

quickly that her name was included as a poet in the *Heian jinbutsu shi*, the Who's Who of Kyoto, as early as 1838.[4] Her name appeared in this directory again in 1852 and 1867. As her reputation as a poet grew, she made ceramic wares in order to support herself. Her pottery products, on which she inscribed her own poems, were mostly for use in preparing steeped tea (*sencha*).

Rengetsu used the imagery of a hazy spring moon in her waka and often painted a partially hidden moon defined by broadly applied, misty ink,[5] as in the present hanging scroll. The moon, an almost full circle, floats above her poem's vertical columns:

Yado kasanu
Hito no tsurasa o
Nasake nite
Oborozuki yo no
Hana no shita fushi.

Refused at the inn —
But I took this unkindness
As a gracious act;
Under the hazy evening moon
I slept beneath blossoms.[6]

This verse, one of her most famous, also graces a number of her small teapots (*kyūsu*).[7] The tiny columnlike signature, "Rengetsu," followed by her age, "nanajū-nana sai" (age seventy-seven), resembles a reclining figure (the author) under a large cherry tree, the image evoked in the poem but not shown in the painting.

Rengetsu's calligraphy, smooth and fluid, is clear and easy to decipher. Her characters have a squat horizontal shape, rooted in her practice of inscribing her poems on compact ceramic surfaces.[8] The brief lyrical poem and simple drawing evoke not only a spring evening but also the sentiments in waka poetry of the Heian period. It is not difficult to understand Rengetsu's great popularity during her own lifetime and the immense demand for her works, which is said to have oppressed her.   M M

1. Fister 1988, p. 143.
2. Fister 1988, p. 9.
3. Main sources for her life are autobiographical notes contained in her letter to a much younger protégé and later a leading *nanga* (literati painting) artist painter Tomioka Tessai (1836–1924). The letter was written when she was eighty-four years old. Other letters also contain information on her life; see Rengetsu 1980. For a chronology of her life, see Kuroda 1961.
4. The *Heian jinbutsu shi* of the ninth year of the Tenpō era (1838); fifth year of the Kaei era (1852); and the third year of the Keiō era (1867).
5. Fister 1988, nos. 69 and 71.
6. Translation by Patricia Fister, in Fister 1988, no. 72.
7. Fister 1988, no. 72.
8. Fister 1988, no. 72.

WRITINGS OF ZEN MONKS

Zhang Jizhi (1186–1266)

34.
Excerpt from "Song of Leyou Park"

Southern Song dynasty
(1127–1279)
Section of a handscroll mounted
as a hanging scroll, 12¾ × 30⅛ in.
(32.4 × 76.5 cm)
Gift of Sylvan Barnet and
William Burto, 2000 (2000.325)
Ex coll.: Tokyo Gallery
Literature: London Gallery,
Tokyo 1995, pp. 6–10

Zhang Jizhi (J: Chō Sokushi), the last important calligrapher of the Song period, came from a family of high officials and brilliant scholars from Liyang (modern He Xian, Anhui province).[1] His father, Zhang Xiaobo (*jinshi*, 1163), attained the rank of Vice Grand Secretary. His father's cousin, Zhang Xiaoxiang (1133–1170), not only took first place in the metropolitan exams of 1154 but was a highly regarded calligrapher noted for his large-character writings.[2]

Because of his father's merit, Zhang Jizhi entered the civil service with the honorary rank of Gentleman for Rendering Service (*chengwulang*) and a nominal appointment in the tax transport bureau of Liangzhe Circuit (parts of modern Zhejiang and Jiangsu provinces). He later obtained his *jinshi* degree, the highest rank in the civil service examination system, and held a number of low administrative posts without rising to high office. Toward the end of his career he was appointed magistrate of Jiaxing, but he declined the post and was allowed to retire, sometime before 1256. His fame as a calligrapher, however, spread beyond the borders of the Song to northern China and to Japan, where his handwriting was particularly prized by Zen monks.[3]

Zhang's own interest in Buddhism is well attested to by the various Buddhist sutras that he transcribed, including a 1253 transcription of the Diamond Sutra that in 1254 he presented to the Chan (J: Zen) monk Xiyan Liaohui (1198–1262), a disciple of Wuzhun Shifan (1177–1249).[4] The Japanese monk Enni Ben'en (1202–1280), who studied with Wuzhun between 1235 and 1241, returned to Kyoto with at least three works by Zhang Jizhi: a Diamond Sutra, a Lotus Sutra, and an Avalokiteshvara Sutra.[5] *Excerpt from "Song of Leyou Park,"* originally part of a long handscroll, bespeaks another side of Zhang's personality. It is one of several works by Zhang, all in large characters,

which transcribe poems by Du Fu (712–770) and others on court life and official service.

Excerpt from "Song of Leyou Park" preserves a portion of a Du Fu poem that describes a springtime outing in one of the imperial preserves of the Tang capital, Chang'an.[6] The poem opens with an account of the revelers partaking of food and drink on a high hill followed by a ride through the park to lakeside halls where dancers perform. In its present fragmentary state, the text preserves only a portion of the

following two couplets (the text of the scroll is in italics):

> Palace gates, open beneath clear skies, reveal a
> vast expanse;
> *By the Serpentine are kingfisher curtains, arrayed*
> *with silver plaques.*
> *Skimming the water, back and forth, the dancers'*
> *sleeves flutter;*
> Climbing to the clouds, crisp and clear, the
> singers' voices rise.[7]

The final section of the poem turns wistful as the poet reflects on his inability to attract the attention of the court and his anxiety over what the future will bring.

Other Du Fu poems transcribed by Zhang also reflect Zhang's interest in official service. A long handscroll in the Liaoning Provincial Museum, brushed in 1250 when Zhang was sixty-four years old, transcribes two poems.[8] The first, "Termination of the Court Audience at the Zichen Palace," describes the pageantry of a morning audience that Du Fu witnessed when he held a minor court appointment.[9] The second poem, "Presented to Reception Officer Tian Cheng," is a flattering request for help in gaining imperial recognition and official advancement.[10] The Liaoning scroll bears no dedication but may have been intended for a high-ranking official, perhaps one who had been helpful as Zhang neared or entered retirement. Du Fu's "Wash the Weapons," a fragment of which survives from Zhang's hand, would also have been suitable for presentation to a high official as it celebrates recent military victories and looks forward to a time when weapons will be put away and never used again.[11]

Zhang's admiration for Du Fu was undoubtedly influenced by the revival of interest in the Tang poet by the leading scholar-officials of the Northern Song period (960–1126), including Su Shi (1037–1101) and Huang Tingjian (1045–1105). This interest led to the intensive study of Du Fu's life and poetry, culminating in an annotated compilation of his poems published by Huang He in 1226, when Zhang Jizhi was forty.[12] On a more personal level, Zhang, like Du Fu, came from a distinguished family of scholar-officials but spent his career in minor official posts and achieved lasting recognition only through his art. In spite of his lackluster career, however, Du Fu continued to hope for opportunities to serve at court; Zhang's selection of poems suggests a similar preoccupation with government service. Like Du Fu, Zhang could also be frank in his advocacy of what he considered to be morally correct. Zhang's biography relates that, although living in retirement, he wrote a letter advocating mercy for the fatherless children of an official who had been wrongly executed due to slander. Zhang even directed his grandnephew to marry the man's orphaned daughter. Zhang's initiative is credited for the eventual rehabilitation of the man's reputation.[13] But it was for his calligraphy that Zhang was best known. His official biography concludes that he "was famed throughout the world for his ability as a calligrapher; the people of Jin especially treasured his calligraphies."[14] Viewed from this perspective,

the poems Zhang chose to transcribe may have been selected with a view to flattering the recipients.[15]

Zhang was particularly proficient in a dynamic version of running regular script also known as Song regular script, which is characterized by delicate connecting ligatures between some of the individual brushstrokes.[16] He utilized this same script in writings of greatly varied scale.[17] In Japan a group of monumental titles suitable for identifying the halls of a Buddhist temple complex is attributed to Zhang. The most famous of these is the two-character inscription "Abbot's Quarters" (C: *fangzhang*; J: *hōjō*), now in the collection of Tōfukuji, the Buddhist temple in Kyoto.[18] This piece and other such titles probably served as models for the carved wooden placards hung above the doors of the various halls. In these writings a single character fills the entire height of the paper. The transcriptions of poems by Du Fu and others are written in characters half the height of a handscroll, so that each column consists of two characters. Zhang's sutra transcriptions are written in medium-size running regular script with from eight to fifteen characters in each column, although most examples have ten-character columns. Letters reveal Zhang at his most informal and exhibit the smallest characters.[19] Regardless of the size, however, Zhang's writing is amazingly consistent in style.

Excerpt from "Song of Leyou Park" consists of four columns in large running regular script. The eight characters were once part of a much longer composition. Since Du Fu's poem is made up of twenty lines, each seven characters in length, Zhang's transcription of the entire poem in two-character columns would consist of a seventy-column handscroll measuring more than forty-five feet (about fourteen meters) in length. This compares closely to the Liaoning Provincial Museum handscroll, which transcribes two Du Fu poems in fifty-six two-character columns (plus a six-column colophon written in three-character columns) and which measures more than forty-one feet (about thirteen meters) in length. Further evidence that *Excerpt from "Song of Leyou Park"* is taken from a longer composition comes from the fact that the second column from the right is bisected by a seam where two sheets of paper are joined. Faint traces of a seal along the lower right edge of this seam show that an early owner attempted to prevent the handscroll from being cut apart by imprinting his seal over each join.[20]

Zhang's writing style is characterized by boldly contrasting blunt and sinuous brushstrokes and fluid ligatures. Bold coarse lines and delicate lines often occur within the same character. The sharp entries or final delicate connecting ligatures used in many strokes contrast with the blunt abrupt endings seen in others, particularly Zhang's powerful vertical strokes. Each character is uniformly dark, but Zhang frequently allows bristles of the brush to separate, giving a streaked quality known as "flying white" that imparts a sense of speed and energy.

In spite of the enormous variations in line width, the individual characters are generally consistent in size—each occupying either an imaginary square or a somewhat elongated rectangle. The spacing around characters is usually generous and the intervals between columns are even more pronounced. The spacing, dark ink, and broad lines impart a sense of monumentality to the characters, yet this is offset by the relaxed informality of the execution. There is not a single straight line in Zhang's writing: each brushstroke curves slightly and varies in thickness, often dramatically, with the brush's entry point or exit often marked by a sharp point or a blunt rough bulge. Plump rounded curving forms also contrast with crisp angular shapes. The result is a dazzlingly complex style that alternates between fluidity and abruptness, delicacy and coarseness, with apparent effortlessness. The angular intersections of the carefully shaped lines also serve to animate the negative spaces between brushstrokes. The diagonal and vertical elements of the radical "man" (*ren*), the lefthand component in each of the characters in the leftmost column of *Excerpt from "Song of Leyou Park,"* meet at nearly a right angle.

Chinese scholars have likened Zhang's writing to that of the Tang masters Chu Suiliang (596–658) and Yan Zhenqing (709–785)—the latter also mentioned in conjunction with the writing of Zhang's relative Zhang Xiaoxiang, whose style shows many

of the same qualities of thickening and thinning brushstrokes found in Zhang Jizhi's works.[21] Both men were also influenced by the individualistic styles of Mi Fu (1052–1107) and Huang Tingjian.[22] While Zhang was undoubtedly influenced by all of these sources, he did not follow any of them in a dogmatic fashion and seems to have succeeded in inventing his own style—a trait that the Ming critic Dong Qichang (1555–1636), himself an ardent lay follower of Chan, greatly appreciated, characterizing Zhang's writing as following no earlier master, but rather conveying "the outflowing of the innermost self."[23]

Given the stylistic consistency of Zhang's extant writings, and the fact that all of his dated calligraphies fall within a ten-year period from 1246 to 1256, it is difficult to assign a date to *Excerpt from "Song of Leyou Park."* A record of a Diamond Sutra written by Zhang in 1263 suggests that he remained active during the last years of his life.[24] Likewise Zhang must have had a long career before 1246. Certainly he was already well known to members of the Chan Buddhist community by 1241, when he was fifty-five years of age (fifty-six *sui*) and the monk Enni returned to Japan with his works. It is even likely that he had gained a reputation in his thirties, like his relative Zhang Xiaoxiang, who died at the age of thirty-seven, since his official biography states that his writings were admired by the people of the Jin dynasty, which was extinguished by the Mongols in 1234, when Zhang would have been forty-eight.[25]

The popularity of Zhang's calligraphy among the people of Jin and the Japanese highlights the unorthodox nature of his writing, which may have been easier for foreigners to appreciate than for his fellow countrymen. While Chinese appraisals of Zhang's calligraphy have been mixed, in the Jin territories of northern China and in Japan his calligraphy was extremely influential, especially among Zen monks, who were less concerned with Chinese orthodox calligraphic traditions.[26] Indeed, it is likely that *Excerpt from "Song of Leyou Park,"* like other fragments in Japanese collections, was cut from a handscroll only after it came to Japan so that it could be remounted as a hanging scroll suitable for display in a tokonoma as part of the tea ceremony.[27] Completely disregarding the poetic phrasing of the original, *Excerpt from "Song of Leyou Park"* was venerated primarily for its aesthetic qualities without regard to its literary content.　　　　M K H

1. For Zhang's birth and death dates see Fu 1976, pp. 43–45 (English summary, pp. 21–23) and the biographical entry by Kanda Kiichirō in *Shodō zenshū* 1954–68, vol. 16 (China, vol. 11), p. 172. While Zhang's family home was in Anhui, one source gives his place of birth as Yin Xian (modern Ningbo, Zhejiang province); see *Songren juanji ziliao suoyin* 1974–76, vol. 3, p. 2398.

2. For Zhang biographical information on Xiaobo and Xiaoxiang see *Songren juanji ziliao suoyin* 1974–76, vol. 3, pp. 2377–76. According to Wen Zhengming's colophon to *Wang shi Baoben'an ji* (Record of Mr. Wang's Hermitage for Requiting One's Ancestors), these men were brothers, not cousins. See *Sung Zhang Jizhi shu "Baoben An ji"* in Liaoning Provincial Museum 1962.

3. For Zhang's official biography see *Song shi* 1977, *juan* 445, p. 13145. See also the biographical summary by Kanda Kiichirō in *Shodō zenshū* 1954–68, vol. 16 (China, vol. 11), p. 172; Fontein and Hickman 1970, pp. 26–28; and Fu 1976.

4. For the 1253 Diamond Sutra, now in the collection of Chishakuin, in Kyoto, and a discussion of Zhang's Buddhist affiliations see Furuta 1962. See also Fu 1976 for a stylistic analysis of Zhang's sutra writings.

5. See Fu 1976, p. 46 (English summary, p. 25).

6. The Leyou Park, first established in 59 B.C. by Han Xuandi (r. 74–49 B.C.) at the site of the highest point in the metropolitan area, was a favorite place for the palace ladies to view the spring and fall scenery on the Double Third and Double Ninth festivals. See *Zhong wen da ci dian* 1973, vol. 9, p. 7403. In Tang times it was expanded to include a meandering lake, the Serpentine, first constructed by Han Wudi (r. 141–87 B.C.); see under *qujiang* in *Zhong wen da ci dian* 1973, vol. 9, p. 6641.

7. The poem was identified and transcribed by Nakata Yūjirō in his entry on "Chō Sokushi sho To Ho Rakuyū koen shi dankan" (Zhang Jizhi's Writing of a Fragmentary Section of Du Fu's "Song of Leyou Park") in London Gallery, Tokyo 1995, pp. 6–9. The present translation benefited from the generous advice and translation of Jonathan Chaves, in a private communication, and from the translation in Hung 1952, pp. 55–56. While the poem cannot be dated with certainty, Hung suggests it was composed between 745 and 749.

8. For a reproduction of the whole scroll see *Zhongguo gu dai shu hua mu lu* 1984– , vol. 15 [Liaoning Provincial Museum], *Liao* 1–046. A section of this scroll is also reproduced in *Song Jin Yuan shu fa* 1986, pl. 73. For a tracing copy of this calligraphy, see "Nan Song Zhang Jizhi shu Du shi," in Shanghai Museum 1964, no. 9.

9. "Zichen Dian tuichao kouhao"; for a translation see Hung 1952, pp. 125–26.

10. "Zeng xian'na shi"; for a translation see Hung 1952, p. 80.

11. See *Shodō zenshū* 1954–68, vol. 16 (China, vol. 11), pls. 71–72. For a translation of this poem ("Xi bingma") see Hung 1952, pp. 126–27.

12. For the Song revival of interest in Du Fu see Hung 1952, pp. 3–4. For biographical information on Huang He and his father, Huang Xi (*jinshi*, 1166), whose compilation of Du Fu poems, *Huang shi buzhu Du shi*, he completed and published, see *Songren juanji ziliao suoyin*, 1974–76, vol. 4, pp. 2841, 2886.

13. See *Song shi* 1977, *juan* 445, p. 13145. For this and similar comments see Fu 1976, pp. 45–46 (English summary, p. 23).

14. See Fu 1976, pp. 45–46 (English summary, p. 23).

15. In addition to the poems by Du Fu, large-character writings by Zhang also include: *Running Script Transcription of Li He's [791–817] Passing a Lofty Hall (Gao xuan guo),* a long handscroll that has lost portions of the poem at both the beginning and end, and *Running Script Transcription of Record of the Waiting on the Clepsydra Courtyard (Dailuo Yuan ji),* a text by Wang Yucheng (954–1001), in *Zhongguo gu dai shu hua mu lu* 1984– , vol. 2 [Shanghai Museum], *Hu* 1–0073–74. Kanda Kiichirō has also mentioned the existence of a handscroll with two-character columns in the Tokugawa collection in Mito; see *Shodō zenshū* 1954–68, vol. 16 (China, vol. 11), nos. 71–72, p. 158.

16. Weng Fanggang (1733–1818) identified this form of running-regular script as Song regular script. See Fu 1976, p. 48 (English summary, p. 26).

17. Fu categorizes Zhang's calligraphy in five groups: giant-size characters for titles and frontispieces; transcriptions of poetry by Du Fu and others in large fluent-regular script; sutras and epitaphs in medium-sized "regular" script; small running-script works; and letters in running-cursive script. See Fu 1976, p. 47 (English summary, p. 25).

18. This title, one of eight such works in Tōfukuji, bears no signature and has been variously attributed. It is believed to have been brought to Japan by Tōfukuji's founder, Enni Ben'en, in 1241. See Fontein and Hickman 1970, no. 9, pp. 26–28; see also Brinker and Kanazawa 1996, no. 35, pp. 272–73.

19. For examples of Zhang's letters see *Song Jin Yuan shu fa* 1986, pl. 71, and *Shodō zenshū* 1954–68, vol. 16 (China, vol. 11), pp. 6–7, pl. 87.

20. The fact that no trace of the seal ink is visible on the left side of the seam suggests that the left sheet of paper may have been slightly trimmed, although no loss or retouching of the characters is evident so the amount of trimming was negligible.

21. Zhang Jizhi's friend the monk Wuwen Daocan (active mid-thirteenth century) mentions a number of earlier masters whose styles influenced Zhang, including Wang Xizhi (303–361) and his son Wang Xianzhi (344–348), as well as the Tang calligraphers Ouyang Xun (557–641) and Chu Suiliang (596–658); see *Shodō zenshū* 1954–68, vol. 16 (China, vol. 11), p. 7. Wen Zhengming (1470–1559) observes that Zhang continued the family tradition established by his relative Zhang Xiaoxiang, whose style was influenced by Yan Zhenqing; see reference in note 2 above. For examples of Zhang Xiaoxiang's calligraphy see *Song Jin Yuan shu fa* 1986, pls. 53–54.

22. According to Matsui Joryū, Zhang Xiaoxiang inscribed a colophon on Huang Tingjian's *Jing Fuboshen Ci shijuan* of 1101, now in the Hosokawa Collection, Tokyo. See Matsui 1962, p. 58.

23. See Amy McNair's entry on Zhang's Diamond Sutra in Harrist and Fong 1999–2001, p. 118.

24. See Fu 1976, pp. 53, 62 (English summary, pp. 29, 37), where it is noted that a sutra dated to 1263 was recorded in the collection of An Qi (1683–ca. 1746); see also Nakata et al. 1983, p. 94.

25. See Fu 1976, p. 46 (English summary, p. 23). Since the Mongols did not proclaim their own Yuan dynasty until 1260, it is also possible that the Chinese living under Mongol rule in the old Jin territories might still have been referred to as "people of Jin" after 1234.

26. See Nakata et al. 1983, p. 94.

27. For a similar fragment, now in the collection of Chisakuin, Kyoto, see *Shodō zenshū* 1954–68, vol. 16 (China, vol. 11), pls. 73–74. The present scroll is accompanied by a Japanese wooden box inscribed on the cover with the title "Ink trace of Zhang Jizhi [*Chō Sokushi bokuseki*]." A seal, now illegible, has been impressed on the inside of this cover. At one end of the box exterior is a paper label that identifies the piece as having been viewed by Yoraku-in, the Buddhist name adopted in 1725 by the well-known calligrapher Konoe Iehiro (1667–1736). This label notes the presence of the inscription on the box cover. It should be noted that the scroll is about one-half inch (1.5 centimeters) shorter than the box interior, so it is not clear if the box was originally made for this piece. I am indebted to Miyeko Murase for these observations.

35.
Portrait of Shun'oku Myōha

Nanbokuchō period (1336–1392)
Hanging scroll, ink, color, and
gold on silk, 40 × 20½ in. (114.3
× 52 cm)
Colophon by Shun'oku Myōha
Seal: illegible
Ex coll.: Henri Vever, Paris
Literature: Sotheby's, London
1994, no. 17; Morse and Morse
1996, no. 34; London Gallery,
Tokyo 2000, no. 117

The Zen master Shun'oku Myōha (1311–1388), one of the preeminent mentors of early Japanese Zen, is depicted here against a neutral background. He is portrayed in three-quarter view, turning his gaze to the right of the beholder. A self-eulogy written by Myōha appears above the figure as four lines of text.

> There are no eyes on the top of the head
> There are eyebrows under the chin.
> This is everything; this is nothing.
> I also could not become a phoenix.[1]

The inscription concludes by stating that the portrait was made for a ritual at the Muryōjuin Hall (the location of this structure is not known).

The master is seated cross-legged on a low-backed chair hung with an elaborately figured textile. He is clad in a formal garb of figured silk with a surplice draped over his left shoulder, fastened by a large ring. In his right hand he holds a staff, while his left is clenched in a fist. His shoes sit neatly on a footstool in front of him.

A disciple of one of the most important Zen priests of Japan, Musō Soseki (1275–1351; cat. no. 36), Shun'oko was a confidante of the first Ashikaga shogun Takauji (1305–1358). His life was recorded in considerable detail, and because of his prestige a handful of his portraits have survived, at least four in Japanese collections. Shun'oko held a series of important positions at leading Zen temples in Japan, such as the abbacy at Tenryūji and, most important, the abbacy at Shōkokuji, the temple

under direct shogunal supervision. Among his disciples were many of the most renowned scholar-poet-monks of the time, including Gyokuen Bonpō (cat. no. 40). It is said that more than 8,500 disciples took tonsure under Shun'oku's supervision.

Portraits of Zen masters are known in Japan as *chinsō* (or *chinzō*). The word's root is *ushnisha* (J: *nikkei*), the Sanskrit term for the fleshy protuberance on top of the Buddha's head, but in Japan the word came to signify paintings and sculptures made to preserve the likeness of Zen masters. *Chinsō* paintings, in particular, have been defined by scholars—most notably historians of Japanese art—as physical proofs of enlightenment, certificates of dharma lineage granted by masters to their disciples. Recently, however, some Buddhologists have challenged this widely held interpretation on the basis of new examinations of texts, including documents from China.[2]

According to these scholars, the term *chinsō* (C: *ding-xiang*) designates a broad range of portraiture, but no textual source has been discovered to prove that the word signifies dharma inheritance. Rather, the importance of *chinsō* was firmly established in the funerary and memorial rites of East Asian Buddhism. In this respect Japanese *chinsō* preserve the venerable Chinese tradition of secular portrait painting. In China portrait images were produced in large numbers to be displayed in rooms, sent home as reminders of the sitter, given to daughters about to be married, or exchanged with friends,[3] as well as to be used in funerary rites and

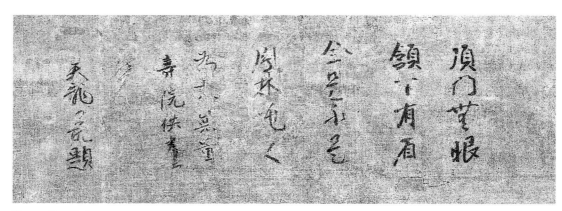

Fig. 21. Detail of cat. no. 35

memorial services. *Chinsō* of monks were disseminated among their followers, both lay and monastic,[4] and many such portraits were brought from Southern Song China to Japan, where iconographic standards for Zen *chinsō* were quickly established.

It has recently been acknowledged, even by Japanese art historians,[5] that the gift of a portrait did not necessarily symbolize successful transfer of the dharma from teacher to pupil. This view is supported by the fact that *chinsō* were often given to Japanese monks who had studied in China for only a brief period; in addition, colophons were inscribed by Chinese monks on portraits that had been painted in Japan and brought to China for that specific purpose.[6]

Past scholarship claimed that the truly naturalistic depiction of the sitter's face in *chinsō* painting was proof of *chinsō*'s function as a certificate of dharma inheritance, but this long-held theory must also be reexamined. It is undeniable that when compared to the imaginary and stereotypical Japanese portrait images of earlier centuries, Muromachi- and post-Muromachi-period *chinsō* reflect a much stronger tendency to depict the physical idiosyncrasies of the individuals portrayed. Yet in some instances a change in the subject's identity has occurred,[7] and it appears that *chinsō* were not necessarily created using living sitters as models. Limbs and other body parts were depicted as traditionally appropriate for the subject's social status, while the faces may have been copied from models painted directly from life.

In summary Chinese textual sources suggest that *chinsō* were produced and disseminated primarily for funerals and memorial services and were not intended as proofs of dharma lineage. The popular belief that *chinsō* paintings represented successful instances of dharma transmission may have arisen because of the well-known Zen practice in which a master's teaching alone helps his disciple to achieve enlightenment.

A countless number of eulogies and self-eulogies inscribed on *chinsō* have survived in literature, some from paintings that are no longer extant. However, numerous *chinsō*, complete with colophons, are still preserved in Japan. Their self-eulogies often poke fun at the subject's own visage, a literary convention taken from the autobiographical writings of Chan figures in China.[8] This *chinsō* of Sun'oku Myōha bears a self-eulogy based on this singular tradition. MM

1. Morse and Morse 1996, p. 90.
2. Foulk and Sharp 1993–94; also see Ide 2001, p. 35.
3. Ebine 2000, p. 31.
4. Foulk and Sharp 1993–94, p. 206.
5. Ide 2001, p. 33.
6. Ide 2001, p. 34.
7. Levine 2001.
8. Foulk and Sharp 1993–94, p. 197.

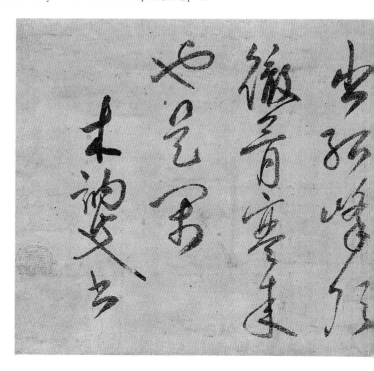

Musō Soseki (1275–1351)

36.
Poem on the Theme of Snow

Nanbokuchō period (1336–1392)
Hanging scroll, ink on paper,
11¾ × 32½ in. (29.9 × 82.6 cm)
Seal: Musō
Ex. coll.: Umezawa Memorial
Museum, Tokyo
Literature: Shimizu and
Rosenfield 1984–85, no. 42

Musō Soseki was a prominent and influential Zen priest active from the late Muromachi to the Nanbokuchō period. Initially he studied Tendai and Shingon Buddhism, but after training under Yishan Yining (1247–1317), the Chinese Chan master living in Japan, he turned to the practice of Zen Buddhism. He was greatly respected and trusted by the most powerful figures of his day, including Emperor Godaigo (1288–1339), from whom he received the special designation "National Master Musō," and Ashikaga Takauji (1305–1358). During his lifetime Musō founded over fifteen temples, including Tenryūji in Kyoto, and in his later years became abbot of Shōkokuji temple in Kyoto, which was built under the sponsorship of the Ashikaga shogunate and was also ranked among the Five Mountains network of Zen temples.

Poem on the Theme of Snow was formerly in the Nagashima collection, famous for its calligraphic works by Zen priests. The text, which describes the first rays of dawn shining forth on a snowy landscape, reads as follows:

On the theme of snow

From heaven fall icy petals;
In the sky not a spot of blue remains.
A dusting of jade covers the ground
And buries the blue mountains.
The sun rises over the mountain peak.
The chill pierces my bones.
Silence prevails.

Written by the Clumsy Old Stutterer[1]

The twenty-plus extant examples of Musō's calligraphy can be divided into two main categories: the first is one-line columns of large characters, generally transcribing Buddhist maxims, and the other is lengthier poems of Buddhist verse in the horizontal hanging scroll format, such as *Poem on the Theme of Snow*. In general Musō's calligraphy is executed in an elegant cursive script, reflecting the influence of his Chinese master, Yishan Yining. Musō's lines, however, are not quite as supple as Yishan's, and he does not share his master's ease

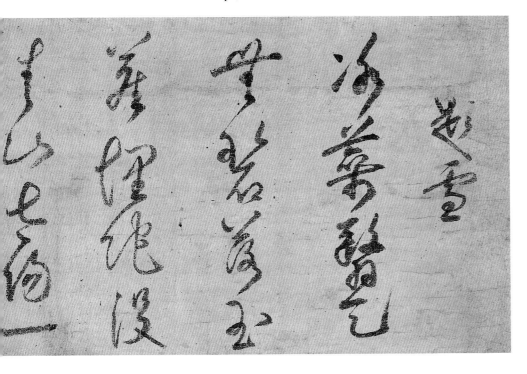

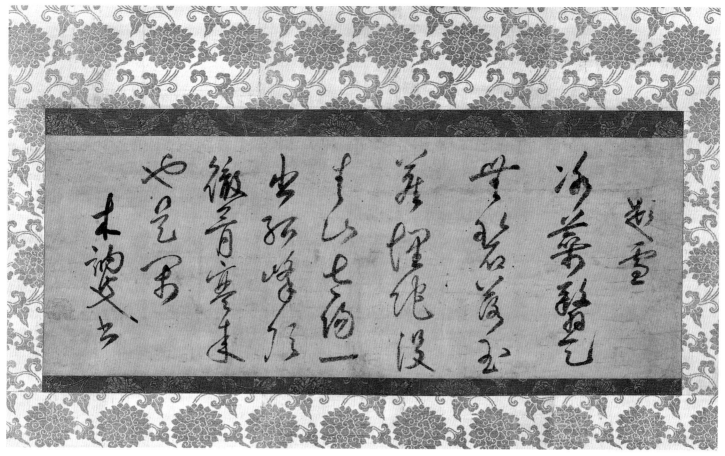

Fig. 22. Detail of mounting of hanging scroll (cat. no. 36)

with the brush or his largeness of scale. Instead Musō's brushwork has a certain conscientiousness, and his characters convey the impression that he has carefully studied classical examples, resulting in a stylized expression. Unlike other *bokuseki* done by Zen monks, Musō's calligraphy does not convey a sense of spontaneity but instead a calm orthodoxy and fidelity to classical styles. In addition, his characters are slightly larger in size than typical examples of Zen calligraphy of this period and tend to angle toward the upper right.

A seal pressed on the work reads "Musō" and matches the seals found on two other Musō works.

TK

1. Translated in Shimizu and Rosenfield 1984–85, p. 126.

Kokan Shiren (1278–1346)

37.
Poem about Sugar

Nanbokuchō period (1336–1392)
Hanging scroll, ink on paper,
12¼ × 18⅝ in. (31.1 × 47.3 cm)
Seal: Kokan
Literature: Shimizu and
Rosenfield 1984–85, no. 43

Born in Kyoto, Kokan Shiren had his early Zen training at temples in that city, among them Kenninji, Nanzenji, and Tōfukuji. He later traveled east to Kamakura, where he stayed at Engakuji and studied under the celebrated Chinese master Yishan Yining. With extensive training in the fundamentals of Zen, Kokan would go on to become a leading figure of Japanese Buddhism, serving as abbot of many important temples, including Entsūji, Tōfukuji, and Nanzenji. Kokan also wrote numerous texts; his *Genkō shakusho* stands out as a richly detailed history of Japanese Buddhism.

Among Kokan's calligraphic works, a transcription of an essay by the Chinese scholar Han Yu (768–824), at Tōfukuji, is perhaps the most

renowned. An outstanding work displaying a fully mature style, the Tōfukuji piece reveals the strong influence of the Northern Song calligrapher Huang Tingjian (1045–1105). In fact, Kokan appears to have owned several of Huang Tingjian's works and to have added colophons to them, singling out this master's calligraphy among the numerous styles current in Song China for emulation (see cat. no. 34). Other notable examples from Kokan's brush — such as those in the Mitsui Bunko Library and the Masaki Museum — also reveal a debt to the Chinese master and share certain appealing characteristics: crisp brushwork, long horizontal strokes brushed with a modulated rhythm, and an overall rightward-leaning tendency. These elements are found in the

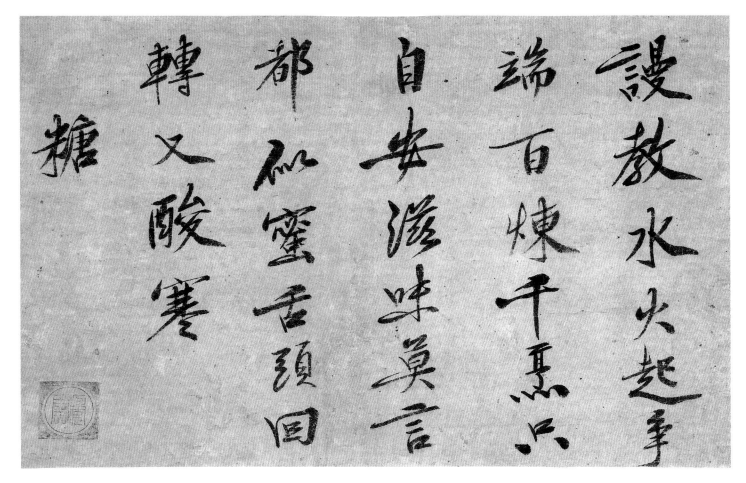

Fig. 23. Detail of cat. no. 37

present seven-character quatrain. A close comparison with Kokan's other works reveals that this calligraphy, formerly in the collection of the Umezawa Memorial Museum, Tokyo, is brushed at a slightly quicker pace.

Kokan's poem reads as follows:

Now let fire and water fight it out:
Heat and boil it many times,
It will form naturally;
Don't say that it always tastes like honey.
When you roll your tongue
It may also taste sour.

Sugar[1]

In addition to calligraphy in the style of Huang Tingjian, Kokan was also known to brush large-scale characters in a bold style, as seen in *Pine Barrier* in the Gotoh Museum. This bold manner was popular among Japanese Zen priests from the Kamakura to the early Muromachi period, but what distinguishes Kokan's calligraphy in this style was the rounded edges of his characters. This rounding had the effect of softening the overall impression and might be thought of as a manifestation of the Japanization of the genre. Since this style became widely practiced only in the mid-Edo period, Kokan's calligraphy was well ahead of its time. At present Kokan's oeuvre, which includes both letters and poetic inscriptions, numbers over twenty works.

T K

1. Translated in Shimizu and Rosenfield 1984–85, p. 127.

Sesson Yūbai (1290–1346)
38.
My Thatched Hut

Nanbokuchō period (1336–1392)
Hanging scroll, ink on paper,
16 × 23⅜ in. (40.6 × 59.4 cm)
Seal: Shaku Yūbai
Ex coll.: Fujii Tokugi, Hyōgo

Sesson Yūbai was a Zen priest of the Rinzai sect who trained under the Chinese émigré monk Yishan Yining who lived in Japan and later studied in China for over twenty years. Because of his tutelage of Ashikaga Tadayoshi (1306–1352), Sesson was appointed to the abbacy of the prestigious Nanzenji temple in Kyoto, and in his later years he retired to the subtemple Seijuin. He is greatly admired for his learning, and his collected sayings and poetry anthologies were widely read.

Sesson's calligraphy displays a careful study of Chinese models. More specifically, his brushwork appears to be influenced by that of the Yuan literatus and calligrapher Zhao Mengfu (1254–1322), who is said to have praised Sesson's calligraphy when they met. It is true that Sesson's master Yishan Yining is less of a direct influence than are contemporary Chinese monks, such as Zhuxian Fanxian (1292–1348), with whom Sesson became friendly during his long sojourn on the continent. His calligraphy thus reveals a close relationship with the latest Chinese styles.

The poem reads:

My thatched hut is woven with disordered layers of clouds.
Already my footprints are washed away with the red dust.
If you ask, this monk has few plans for his life:
Before my window, flowing waters; facing my pillow, books.[1]

Sesson's oeuvre includes only *Poem on Flowering Plum* in the Hoppō Bunka Museum (Niigata prefecture), a one-column calligraphy in a private collection, and the present poem. Four other works that have been traditionally thought to be from Sesson's hand are in all likelihood misattributions.

When the three standard works by Sesson are compared, however, all appear rather different, employing varied brush methods. In addition, all three bear different combinations of seals, rendering difficult any overall characterization of Sesson's

Fig. 24. Detail of cat. no. 38

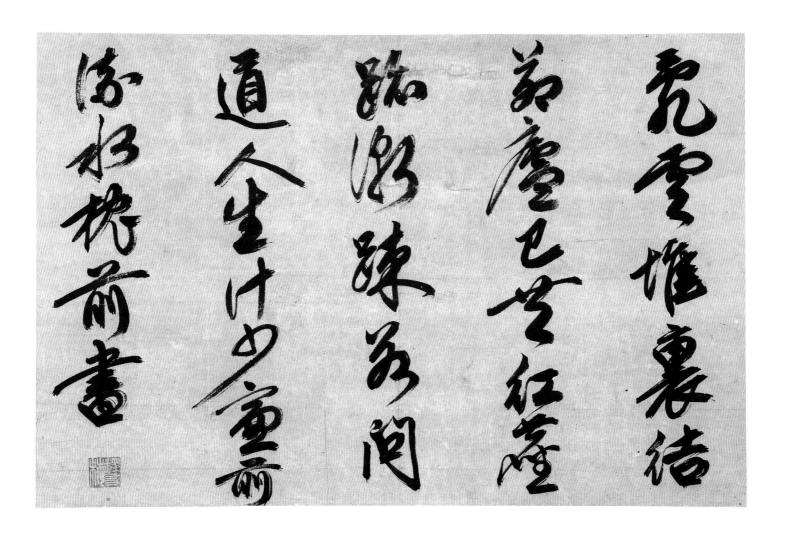

style.[2] Of the three, *My Thatched Hut* is the boldest and most vigorous. The brush is loaded with ink and approaches its task one character at a time, moving forward with sureness and consistency. The relatively large space between columns gives the longer horizontal strokes and pronounced diagonals more elbow room. The characters lean toward the upper right, allowing the calligraphy to proceed smoothly down each column.

Razor-thin strokes punctuate the work here and there, revealing the energy and speed of the brush as well as the keen sensibility of the calligrapher. In contrast to these thin strokes, the majority of thick ones are soft and gentle, almost capering, because of the pressure applied directly down the brush's axis (the thin strokes are created by the relaxation of this pressure). The resulting calligraphy carefully coordinates the ratio of thick to thin strokes. Much of this technique takes advantage of both the brush's sharp tip and thick body, using them for expressive ends.

TK

1. Translation by Stephen Addiss. The same poem is recorded in the 900-volume collection of Chinese poetry compiled in China in 1705, during the Qing dynasty, with slight differences, including the use of the word "rustic" instead of "monk."
2. These three works are reproduced in Tamaya 1961, vol. 1, no. 142. Only *My Thatched Hut* has the square seal "Shaku Yūbai," while the other two works bear the tripod-shaped "Sesson" seal; *Poem on Flowering Plum* includes in addition a square reserve seal reading "Shaku Yūbai."

Zekkai Chūshin (1336–1405)

39.
"There Is No One in the Mountain . . ."

Muromachi period (1392–1573)
Hanging scroll, ink on paper,
34½ × 8⅝ in. (87.6 × 21.9 cm)
Seals: Zekkai; Chūshin

"There is no one in the mountain and I can only hear the sound of the pinecones falling" (*Yama munashiku shite, shōshi otsu*): this one line from a longer poem is complete as a work of calligraphy and is accompanied by a certificate (*kiwame fuda*) dated 1761 by the eighteenth-century calligraphy connoisseur Kohitsu Ryōen. Two seals are found in the lower left corner, the one above a tripod-shaped seal reading "Zekkai," below which is a square relief seal reading "Chūshin." It is rare for both seals to be found on the same work by Zekkai Chūshin. Comparison with other works by this Zen priest proves difficult because his most famous examples are executed in an orderly regular script, as opposed to the running script of this scroll.

The verse captures the experience of deep solitude in the mountains. Without any other human presence, the only sounds are those of the falling pinecones. The line is taken from a poem by Wei Yingwu (737–790), who along with Wang Wei (701–761) was one of the most renowned poets of the Tang dynasty (618–907). The verse selected is the third of a four-line poem, effecting a transition from the opening subject to the concluding one. The choice of a verse loaded with such semantic movement indicates how deeply Zekkai understood the aesthetic dimensions of the art of calligraphy. On the flat surface of the two-dimensional paper ground, the brushwork dances in a lively manner, as if the kinetic movement of the ink were corresponding to the semantic movement of the verse.

"There Is No One in the Mountain" takes full advantage of the brush's physical properties. Its relaxed, leisurely tone is created by a rhythmical placement of brushstrokes, which repeatedly angle down from upper right to lower left. These diagonal strokes are especially prominent in the transition between characters. In four instances the brush does not leave the paper but floats in a thin line before entering the next character with great vigor. It takes immense skill to use the ink reserves in the brush head to connect the characters in this manner. Furthermore, while Zekkai

repeatedly employs softly arching diagonals, he expresses each in a slightly different way, again revealing his marvelous skill and control.

The quality of line is quite straightforward and clear. This clarity results not only from the consistent ink gradation but also from the balance between the physical quality of the brush, the type of brush hair employed, and the handling of the brush. While the ink lines are full of variation, they do not change abruptly. The strokes are stable, covering relatively long distances with great sureness. When making a circular motion, the brush tip sometimes becomes distorted, but it continues to move forward, wonderfully varying the line's appearance. The first character, "mountain," and the upper portion of the second character, "empty," are brushed as if to suggest a single deep breath. The bottom portion of "empty" is quite abbreviated, and the brush does not stop until the third character, "pine," is completed.

The multiple changes in brush pressure deserve special notice. At times the brush moves over the paper with force and at other times quite gently, as if the calligrapher were sliding his finger across its surface, barely creating a sound. This movement is like the minute reverberations produced by plucking a taut string. The brush's movement dictates the thickness (or thinness) of the line, and at times the traces of individual hairs are evident, creating a scratchy appearance.

At the age of thirteen Zekkai entered Tenryūji in Kyoto and afterward moved to Saihōji to study under the famous priest Musō Soseki (see cat. no. 36). In his thirties he traveled to China, where he spent over ten years studying at Zen monasteries, including the famed Lingyin and Wanshou temples. Upon his return, Zekkai took up a life of seclusion, against the wishes of the reigning shogun, Ashikaga Yoshimitsu (1358–1409). However, he eventually returned to Kyoto to serve as abbot of Tōjiji and Shōkokuji temples. With numerous anthologies of poetry and recorded sayings to his credit, Zekkai was also known for his literary achievements.   T K

Fig. 25. Detail of cat. no. 39

Gyokuen Bonpō (ca. 1348—after 1420)

40.
Orchids, Bamboo, and Brambles

Muromachi period (1392–1573),
fifteenth century
Hanging scroll, ink on paper
34½ × 13¾ in. (87.6 × 34.9 cm)
Signed: Gyokuenshi
Seals: Gyokuen; Shōrin
Ex coll.: Fujioka Kaoru, Kyoto
Literature: Fontein and
Hickman 1970, no. 41

Evidence suggests that the Zen priest Gyokuen Bonpō died in his seventies, sometime after 1420. Other biographical details hint at his unique personality, which stood out within the highly bureaucratized Zen monastic system of the period.[1] As a teenager, Bonpō studied at Nanzenji temple in Kyoto under the high priest Shun'oku Myōha (1311–1388), a superb portrait of whom is in the Barnet and Burto collection (see cat. no. 35). Although Bonpō's painting and the portrait of Shun'oku were purchased separately, their entrance into the same American collection unites master and disciple some six hundred years after their deaths.

His connection to Shun'oku gave Bonpō direct access to Ashikaga shogunal power and placed him in a position to move rapidly up the Rinzai Zen hierarchy. After serving as abbot of Manjuji temple in Bungo province in Kyushu and Kenninji temple in Kyoto, Bonpō was appointed to the abbacy of Nanzenji in 1413, the most powerful position within the Rinzai Zen community. Although records indicate that the reigning shogun Ashikaga Yoshimochi attended the inauguration ceremony, Yoshimochi and Bonpō would later have a falling-out; Bonpō resigned his abbacy and went into reclusion. While various theories have been proposed, Bonpō's activities and whereabouts after leaving Nanzenji remain unclear.

During his twenties Bonpō had left Kyoto to study with other masters besides Shun'oku, first with Jakushitsu Genkō (1290–1367) at Eigenji temple (Ōmi province) and subsequently with Gidō Shūshin (1325–1388) at Zuisenji temple in Kamakura. His encounters with these learned and reclusive monks proved to be of decisive influence for his later development. The large number of orchid paintings he left speaks eloquently of his desire to emulate the lofty reclusion of Chinese literati. Orchids are symbolic of literati who, while inhabiting inner circles of power and authority,

never compromise their virtuous character. During Bonpō's youth the orchid paintings of the Chinese Yuan-period monk Xuechuang Puming (active mid-14th century) were imported to Japan, where they proved to be highly popular. The Japanese monks Chōun Reihō (dates unknown) and Tesshū Tokusai (d. 1366), who went to China and studied under Xuechuang, had already championed the orchid as a painting subject closely associated with lofty amateurism.

Bonpō painted orchids throughout his life; his twenty or so surviving paintings of this subject constitute an unusually large corpus, demonstrating how focused the artist was on it. These paintings can vary greatly from formal, rather stiff versions, such as the work in the Tokyo National Museum, to examples that are much more improvisational and relaxed in nature.[2] The present painting can be placed somewhere between these two poles.

Bonpō inscribes a poem toward the bottom of the scroll, but damage to the paper has rendered some of the passages illegible. Such phrases as "crane curtain," "the recluse of North Mountain," and "dew on the orchids," however, make it clear that Bonpō was aware of Kong Zhigui's *Beishan yiwen*, a classic of Chinese reclusive literature from the Southern Qi period (479–502). Whatever the exact nature of its content, Bonpō's poem is not mentioned in the lengthy inscription added to the scroll box by the painter Tomioka Tessai (1837–1924), who is known to have felt a close connection to Bonpō. Apparently even someone as steeped in Chinese learning as Tessai found the poem difficult to comprehend.   Y Y

1. See Tamamura 1983, pp. 112–13. Hoshiyama Shin'ya, in his catalogue entry in *Zenrin gasan—Chūsei suibokuga o yomu* 1987, pp. 413–17, gives Bonpō's dates as 1348–1420 but provides no documentation.
2. Shimizu and Wheelwright 1976, pp. 244–51.

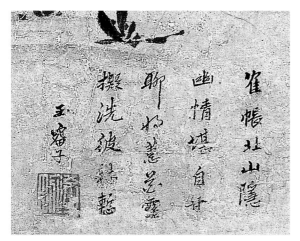

Fig. 25. Detail of cat. no. 40

Shunpo Sōki (1416–1496)

41.
Preface and Poem in Chinese

Muromachi period (1392–1573)
Hanging scroll, ink on paper,
10¼ × 12¼ in. (26 × 31.1 cm)
Signed: Shunpo Sōki hai keisō
Seals: Shunpo; Sōki

Shunpo Sōki was a Zen priest of the Rinzai sect. A disciple of the Daitokuji priest Yōsō Sōi (1376–1458), Shunpo became the fortieth abbot of Daitokuji and was famous for his efforts in reconstructing the temple in the aftermath of the devastation of the Ōnin War (1467–77).

The few examples of Shunpo's calligraphy that survive reveal tenacious brushwork, the use of very black ink, and a sensitivity that somehow produces the sensation of a relaxed space in the interior of each character, a quality not always found in the works of professional calligraphers. Although they lack a high level of technical skill, Shunpo's brushstrokes are laid down thoughtfully and result in a highly original style, allowing the viewer to imagine the calligrapher breathing as he brushes the characters on the paper. Shunpo's calligraphy is best appreciated not one character at a time, when minute technical faults might be noted, but in units of several characters or even one column at a time; when viewed in this way, the brushwork conveys a lyrical quality and even gives rise to melancholy feelings.

The calligraphy here is quite elegant, possibly because it transcribes a farewell poem. The characters are on the small side and brushed rather serenely, reminding one of the delicate sense of coloration found in the ink painting of the Muromachi period.

The ink used is light and does not jump out aggressively at the viewer. The effect is similar to the calligraphy of another Zen priest, Sakugen Shūryō (cat. no. 43).

The preface reads as follows: "The monk Kai'ō composed a short poem on the day he retired from the abbacy of Daitokuji. His poem, an outstanding work, so touched my heart that, based on it, I composed a poem honoring his return to the old hermitage in Tajima. May my repeated bows of salutation bring him good fortune." The accompanying poem reads as follows:

> The working of your spirit is like the Heavenly
>   Horse free of earthly halter.
> Though I may provide a pavilion for you to play
>   your long flute,
> I cannot stop your journey over layered hills and
>   mountains.
> For your departure I break a bough from a thin
>   branch of plum
> Under the moonlight in the capital.
>
> The aged Shunpo Sōki, bowing deeply.[1]

T K

1. Translated in Shimizu and Rosenfield 1984–85, p. 146.

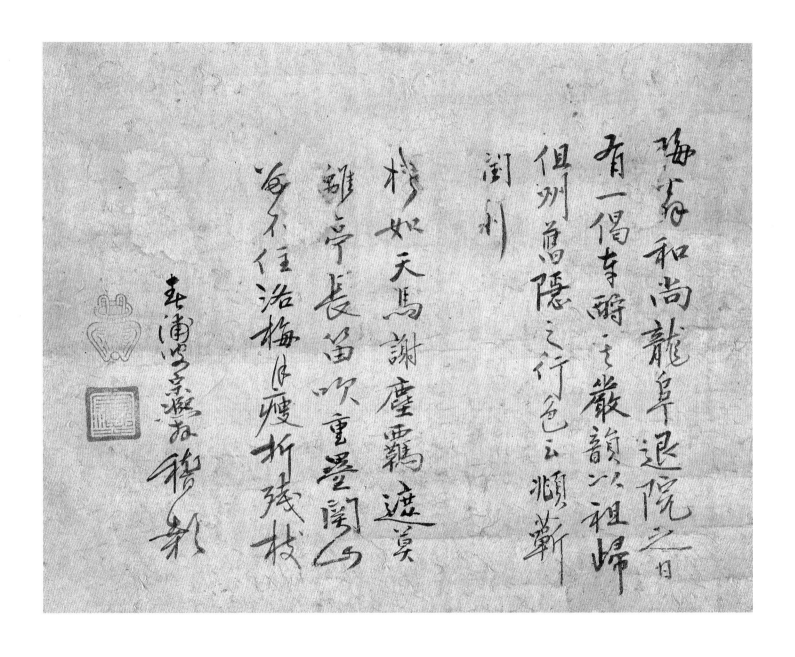

海翁和尚龍阜退院之日
有一偈專辭之嚴韻次祖嶠
但州昌隱之行色云兆新
闍梨

杉如天馬謝塵羈遊莫
離亭長笛吹重疊關山
海不住洛梅但瘦折殘枝

玉浦沙宗瀛拜稽首

Gukyoku Reisai (ca. 1369–1452)

42.
Two Buddhist Maxims

Muromachi period (1392–1573)
Pair of hanging scrolls, ink on
paper; both: 36¼ × 8¾ in. (93.4 ×
22.2 cm);
Seals (on both): Fūgetsu shujin;
Gukyoku
Ex coll.: Nakamura Fujitarō,
Tokyo
Literature: Tamaya 1965, pl. 243;
Kyoto National Museum 1967,
pl. 142; Shimizu and Rosenfield
1984–85, no. 48

These two scrolls present the fundamental doctrine
of Pure Land Buddhism: by invoking the name of
Amida, the believer will be forgiven every sin, no
matter how severe, and will be reborn in the
Western Pure Land. They read: "For those who
commit the most evil deeds, there is no other way"
(left) and "Chant the name of Mida to gain
birth in Paradise" (right).[1] Here "Mida" is an abbre-
viation for Amida Buddha, the Buddha of Immeasurable Light, who presides over the Western Paradise,
or Pure Land, where he preaches the dharma, or
Buddhist law.

The seals indicate that the author of the calligraphy is Gukyoku Reisai, a renowned Zen priest of
the Rinzai sect, who was also known as Master of
the Wind and Moon (Fūgetsu shujin).[2] Reisai
belonged to the dharma lineage of Enni Ben'en
(1202–1280), the founder of Tōfukuji in Kyoto, and
he served as the 149th abbot of that temple. He also
served as the 145th abbot of Nanzenji, and died at
the age of eighty-three.

It is said that examples of Reisai's calligraphy
were much sought after in his own time, because it
was believed that temples with name plaques or
tablets (*hengaku*) inscribed by him were safe from
fire. Although none of these plaques is extant, more
than ten examples of his calligraphy in other genres
are known. Works in the Eisei Bunko in Tokyo and
Chōshōin collections at Nanzenji are considered to
be his masterpieces.

The border of the paper on which the present
scrolls are inscribed is decorated in a rubbed-wax
technique known as *rōsen*. A desired design is carved
in relief on a woodblock, and the paper is placed on
top and vigorously rubbed with colored wax until

a glossy pattern appears. Wax-rubbed paper from
China was employed for calligraphy in Japan as
early as the Heian period, when the paper's entire
surface was decorated. From the Kamakura period
onward, however, the decoration came to be limited
to the edges of the paper, as in the present scrolls.
The border here employs the dragon motif, the
decorative pattern on almost all the *rōsen* paper
imported from China. The paper itself dates to the
Ming period, and its use demonstrates the Japanese
admiration of Chinese Zen masters. In fact, most
calligraphy by Muromachi-period Japanese Zen
priests is based upon Chinese styles and techniques.
Reisai's calligraphy, however, resembles instead the
so-called Shōren'in style, an indigenous style developed by Prince Son'en (1298–1356) and practiced
by courtiers, which became the basis for one of
the standard schools of Japanese calligraphy. (See
the appendix for a discussion of the mountings of
these scrolls.)

In the earlier Kamakura period, Chinese styles
were assiduously copied within Japanese Zen circles, but Zen calligraphy of the Muromachi period
had to be from the hand of a famous priest to be of
value. As long as the calligraphy demonstrated a
practiced hand, it did not necessarily have to reflect
a Chinese calligraphic style. ᴛ ᴋ

1. Translated in Shimizu and Rosenfield 1984–85, p. 138.
2. The position of the seals in this pair of scrolls is somewhat
   unnatural, problematizing the attribution of the scrolls to
   Reisai. It is possible that the works are from the hand of a
   different calligrapher, whose identity became confused with
   Reisai's in later periods. The style is similar, for instance, to
   that in *Lin Hejing's Poem on Plum Flowers* by the Zen priest
   Musō Soseki (1275–1351) in the Idemitsu Museum collection in
   Tokyo, a relationship that requires further study.

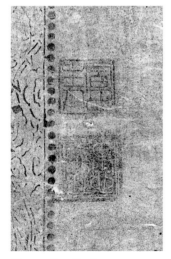

Fig. 27. Detail of cat. no. 42

Sakugen Shūryō (1501–1579)

43.
Account of the Three Springs of Jiangsu

Muromachi period (1392–1573)
Hanging scroll, ink on paper,
11¼ × 16¾ in. (29.2 × 42.5 cm)
Seal: Sakugen
Literature: Shimizu and
Rosenfield 1984–85, no. 55;
Richardson 1992–93, p. 50

Sakugen Shūryō, the artist of the present piece, was among the small number of Japanese who had the opportunity to visit China during the Muromachi period. Sakugen did not make the voyage to study Buddhism, although he had begun Buddhist training at the age of nine. A gifted child, he soon became known as a prodigy with a special talent for Chinese-style poetry.[1] Ordained at age eighteen at Tenryūji in Kyoto, one of the leading Zen temples of Japan, Sakugen's reputation in Zen circles as a learned monk was soon firmly established.

In 1530 the Ashikaga shogun Yoshiharu (r. 1523–1545) directed Ōuchi Yoshioki (1477–1528), lord of Suō province (modern Yamaguchi prefecture), to organize a mission for *kangō bōeki* (tally trade) with Ming-dynasty China. This type of restricted trade involved the issuance of a *kangō* — proof of permission to conduct commerce — to the Japanese trade mission by the Ming government. Sakugen was chosen as an aide to the chief envoy and stayed in China for almost two years, returning home in 1541. In 1547 he served as chief envoy for another mission and was granted an audience with the Ming emperor, before returning to Japan in 1550. Sakugen was able to bring back many rare objects and books, and during his years in China he also visited well-known sites and met prominent men of letters with whom he exchanged poetic and calligraphic works.[2] He kept daily records of his travels, the *Sakugen Oshō shotoshū* (The First Voyage to China of the Monk Sakugen) and the *Sakugen Oshō Saitoshū* (The Monk Sakugen's Second Voyage to China).[3]

In the present work Sakugen displays his intimate knowledge of the comparative merits of spring water in south China, a region that he and many other Japanese pilgrims had visited. The text reads:

> The spring named Zhong Lingquan on Mount
>   Jin at the heart of the Yangzi River is called the
>   Number One source of water under Heaven.

That of the Huishan Temple at the Jinlong Feng
    is called Number Two.
Jianchi Pond at Huqiu Temple in Suzhou is called
    Number Three.

> Ki'in Kensai sho [written by
>   Ki'in Kensai], seal [Sakugen]

Sakugen had visited all three springs and recorded the proclamations inscribed on the ubiquitous plaques and tablets located at these famous sites.[4] His visits to these places, all in the Jiangsu region north of Ningbo, where he landed, took place during his first China trip and are recorded in his diary: Number Two spring at Huishan temple on November 21, 1539, Number One spring at Zhong Lingquan, on December 3 of the same year, and Number Three spring at Huqiu temple, on August 23, 1540, just before his return to Japan.

Sakugen's firsthand knowledge of south China's famous places, which had been immortalized in literature, made his descriptions of the sites — inscribed in his own hand — desirable to collectors who were unable to travel. He created other calligraphic pieces on request, describing such sites as the famous West Lake;[5] other examples of his calligraphy contain transcriptions of well-known Chinese poems, suggesting that there was a demand for such works.

Like the present piece, most of Sakugen's calligraphy features well-controlled movement of the brush; every character is well formed and maintains its independence. The clarity and restrained quality of the writing create a sense of solemnity and orthodoxy. For this work, written in a combination of cursive and semicursive scripts, Sakugen manipulated the brush carefully, maintaining a consistency of speed and motion. Formal and precisely modulated, each letter possesses a singular rhythm that contributes to the overall balance of the composition.   M M

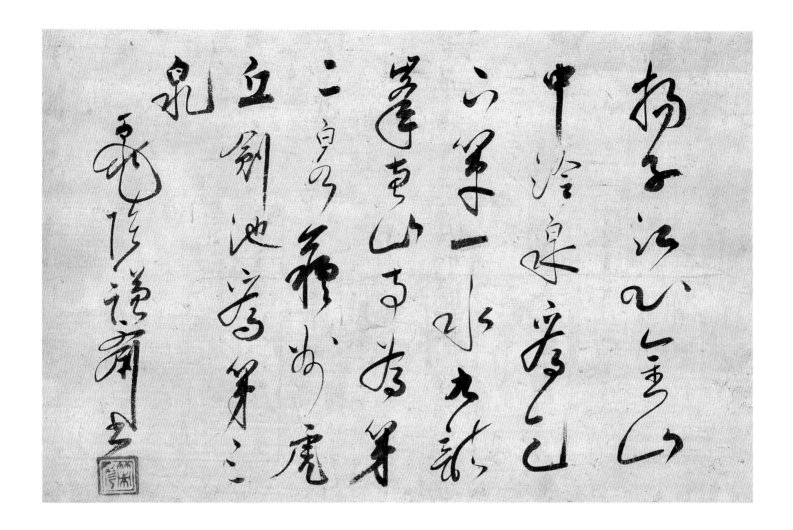

1. For his poetry, see *Sakugen Oshō shishū* (Collection of Monk
Sakugen's Poems) in *Zoku Gunshoruijū* 1926, no. 352, pp. 811–85.

2. Murase 1970.

3. Reprints in Makita 1955–59, vol. 1.

4. These visits are entered in his diary. See Makita 1955–59, vol. 1,
pp. 107, 110, and 146, respectively; also the map of his travels
after p. 396.

5. Komatsu, ed. 1978–80, vol. 10, no. 116.

Yinyuan Longqi (J: Ingen Ryūki) (1592–1673)

44.
Mind and Moon

Edo period (1615–1868)
Hanging scroll, ink on paper,
11¼ × 23 in. (28.6 × 60.8 cm)
Signed: Huangbo Yinyuan
Seals: Linji Zhengzong; Boshan
Zhuren; Yinyuan zhi yin

The two characters here, *shingatsu*, describe the heart of one who has realized enlightenment.[1] In Esoteric Buddhist thought, from the perspective of the enlightened Diamond Realm (J: Kongōkai), the heart of a sentient being is seen as the round disk of the moon, while the "heart moon disk" (J: *shin gachirin*) symbolizes the completely clear heart of a bodhisattva. The term "heart moon" likens the original enlightened nature of the heart to the form of the moon.

Yinyuan Longqi, a monk who came to Japan from Fuzhou province in China, was the founder of the Ōbaku (C: Huangbo) sect of Buddhism in Japan. Escaping the strife that was tearing China apart at the end of the Ming and the beginning of the Qing dynasty, he was accompanied by many monks who spread this new form of Buddhism in Japan. In 1654 Yinyuan received an invitation from Kōfukuji in Nagasaki, and nine years later he established Manpukuji temple in Uji, near Kyoto, as the center of the Ōbaku sect.

Yinyuan was an important figure in fanning the rage for the Chinese style (J: *karayō*) that gripped Edo-period Japan and that underlay the calligraphy of the Ōbaku sect. The free touch of the brush in the present work is typical of Yinyuan's hand, a style said to have been influenced by the late Ming artist Dong Qichang (1555–1636). Through his extended lines and expansive strokes, Yinyuan denies the confining effects of a small scale. Writing characters with only a few brushstrokes, he has tried to reveal the state of a complete and serene state of mind that is the true subject of the piece.

The combination of the two seals at the left is relatively rare but is found on a Buddhist poem of four seven-character lines (now in Ryūkōin collection) that Yinyuan wrote for Duzhi Xinji (J: Dokuchi Seiki) when he assumed office as the first abbot of Butsunichiji in 1661.

T K

1. This term is found in such texts as the ritual manual Abbreviated Method for Chanting the Mahavairochana Sutra (J: *Dainichikyō,* eighth century), the Recorded Sayings of the Master of Mount Tong (C: *Tongshan yulu,* ninth century), and the *Hogoshū,* a collection of writings found on the back of other texts.

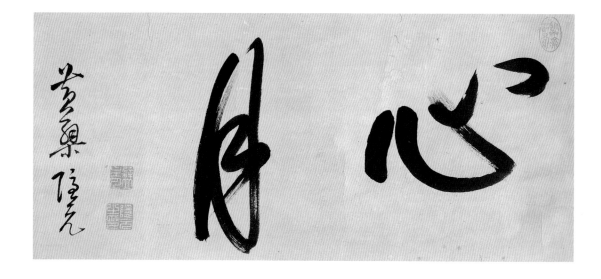

Muan Xingtao (J: Mokuan Shōtō) (1611–1684)

45.
Branch

Edo period (1615–1868)
Hanging scroll, ink on paper,
14⅜ × 27¼ in. (36.5 × 69.2 cm)
Signed: Huangbo Muan
Laoseng shu
Seals: Linji Zhengzong; Shi
Jietao yin; Muan shi

The calligrapher of this work, Muan Xingtao, was born in China. His family name was Wu, and Muan was his courtesy name. He took holy orders by the age of nineteen; soon after he traveled to Mount Huangbo where he studied Chan under Yinyuan Longqi (cat. no. 44). Following Yinyuan, Muan accepted an invitation to go to Japan in 1655, took up residence at Fukusaiji, a Nagasaki temple, and was active in promoting the Ōbaku sect in Japan. In 1664 he followed Yinyuan as abbot at Manpukuji, outside Kyoto, the headquarters of the Ōbaku Zen school in Japan.

Here the large character for "branch" appears at the right end of the paper. A fourteen-character verse in three columns follows to the left. The text, in Chinese, reads:

Branch
The garden full of spring color will not stay closed.
A branch of red apricots comes over the fence.
Written by the old monk of Ōbaku, Muan

Since Muan signs the calligraphy as "the old monk," this is probably one of his later works.

The couplet's author stands before a scene redolent with spring, his sight dazzled by the season's profusion. Then a branch of rosy-hued apricots catches his eye. As the branch crosses the fence and leans toward him, it seems that the rich bounty of fruit—the essence of spring—is being offered to him.

This composition—one large character accompanied by smaller characters—is common in the calligraphy of Ōbaku Zen monks. The large character thus expresses the essence of the poetic passage, and the work as a whole speaks to how people overcome limits and restraints, despite invisible barriers and unspoken assumptions in their hearts. The "branch" has overcome all "fences" (that is, obstacles) in the myriad phenomena of the world. The unrestrained calligraphic style also embodies the meaning of the words. TK

Muan Xingtao (J: Mokuan Shōtō) (1611–1684)

46.
"In the Pot There Is a Separate Heaven"

Edo period (1615–1868)
Hanging scroll, ink on paper,
52⅛ × 14¼ in. (132.4 × 36.2 cm)
Signed: Huangbo Muan shu
Seals: Linji Zhengzong; Muan
Zhi yin

This scroll reads: "In the pot there is a separate heaven." The same idea is expressed in the phrase "heaven in a pot," which makes reference to a famous story found in the section on Fei Changfang in the *Hou Hanshu* (History of the Latter Han Dynasty, compiled ca. 432). Since this saying has been taken to refer to the world inhabited by immortals, it was a favorite and oft-discussed phrase among literati who, in times of corruption, aspired to separate themselves from the mundane world.

The story from which this line comes concerns a townsman named Fei Changfang and a man who sold medicine during China's Han dynasty (25–220). Every day at the close of business the old pharmacist would disappear in a wink into a pot that hung at the top of his store. One day Fei Changfang visited the old man and asked to go into the pot as well.

The man took him into the pot, and there Fei saw a vast space — the realm of the immortals — spread out before him. With its soaring palaces and rich food and drink it was truly "a separate heaven."

Muan's calligraphic style resembles that of his teacher Yinyuan Longqi (cat. no. 44), but it lacks the volumetric and expansive feel of Yinyuan's hand. The calligraphy races from one stroke to the next. Indeed, more than in Yinyuan's calligraphy, one can sense Muan's intensity in the pronounced slant of the characters to the upper right. Muan's approach is also distinctive in that he employed a "short peak" brush (J: *tanpō*) — one with a short tip and stout body — that was saturated with ink. Firmly maintaining a vertical alignment, he would write in a single burst without stopping. The present work displays his characteristic method clearly.

TK

壺中別有天

Seigan Sōi (1588–1661)

47.
Hell

Edo period (1615–1868)
Hanging scroll, ink on paper,
12 × 35½ in. (30.5 × 90.2 cm)
Signed: Seigan sho
Seals: Seigan; Sōi
Ex coll.: Daitokuji, Kyoto;
Sakamoto Shūsai

Seigan Sōi was the 170th abbot of Daitokuji in Kyoto. Also known as Jishōshi or Korō, he founded Zen temples throughout Japan and was invited by the shogun Tokugawa Iemitsu (1604–1651) to assume the abbacy of Tōkaiji in Shinagawa, Edo (Tokyo) in 1649, after the death of the eminent monk Takuan Sōhō (1573–1645).

Seigan was strongly influenced by the brush styles of the Southern Song in China, and he used a stiff brush to achieve a sharp line. The almost explosive thrust of his strokes, the flares that arise where the brush pauses, and the long sweep of his lines are distinctive characteristics of his work. Seigan's vigorous style often gives the impression of a sharp blade cutting through the paper.

Hell was thought to be a place in the netherworld for the wicked dead where they made restitution for the evil deeds they had committed in this world. In Buddhist cosmology hell (J: *jigoku*) is one of the Six Paths (J: *rokudō*) of existence through which all living creatures are reincarnated, moving up or down according to their karma. These include hell, the hungry ghosts, animals, the Asuras who continuously fight the gods, humans, and gods. Hell is thought to be a world adjacent to, but in tension with, the world of humans. The Hell of No Interval (S: Avuci; J: Muken) is named for the constant torment to which its inhabitants are subject, symbolic of the limitlessness of all the hells. In like manner the myriad phenomena of the human realm are limitless, as are the spiritual practices that may liberate humans from suffering.

This calligraphy was probably hung in a room reserved for tea ceremonies and was likely the subject of much conversation. In the hushed silence of the tea preparation, one hears only the soft sounds of the host's movements. The guests in such a highly charged atmosphere try to achieve a state of mental clarity and calm their hearts. For both guests and host the theme of hell would have illuminated worldly affairs of the time or perhaps would have been a catalyst for an individual guest to reflect on his or her conduct.

The practice of brushing phrases that had only a few characters was quite popular in the early Edo period. Other notable examples include the single line of calligraphy owned by the Urasenke school of tea ceremony that reads, "It is right in front of your eyes, [but] if you search for it, it is nowhere [to be found]" (J: *Tada mokuzen ni ari, tazunuru ni tokoro nashi*), and a piece owned by the Sanritsu Hattori Museum of Art in Nagano prefecture that reads, "Void is exactly the dharma body" (J: *Kokū soku hōshin*). TK

Hakuin Ekaku (1685–1768)

48.
Posthumous Name of Prince Shōtoku

Edo period (1615–1868)
Hanging scroll, ink on paper,
38½ × 10¾ in (97.8 × 27.3 cm)
Seals: Kokan'i; Hakuin; Ekaku
Literature: Morse and Morse
1996, no. 48; Perkins et al. 2000–
2001, fig. 36

This work is a name scroll (J: *myōgō*)on which the name of a Buddhist or Shinto deity was brushed in a simple manner and which was then hung and revered. In contrast to Buddhist paintings of the late Heian period, which were commissioned by patrons from professional painters for great sums of money, name scrolls were easily reproducible religious objects. From the Kamakura period onward they were created in large numbers by those Buddhist sects — particularly the Nichiren and True Pure Land sects — that sought to appeal to commoners. Only a small fraction of these scrolls have survived.

In the early Edo period most religious institutions were incorporated into a national administrative structure, thereby neutralizing the antiestablishment tendencies of many monasteries. One consequence of this bureaucratization was a sharp decline in the production of name scrolls. Only some eccentric Buddhist priests, especially Zen priests, who sought to work independently for the salvation of ordinary people, continued to create name scrolls and give them to believers. Because such scrolls required only the brushing of the name of a deity, such as Namu Amida Butsu in a single vertical column, dozens of works could be produced in a single day. The Zen priest Hakuin no doubt created this calligraphy in a matter of minutes.

Born with the surname Nagasawa, Hakuin was the son of a stationmaster at Hara (modern Numazu, Shizuoka prefecture), one of fifty-three stations along the famous Tokaidō highway that ran between Edo and Kyoto. He took Buddhist vows at the age of fifteen and initially studied under the priest Tanrei Soden at Shōinji. During the peripatetic period that ensued, Hakuin traveled through the provinces of Mino, Iyo, Echigo, Shinshū, the city of Kyoto, and elsewhere. This itinerant lifestyle was the result of both Hakuin's rigorous Zen training and his constant search for new spiritual masters. Among those whom he met along the way, the priest Dōkyō Ezui of Shōjuan temple in Iiyama city

(Shinshū province) would be a particularly decisive influence.

After assuming the abbacy of his hometown temple Shōinji at the age of thirty-three, Hakuin embarked upon a period of concerted proselytization, though not simply to gain converts for the Rinzai sect of Zen Buddhism to which he belonged. Hakuin's missionary activity transcended narrow religious views and reflected an extremely broad humanistic outlook, and these efforts eventually caught the attention of conservative sectarian leaders, who invited him to take up a position at Myōshinji, one of the headquarters of the Rinzai sect. He refused this invitation, however, and continued to work tirelessly for the salvation of common people until he died at eighty-four.

The name inscribed on this scroll, Jōgūhōsōōji (which can also be read Kamitsumiya toyoto miko), refers to the posthumous name of the legendary Prince Shōtoku (574–622), a prince regent of the Asuka period and an important early patron of Buddhism. In later centuries he was deified and widely worshiped, as the survival of a great number of iconic portraits attests. His cult even continues into the modern period, as demonstrated by the inclusion of a portrait of Prince Shōtoku on an earlier version of the ten-thousand-yen note that was in circulation until about twenty years ago.

The oozing quality of the ink is characteristic of Hakuin's calligraphy. The initial characters at the top of the scroll are brushed with such vigor that the third character, "hō," is too large, and Hakuin was forced to shrink the size of the final three characters in order to fit them on the scroll. This gradual diminution of the characters' scale is evident in much of his calligraphy. Hakuin was a prolific calligrapher from his sixties onward, and *Posthumous Name of Prince Shōtoku* dates to approximately his eightieth year. Similar works are quite rare, and this particular name scroll was not included in the Japanese catalogue raisonné of Hakuin's work published in 1964.[1] Recently, however, it has received increasing attention and has been included in two exhibitions in the last several years.[2]

Y Y

1. Takeuchi 1964.
2. Morse and Morse 1996; Perkins et al. 2000–2001.

Fig. 28. Detail of cat. no. 48

Fig. 29. Detail of cat. no. 48

Jiun Onkō (1718–1804)

49.
Daruma

Edo period (1615–1868)
Hanging scroll, ink on paper,
48⅛ × 21¾ in. (123.4 × 55.4 cm)
Signed: Jiun keisho su
Seals: Zenga no nagare;
Katsuragi Sanjin; Jiun
Literature: *Bokubi* 1953; Furuta
1959; Yabumoto 1980; Smith
1979, p. 7

The subject of this painting, the first Zen patriarch, is often referred to as Daruma in Japanese and Damo in Chinese, but he is more properly called by his Sanskrit name "Bodhidharma." He is believed to have been active in India from the latter part of the fifth and early sixth century and is said to have traveled to the Kingdom of Wei (386–ca. 534) in China, where he established himself at the Shaolinsi temple on Mount Song. There he deepened his understanding of the Buddhist law (S: *dharma*) through intensive sitting meditation. Images of Bodhidharma in meditation express his effort to establish continuity with Zen Buddhist teachings. This painting belongs to that tradition. Surveying the development of representations of Bodhidharma, one can trace a general trend from concrete to abstract in the various portraits that have survived. This work is a highly abstract representation, using only three brushstrokes, though the form of the sage's back can still be discerned as he faces a wall, deep in meditation. This subject, often called "Bodhidharma facing a wall" (J: *Menpeki Daruma*), refers to the patriarch's nine-year meditation while facing a cave wall and recalls the severity of the quest for truth in Buddhist practice.

This image is inscribed with two characters that mean "Don't know" (J: *fushiki*), a terse phrase that captures the essence of Zen Buddhism. These words occurred in a conversation between Bodhidharma and Emperor Wu of the Liang dynasty (502–557) in 520, which is recorded in the first section of the fundamental Zen compendium, Blue Cliff Record (C: *Biyanlu,* J: *Hekiganroku,* published 1300). The emperor asked how much merit he had gained from his lavish sponsorship of Buddhism, to which Bodhidharma replied, "No merit at all." The emperor then asked what Buddhism's core was. Again a cryptic reply: "Vast emptiness, and nothing sacred." Finally he asked, "Who is before me now?" Bodhidharma simply answered "I don't know."

The Osaka Municipal Museum has a very similar image of Bodhidharma, brushed in an abstract way with the same inscription as the piece here, and other paintings of the Zen patriarch are also inscribed with similar phrases.[1] However, the present work is unique in being the only one of this group of paintings with the signature "Respectfully written by Jiun."

TK

1. For instance, two in Blue Cliff Record 17: "from the west" (Records of Zhaozhou [C: *Zhaozhoulu*] 1, *Wumenguan* 37, etc.); and "one's face follows the grand coming of the dew" (*Wumenguan* 23). Two others are those found in the last fascicle of the Platform Sutra of the Sixth Patriarch (C: *Liuzu tanjing,* mid-ninth century): "no merit" and "five petals open on one flower" (referring to the five schools of Zen).

Jiun Onkō (1718–1804)

50.
Ensō

Edo period (1615–1868)
Hanging scroll, ink on paper,
25⅜ × 10½ in. (64.6 × 26.7 cm)
Seals: Jiun; Onkō
Literature: Yabumoto 1980

The so-called single circle sign (J: *ichi ensō*) symbolizes the enlightened state and, as such, is revered most highly in the Zen world. The tradition of brushing such circles goes all the way back to the eighth century in China.

The thirtieth fascicle of the important Zen chronicle Jingde Record of the Transmission of the Lamp (C: *Jingde chuandeng lu,* 1004) contains a long-treasured text called the Inscription of Faithful Hearts (C: *Xinxinming*). One of its lines helps us interpret the meaning of brushing a circle in ink: "Circles are like the great void — there is nothing lacking and no excess." That is, since drawing a perfect circle is exceedingly difficult, the way it is realized reveals one's state of mind at the time one makes it. One cannot call it a circle if some part is missing or if anything else is added to it. The highest ideal is to make a circle without any imperfections or wrong turns. If one gives oneself completely over to this ideal, the very act of taking the brush in hand and drawing a circle can itself become a means of spiritual cultivation.

The last part of the Inscription of Faithful Hearts contains a line that further clarifies the image: "The faithful heart is nonduality. Nonduality is the faithful heart." In other words, when the faithful heart and the object of that faith are completely unified, awareness of duality and opposition vanishes. The most desirable state is one of indivisibility,

where both aspects completely comprehend each other and achieve a natural balance. This is the consciousness of "nothing lacking and no excess."

In this work the inscription at the top reads, "How many people can pass through?" The phrase "pass through" refers to pushing beyond the barriers of delusion. Students of Zen are taught to endeavor in the kind of strict spiritual training in which, even if one achieves a state of enlightenment, one still must devote oneself to realizing "great enlightenment." Even after that, one must devote oneself to yet more exhaustive spiritual exercises so that one finally enters a state of utter completeness. This process has strong parallels to the spiritual practice of making a single circle in ink.

Jiun Onkō's image of the single circle is brushed in one deft swath, in the space of a single breath. Although it may show some irregularity, the resulting white space inside the circle stands out clearly — perhaps such a creation can only come from the brush of one who has lived a long time. The inscription, with its sublimely artless expression, gives one a sense of an old man's hand. Though this work is slightly different from what we have come to know as Jiun's typical calligraphic expression, it excels in the powerful and spirited movement of the brush and deeply communicates the sense of transport and abundance that marks one who has achieved an enlightened state.   TK

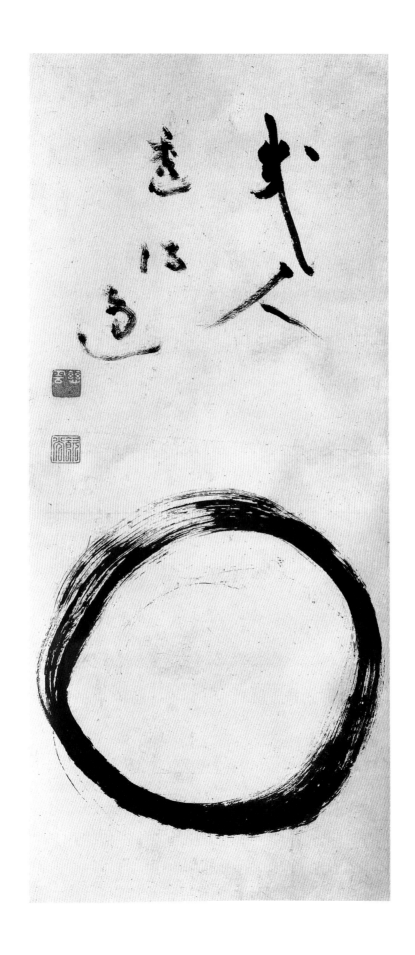

Jiun Onkō (1718–1804)

51.

Sukuna Hikona no Mikoto (God of Medicine and Wine)

Edo period (1615–1868)
Hanging scroll, ink on paper,
52¾ × 18⅝ in. (134 × 47.3 cm)
Seals: Bon'on Kayō kokoni iu
Kishi; Shōji Jiun
Literature: Yabumoto 1980

From about the time Jiun Onkō turned seventy, he dedicated himself to the study of Shinto. As a result, he wrote more than thirty volumes related to the worship of Japan's indigenous gods, or kami (see volume ten of his collected works, *Jiun Sonja zenshū*).

In the calligraphy of this scroll he has conflated two gods. One is the ancient Shinto deity Takami Musubi no Kami, the last character in whose name is also used as a variant for the final character in this scroll for the god Sukuna Hikona no Mikoto. The latter's name can be translated as "Little-Man-Shining-Deity," and he is represented as a dwarf of marvelous agility and endurance. He is often enshrined with Ōkuninushi no Mikoto, a major local deity of Izumo province on the coast of the Sea of Japan. Together these two mythic figures are thought to protect the realm, manage and develop the land, and give humans wisdom and practical knowledge in areas such as medicine, thereby maintaining a well-governed world.

The cursive form of the first character (meaning "small" or "few") in this work, which irrepressibly cuts a powerful swath from the upper right to lower left of the page, occupies two thirds of the paper.

This exceedingly distinctive character traces a right spiral, spinning like the Japanese phonetic character "no." In brushing it, Jiun maintained a continuous movement with constant pressure on the brush throughout. Though the line's jet black core has the weightiness of a steel club, the tail of the stroke reveals dry brush ends. Here and there one can see textures that reveal that the paper was laid on reed matting (J: *tatami*) when the character was brushed. The weave pattern caused by the pressure of the brush gives much the same impression as a woodblock print made with a rubbing pad. Jiun's line, overflowing with a spirited sense of power, might bring to mind crashing waves or the spray of rapids. The final three characters emerge from this chaos and are arrayed in an orderly, light, and measured manner. Their strength gradually increases, as if their power surges out internally from each character. Even the exaggerated form of the character for "Sukuna," while displaying a spatial sensibility unique to calligraphy, shares in this sense of balance. The round dot in the upper right unifies the entire page and seems to echo the two red seals in the lower left.   TK

Jiun Onkō (1718–1804)

52.
Like a Dream

Edo period (1615–1868)
Hanging scroll, ink on paper,
10⅝ × 16⅞ in. (27 × 43 cm)
Seals: Jiun; Onkō no in
Literature: Yabumoto 1980

The text of this scroll, read as either "nyogen" or "maboroshi no gotoshi" in Japanese, means "like a phantasm." The sixth chapter of the immense Commentary on the Greater Sutra of the Perfection of Wisdom (S: *Mahaprajnaparamitopadesha Sutra*; J: *Daichidoron*), observes that existence is "like a phantasm, like a transformation." Probably based on that line, Jiun's calligraphy expresses the transience of human life.

Since the characters are brushed from right to left, rather than the usual top-to-bottom arrangement, the composition emphasizes a sense of lateral balance. The calligraphy is dark and weighty overall. The intertwining of the two characters in a subtle interplay of strong and weak lines engenders a tranquil feeling. Such a thoroughly careful expressive style is Jiun's specialty. In this horizontal arrangement each character constitutes its own world. These two characters were brushed so as to give predominance to their formal qualities rather than to their meaning. Thus, just "like a phantasm," Jiun's calligraphy has something of a miragelike presence.

Jiun's attempt to distance the characters from their semantic qualities is not limited to such elements as arrangement, overall composition, or brush handling. He goes a step farther by violating the normal prescriptions for writing the character for "phantasm" (J: *gen* or *maboroshi*), which appears on the left. Jiun situates the left radical of this character inside and underneath the right element, which is shaped like an inverted L. This placement makes the character difficult to decipher. As the viewer scours one's memory of Chinese characters, trying to make sense of this form, the artist's contrivance leads the viewer to be aware of the ambiguity of vision. The meaning of this confusing set may seem to become more and more elusive as one is led to the true meaning of "like a phantasm." TK

Tōrei Enji (1721–1792)

53.
Master

Edo period (1615–1868)
Hanging scroll, ink on paper,
46¾ × 11¼ in. (118.7 × 28.6 cm)
Signature: Fubuan shu
Seals: illegible; Enpei no in;
Tōrei
Literature: Yoshii 1959, fig. 35;
Shibayama 1974, pp. 91–98;
Guth 1992–93, fig. 14

This scroll is an example of a rebus image, known in Japanese as a "word picture" (*moji-e*). The dispersal and reassembly of the three characters of the word "master" (*shujinkō*), results in the profile of a seated figure. The stroke at the top of the first character (*shu*) forms the vertical portion of a courtier's hat (*eboshi*), indicating that the figure is a member of the aristocracy. The second character (*jin*) forms the two vertical lines of the figure's shoulder, arm, and back, while the various lines of the final character (*kō*) articulate the figure's lower half.

Although in contemporary Japanese *shujinkō* generally means the "primary character or protagonist of a play," in the Zen lexicon it refers to an anecdote related in the Wumenguan (J: *Mumonkan*), a collection of Zen riddles by the Southern Song Zen priest Wumen Huikai (1183–1228). The Zen priest Ruiyan Shiyan (J: Zuigan Shigen) would address himself out loud as "master" and then proceed to answer his salutation with "yes?" This dialogue with himself would continue with such questions as "Are you fully awake?" or comments like "Don't be fooled by others," to which he would consistently answer himself with a "yes." The anecdote illuminates both the difficulty and importance of continuing to be oneself.

While the inscription at the top of the scroll cites the Wumenguan, its meaning is obscure, and viewers of the time without a specialized knowledge of Zen must have had difficulty comprehending it. It reads: "If you draw a sword to your head, refine pills of immortality with your feet, dispel past, present, and future, and see in the ten directions, are you more likely to be mastered or master? Don't be deceived by the body, mind, world, or Buddhist teachings."[1] This work resembles the kind of Buddhist paintings for which raconteur-priests, known as *etoki*, provided oral explanations within a temple setting. The process of deciphering the graphic puzzle posed by the word picture would reveal the meaning of the aphorism.

Tōrei Enji was born in Ōmi province and entered the Buddhist priesthood in his youth. At seventeen he made pilgrimages to various parts of the country. Encountering his lifelong master Hakuin at the age of twenty-three, Tōrei received his certificate of enlightenment from him at twenty-nine. From middle age onward Tōrei followed Hakuin's practice of working for the salvation of commoners. At the same time, however, because of his managerial and financial skills he was able to carry out many important projects, including the construction of Ryūtakuji temple on Mishima island and the rebuilding of Shidōan temple in Edo.

The aristocratic headgear of the figure in the word picture, along with the existence of many other versions with the same image and inscription, suggests that this scroll was produced on the occasion of Tōrei's legendary 1768 sermon at Tōjiin in Kyoto, when he lectured on the nature of the Buddhist law to more than seven hundred courtiers and daimyos.[2] Unlike Hakuin, who avoided such elite assemblies, Tōrei directed his efforts toward many different social groups. Were it not for him, Hakuin's dharma lineage would have had no real successor and would not enjoy its present prestige. (Every Rinzai priest traces his dharma ancestry to Hakuin.)

In terms of his skill in painting and calligraphy, Tōrei fell far short of Hakuin. Much of his work consists of poor imitations of his master's oeuvre and tends to exaggerate Hakuin's expressionistic tendencies. While the limits of Tōrei's ability are made clear by such a comparison, his best works display a pleasantly humorous satirical quality.   Y Y

---

1. Translation from Shibayama 1974, pp. 91–98. The same piece is reproduced in Guth 1992, which cites the Shibayama translation as well.
2. Sano Museum and Shiga Prefectural Lake Biwa Cultural Center 1993, pl. 42.

Daigu Ryōkan (1758–1831)

54.
Poem about a Crazy Monk

Edo period (1615–1868), nine-
teenth century
Hanging scroll, ink on paper,
21¾ × 35⅜ in. (55.3 × 89.7 cm)
Signed: Ryōkan sho
Literature: Shimizu and
Rosenfield 1984–85, no. 71

A fundamental concept long employed in the appreciation and evaluation of East Asian calligraphy
concerns the "bone" of each character. One way to
evaluate a calligrapher's grasp of the bone of a given
character is the extent to which he is faithful to its
structural (or skeletal) integrity, no matter how
abbreviated the character becomes. Thus, some connoisseurs might give high marks to the calligraphy
of *Poem about a Crazy Monk* because its monk-
author had so mastered and internalized the bones
of the characters that he was able to deviate from
them and brush in this wild and free manner.
Others, however, might suggest that Ryōkan had
purposefully ignored the bones of the characters
precisely in order to brush in an untrammeled manner. In fact, both of these contrasting evaluations of
his calligraphy are equally valid.

Born in Echigo province (modern Niigata prefecture), Ryōkan became a Zen priest of the Sōtō sect
and spent a great deal of time wandering about
before settling in his hometown. There his fame
spread and he began to attract large numbers of followers. From a young age Ryōkan studied the classical calligraphic traditions of both China and Japan;
he did not simply copy earlier models, however, but
produced works famous for their transcendence of
the bone of the characters. These works exhibit the
loose and relaxed appearance of *Poem about a Crazy
Monk.* To a connoisseur the twenty-eight characters
of this poem appear as common linguistic signifiers
transmitting fixed meanings. For most Japanese and
Westerners, who are unfamiliar with the standards
for evaluating East Asian calligraphy, these meanings
remain impossible to understand. At the same time
the agreeable sense of rhythm that is created by the
texture of the paper and the brush traces that are visible upon it transcend national boundaries and appeal
to viewers everywhere. Without understanding the
meaning, one may focus attention upon the beauty of
the ink lines themselves, instead of the semantic or

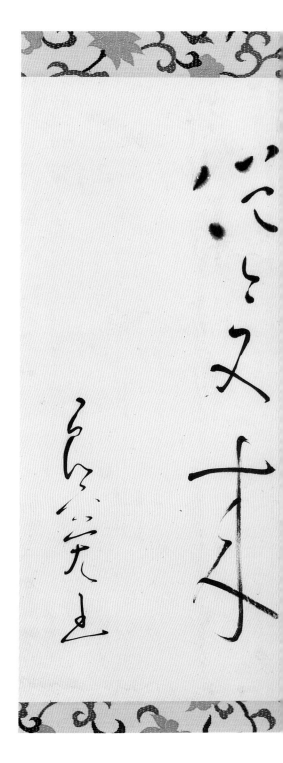

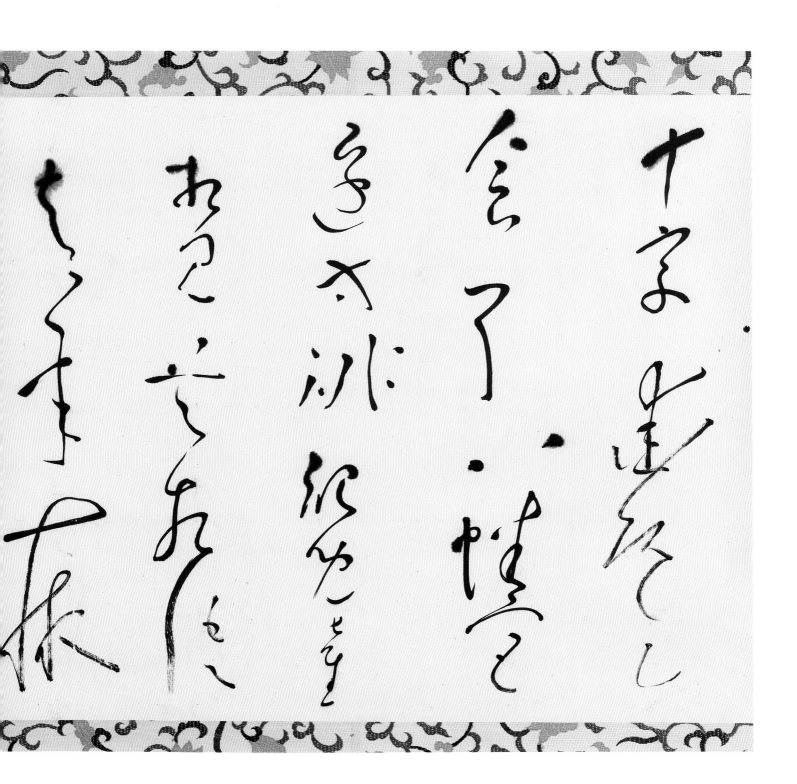

representational content, much as when viewing a Jackson Pollock painting. The inscription reads:

> Finished begging at the village crossroads,
> Now I stroll through the Hachiman shrine.
> When children spot me, they call to each other.
> "That crazy monk from last year is back again."[1]

Ryōkan's calligraphy was highly esteemed in his own lifetime among a small group of connoisseurs, but today it has achieved popular, almost mythic, status. In 2000–2001, a large landmark exhibition entitled *Ryōkansan* (Dear Ryōkan) was held in Kyoto and Tokyo,[2] in which many rare objects were on display. The title of the exhibition reflected how familiar this priest had become to the general public, being on a par with such popular cultural figures as the Zen priests Ikkyū Sōjun (1394–1481) and Hakuin Ekaku (1685–1768).

YY

1. The same poem is inscribed in a separate calligraphic work, reproduced in Tokyo and Osaka 1980, pl. 104.
2. *Botsugo 170-nen kinen ten Ryōkan san* (Dear Ryōkan: 170th Anniversary of His Death) (Kyoto and Tokyo: Kyoto bunka hakubutsukan and Bunkamura, 2000–2001).

ECCENTRIC MASTERS

Konoe Nobutada (1565–1614)

55.
Tenjin Returning from China

Momoyama period (1573–1615),
dated 1610
Hanging scroll, ink on paper,
36¼ × 12½ in. (91.8 × 31.8 cm)
Signature: Sugi
Seals: two illegible seals
Literature: Addiss 1989, fig. 9;
Kaikodo Journal 2000, fig. 4

This figure rendered with an almost minimalist economy of brushstrokes consists of two Chinese letters. The character *ten* (heaven or heavenly), written in *tensho* (seal script), is made up of two short horizontal strokes in dark ink which delineate the male figure's cap. This cap is supported by a bracket-like inverted U that forms the head. The second character, *jin*, written in *sōsho* (running script), begins as a short horizontal stroke at the left of the head to represent a dot in the radical of the character for "kami" (god, pronounced "jin" in this instance). The longer diagonal stroke immediately below the dot changes direction three times to form the figure's right sleeve and continues upward toward the shoulder, ending with a relatively dry brush. The left sleeve was formed next with a long curving hook. Finally the vertical stroke that outlines the torso changes direction to create the hem of the robe before terminating with a flourish as the dry brush hooks upward, completing the right half of the character *jin*. This character, with its three rhythmic flowing brushstrokes, must have taken less than a minute of the artist's time to inscribe.

The facial features of the Tenjin and his mustache and beard were delineated with sharp thin strokes in a style derived from the time-honored Chinese tradition of figure painting in ink. Technically the figure recalls the renowned ink drawing in the Tokyo National Museum depicting the Tang Chinese poet Li Bo (701–762), attributed to the Southern Song painter Liang Kai (active early thirteenth century).

Rebuslike painted images created from Chinese or Japanese kana characters are called *moji-e* (writing pictures). Such word pictures had their origins in the word images of the Heian period (794–1185), which generally used kana script but often included some kanji as well. The practice of creating *moji-e* became extremely popular during the late Edo period at a time when education became more widespread among the masses, making a broad appreciation of *moji-e* possible with creator and viewer sharing a similar cultural background. For this very reason the unsuspecting Western viewer, with an educational background greatly different from that of the *moji-e* artist, can easily miss the true meanings behind these rebus pictures.

The popularity of *moji-e* and a related genre of painting called *e-moji* (picture-words) during the late Edo period led to the publication of numerous books reproducing examples of both types of imagery.[1] One such publication, the *Kiyū shōran* (a collection of essays on music, dance, and manners) of 1830 by Kitamura Nobuyo, refers to a Tenjin image like the present example as one of the older instances of *moji-e*.[2]

The poem written in four lines above the figure reads:

With my plum trees,
Supported by the donations of everyday people,
I serve as a barrier,
Against the demons of the entire world.[3]

The fifth line, at the left, records the date of the fifteenth year of the Keichō era (1610).

Tenjin—Heavenly [*ten*] Deity [*jin*]—was the posthumous honorific title accorded to the ninth-century scholar-statesman Sugawara Michizane (845–903). At the pinnacle of his career Michizane was undone by the slanderous accusations of a political adversary, and he met an untimely death in exile. A bloody medieval tale recounted his vengeful spirit wreaking havoc within the capital and the imperial palace. Such destruction may seem unlikely for a revered man of letters, but the story of Michizane's profound rage against those who had wronged him was believed by men of the time. To pacify his angry soul, the court gave the deceased Michizane the title of Tenjin and ordered a Shinto shrine, the

Tenmangū, built in his honor. Thus appeased, Tenjin ended his destructive rampage and eventually came to be worshiped as the tutelary god of poetry, learning, and calligraphy.

A fantastical story, which recounted that Tenjin traveled to China almost three hundred years after his demise to study Zen Buddhism with Wuzhun Shifan (1177–1249) at Jingshan monastery near Hangzhou, was actively promoted by monks of Tōfukuji, a major Zen temple in Kyoto. According to the legend, Michizane, ensconsed at his main shrine in Dazaifu in northern Kyushu, actually met and studied Zen with Enni Ben'en (1202–1280), the founder of Tōfukuji. Enni had just returned to Japan after studying Zen in China with Wuzhun, and this encounter inspired Tenjin to travel to China himself. As many Japanese monks from Tōfukuji had also studied under Wuzhun, this story expressed a political motive — to increase the Tōfukuji sphere of influence and, because Zen clerics wished to proselytize in provinces where a large number of Tenjin shrines had been erected, to incorporate the popular Tenjin into the Tōfukuji orbit. The origin of the tale about Tenjin's voyage to China to study Zen can therefore be attributed to Tōfukuji circles.[4]

A dream was cited as the source for the pictorial prototype of *Tenjin Returning from China*,[5] but in fact traditional Chinese depictions of scholars and poets helped to inspire this type of Tenjin iconography. The earliest known record of a *Tenjin Returning from China* painting dates from 1394.[6] Popular images of *Tenjin Returning from China* depict the statesman as a frontally oriented devotional image, garbed like a Confucian scholar in robes and headgear often found in paintings of Chinese literati. He carries a pouch containing a robe said to have been given him by Wuzhun and holds a branch of red plum, his favorite flower. It is interesting that this particular type of Tenjin iconography was featured in paintings produced by Chinese artists in Ningbo for sale to Japanese pilgrims.[7] The emergence of this singular iconography coincided with the waning popularity of images of Zen eccentrics in the late fourteenth century. This new type of Tenjin picture must have been popular because of its appeal as a

portrait of an indigenous Japanese hero; at the same time it reflected the growing trend within Zen circles of favoring literary activities over purely religious exercise.[8]

The Tenjin seen here is presented in a dramatically simplified manner. The artist chose to eliminate such ubiquitous attributes as the plum branch. The signature reading "Sugi" (Cypress) at the lower right belongs to Konoe Nobutada, an idiosyncratic nobleman from an exalted family, one of five clans whose members were entitled to serve as imperial regents. As one of the highest-ranking members of the aristocracy, the young Nobutada was quickly promoted through the ranks of the imperial court. During his lifetime, however, warlords like Oda Nobunaga and Toyotomi Hideyoshi held the reins of power, while the imperial household and aristocratic class were mere figureheads on the periphery of political activity. A passionate and strong-minded youth, Nobutada volunteered to join the military forces Hideyoshi was assembling to invade Korea. It is likely that this decision resulted from his frustration over his lack of power rather than a fervent desire to participate in a war. Undaunted by the emperor's refusal to let him join Hideyoshi's army, Nobutada traveled to Nagoya in northern Kyushu, where Hideyoshi had established his military headquarters. The emperor was enraged and ordered Nobutada exiled to Bōnotsu at the southern tip of Kyushu in 1594. He remained there until 1596, when he was pardoned and permitted to return to the capital.

It is believed that Nobutada resolved to paint one thousand images of Tenjin, working every day in order to accomplish his goal. In 1609 alone he is said to have produced one hundred Tenjin paintings. Perhaps for reasons of economy he used rough, coarse paper with visible fibers, such as the example seen here.[9] The actual motive behind Nobutada's seemingly pious resolution is not known. *Moji-e* production had always been closely tied to religious zeal, particularly in connection with pictures created through the use of religious texts.[10] The letters or characters used in *moji-e* were regarded as sacred in themselves, and a Tenjin image like this piece, fashioned from the characters *ten* and *jin*, must have had—at least for Nobutada—a doubly sacred meaning.

Familiarly known in Japan by the posthumous name San'myaku-in, Nobutada is often grouped with the calligraphers Hon'ami Kōetsu (1558–1637; cat. nos. 31, 32) and Shōkadō Shōjō (1584–1639; cat. no. 56). These masters were known collectively as the Three Great Brushes of the Kan'ei Era (1624–44), although Nobutada himself died before the era began. Known primarily for his calligraphic works, he left relatively few paintings. Notable exceptions include his numerous *moji-e* Tenjin images that combine calligraphy and painting, a *moji-e* portrait of the eighth-century poet Kakinomoto no Hitomaro, and a simple drawing of Daruma. The predominance of *moji-e* in Nobutada's oeuvre may have been due to his Zen training at Daitokuji. It was common practice for Zen masters to use *moji-e* as a teaching device, enabling pupils to probe beneath the surface appearance of things to transcend the duality of word and image. *Moji-e* seems to have been regarded as something akin to the paradoxical questions (koan) traditionally posed by Zen masters.[11]

M M

1. *Moji-e* and *e-moji* are not easily distinguished; nor are the terms and their definitions standardized. *Moji-e* is generally considered a writing that is used to construct imagery, while *e-moji* is a painting that is fashioned out of writing, with stronger resemblance to the initials in medieval European manuscripts. See Guth 1992–93 and Inagaki Shin'ichi 1996.
2. This book is in Kitamura 1995, chap. 3, pp. 31–32.
3. Translation in Addiss 1989, p. 25.
4. Etō 1973, p. 146.
5. See cat. no. 25 on portraits of poets for the similar instances of dream-inspired models.
6. See Kitanosha, ed. 1910, pp. 423–34.
7. Suzuki H. 1995.
8. Tokunaga 1980.
9. Komatsu claims to have seen almost twenty of them. Komatsu, ed. 1981b, p. 101.
10. See Katō Nobukiyo's paintings such as *Ten Rakan Examining a Painting of White-Robed Kannon*, in Murase 2000, no. 113.
11. Guth 1992–93, p. 30.

Shōkadō Shōjō (1584–1639)

56.
"Composed under Moonlight at the Western Tower in the City of Jin Ling Castle" by Li Bo

Edo period (1615–1868), dated
February 1635
Hanging scroll, ink on silk, 10⅝ ×
31¼ in. (27 × 80.6 cm)
Signed: Otokoyama biku Shōjō
Seals: Seiō; Shōjō

This poem was composed by the renowned Tang-dynasty Chinese poet Li Bo (701–762). Entitled "Composed under Moonlight at the Western Tower of the City of Jin Ling [modern Nanjing]," it reads as follows (with the title written at the right):

> The night is still in Jin Ling, a cool wind blows.
> I am alone in a high room, gazing over the districts of Wu and Yue.
> White clouds shine on the water and blur the reflection of the still city.
> The cold dew soaks my garments, with drippings like pearls from the autumn moon.
> In the moonlight, murmuring poems, I do not return home for a long time.

It's rare to meet someone that you constantly think about.
Those who can recite the poem "Clear River Is as Bright as Silk" by Xie Tiao,
Always remember the poet.[1]

The signature at the left reads "Otokoyama Biku Shōjō [The Monk Shōjō of Otokoyama wrote this as a gift for a young boy]," followed by the date "a day in *chūshun* [February] (Kan'ei *otsugai* [1635])" and two seals "Seiō" and "Shōjō."

Shōjō was the priestly name of a tea master, poet, painter, and calligrapher who resided at the Otokoyama (also called Iwashimizu) Hachimangū, a Shinto-Shingon Buddhist establishment in

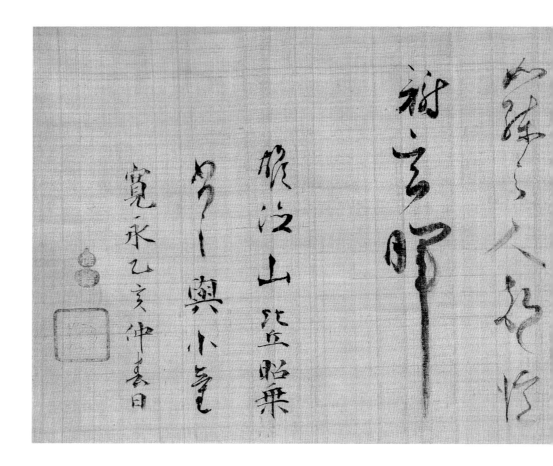

southeastern Kyoto. His reputation as a painter of simple, spare, and spontaneous ink drawings of a variety of subjects — portraits, flowers and birds, and landscapes — has endured to the present day. As a calligrapher he is also revered as one of the Three Great Brushes of the Kan'ei Era (1624–1644), the other two being Konoe Nobutada (1565–1614; cat. no. 55) and Hon'ami Kōetsu (1558–1637; cat. nos. 31, 32). He was the most influential of the three masters, and his impact upon the art of calligraphy has lasted well into modern times.[2]

Shōjō is also widely known as Shōkadō Shōjō, "Shōkadō" being derived from the name of the retirement residence he built in 1637 at the Takino-moto subtemple at Otokoyama, where he served as

abbot for a period of ten years beginning in 1627. In spite of his popularity and fame, his origins remain obscure; the principal source for information on his early life is the *Shōkadō gyōjōki* (Annals of Shōkadō Shōjō), written in 1639 by his tea-master friend Sagawada Masatoshi (1579–1643).[3] Shōjō began his Buddhist training at Otokoyama Hachimangū at seventeen. He seems to have received orthodox Esoteric Buddhism training which included instruction in painting traditional Buddhist icons. A small number of his Buddhist paintings have been preserved; one of the major works in this genre, a set of Portraits of Eight Shingon Patriarchs, was destroyed by fire in 1947, and only copies remain.[4] Shōjō was a versatile artist, adept in the areas of *yamato-e* (literally,

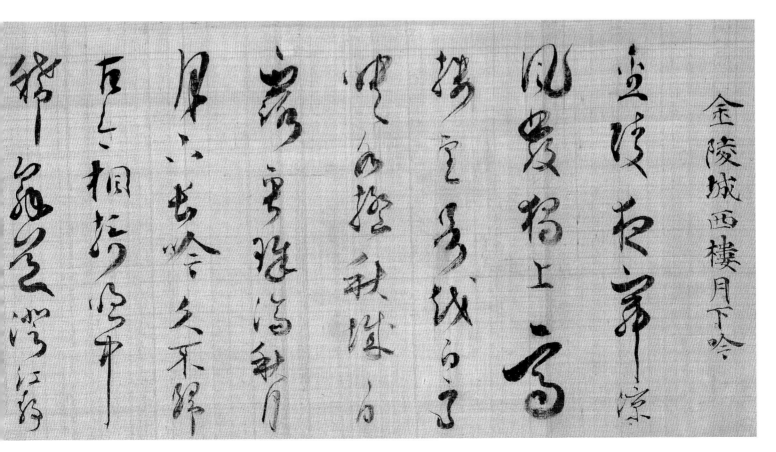

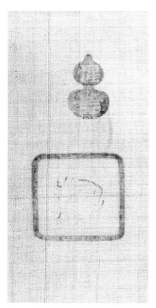

Fig. 30. Detail of cat. no. 56

Japanese painting that departed from *kara-e*, or Chinese painting), ink landscape painting, and polychrome flowers-and-birds painting in the Song Academy style.[5] His paintings were apparently valued highly; Emperor Gomizunoo (r. 1611–1628) once commissioned him to produce *Shokunin zukushi-e* (Portraits of Various Craftsmen), a traditional subject frequently addressed by professional painters of varying artistic backgrounds.[6]

It has been claimed that Shōjō received painting instruction from Kano Sanraku (1559–1635), when the latter took refuge at Otokoyama in 1615 after the fall of Osaka Castle. While Shōjō's friendship with and generosity to Sanraku are well known, it is difficult to discern any influence of Sanraku's painting style in Shōjō's work. What is certain is that Shōjō was an avid collector of arts; the catalogue of his collection, the *Hachiman Takinomotobō zōchō* (Record of the Collection at the Subtemple Takinomoto at Hachiman), lists paintings attributed to the Chinese artists Muqi and Li Di, as well as Japanese painters of the Muromachi period such as Mokuan, Minchō, Shūbun, Sesshū, and Sesson. Works of decorative art and calligraphy were also included in this compendium.

Shōjō was adept at different styles of calligraphy and changed his calligraphic style according to the type of work he was engaged in. His calligraphy on *shikishi* (square poem cards), on handscrolls, and in correspondence displays his versatility. His fame as a great calligrapher was firmly established by the time he reached the age of thirty.[7] He was also so prolific that an enormous number of his calligraphic works is known today, although it is likely that some of the pieces attributed to him were actually produced by his followers.

The present work is written in a mixture of three script styles: *kaisho, gyōsho,* and *sōsho.* Mixed in with these are many characters written in the so-called Taishiryū (Kōbō Daishi style) mode, in which the brush was often twisted and deliberately slowed. The Taishiryū brushline has a quavering quality, exaggerating characteristics widely associated in the popular mind with calligraphy executed by Kūkai (774–835; posthumously known as Kōbō Daishi), who was regarded as the greatest calligrapher of ancient Japan.[8] In this piece such letters as *shuku* ("quiet," the fourth letter from the top in the first line), *fū* ("wind," the top letter in the second line), *kō* ("high," the last letter on the second line), and the final word *ki* ("shine") are eloquent examples of what was broadly regarded as Taishiryū.

Shōjō's older brother was in the service of Konoe Nobutada (cat. no. 55) and it was probably through this connection that Shōjō worked for both Nobutada and his father, Sakihisa (1536–1612), also a noted calligrapher. However, Shōjō's calligraphy has little of Nobutada's bold, powerful style. His own brushwork is more urbane, sophisticated, and gentle, and these features were probably the reason for the enormous popularity he enjoyed among his contemporaries.   MM

1. Xie Tiao was an eminent poet of the fifth century whom Li Bo admired and quoted frequently. The translation of the poem was adapted from Ayscough 1921, p. 70. I am grateful for the suggestions made by Dr. Jason Sun, Associate Curator of the Department of Asian Art, The Metropolitan Museum of Art.
2. Masuda 1978a, p. 48.
3. Reprint is in Yabe 1937.
4. See Nakabe 1993, no. 42.
5. Nakabe 1993, nos. 5–7.
6. Shōjō's letter to Kise Kichijūrō, a retainer working for Konoe Nobuhiro (Nobutada's son, 1598–1649), which is now in the collection of the Yōmei Bunko in Kyoto, refers to this commission. See Yazaki 1974, p. 84.
7. Masuda 1978b, p. 52.
8. For examples of Kūkai's calligraphy reflecting the so-called Taishiryū, see Komatsu, ed. 1981a, nos. 2–4.

Ike Taiga (1723–1776)

57.
Waiting for Hanshan

Edo period (1615–1868)
Hanging scroll, ink on paper,
11⅛ × 23 in. (28.3 × 58.4 cm)
Signed: Kyūka shai
Seals: Kashō; Zenshin sōma no
kata kyūkō

The roughly sketched subject of this painting faces sideways. The eyes, nose, mouth, and other portions of the face are not represented; instead, uncombed hair completely covers the countenance. The figure seems to hold a fishing pole, but this sticklike object is in fact a broom handle. The bushy end of the broom, which provides an important clue to the figure's identity, can be seen at the right edge, as if projecting out of the figure's backside.

The figure is Shide (J: Jittoku), who is commonly depicted with his companion Hanshan (J: Kanzan). As the inscription states, however, "Hanshan has not yet arrived." These legendary Chinese recluses from the late Tang dynasty (618–907) were said to have lived in Guoqing monastery on Mount Tiantai. Their unkempt appearance and eccentric manner of life were much admired in Zen circles where the recluses were regarded as enlightened individuals free of social inhibitions. In China they were pictorialized as early as the Northern Song period (960–1127). Slightly later examples dating to

the Southern Song (1127–1272) and Yuan (1272–1368) periods were imported to Japan, where they served as models for Japanese paintings and where Hanshan and Shide proved to be even more popular painting subjects than in China.

Hanshan and Shide were typically depicted in pairs of paintings in which the former was depicted holding a sutra and the latter a broom, a symbol of the humble act of cleaning a temple but also a metaphor for the clearing of the mind necessary for the practice of meditation. The theme had creative variations in the Edo period. During the eighteenth century, when such parodic variations on traditional themes became widespread, ukiyo-e artists began to depict contemporary figures acting out the roles of the two Zen eccentrics.

The signature, "Kyūka Shai [Kyūka sketches the idea]," is that of the Edo painter Ike Taiga. The seal that accompanies it, however, does not match any of those that Taiga ordinarily employed, and it is difficult to determine how this discrepancy between the authentic signature and the inauthentic seal should be interpreted.

Taiga is widely considered to be the greatest talent of the so-called *nanga* or southern painting school, which flourished during the eighteenth century and was based on Chinese painting styles of the Ming (1368–1644) and Qing (1644–1911) periods. Along with his natural technical facility—in his youth Taiga was considered a prodigy—his best works demonstrate sure brushwork and thorough familiarity with traditional Chinese learning. He was famous in his own lifetime, and today he is regarded as preeminent among Japanese painters of his time. The works by Taiga that have received the highest acclaim in Japan are landscapes in ink and light colors.[1]

The improvisational brushwork found in *Waiting for Hanshan* reveals the strong influence of paintings by the Zen priest-painter Hakuin Ekaku (cat. no. 48). This aspect of Taiga's work has not received scholarly attention from researchers but is crucial in any consideration of the influence of Hakuin's Zen paintings on the leading Kyoto painters of the eighteenth century, including Taiga, Soga Shōhaku (1730–1781), and Nagasawa Rosetsu (1754–1799). In 1751, at the age of twenty-nine, Taiga studied Zen under Hakuin, who had recently arrived in Kyoto, the cultural capital of Japan.

A close examination of the brushwork reveals the faint imprint of tatami flooring, indicating that the work may not have been painted in the artist's studio but perhaps immediately upon request at the house of a patron, in a matter of minutes. The American taste for this style is demonstrated by the many Taiga paintings found in collections in the United States.
YY

1. See, for instance, the selection made in a recent important survey of Taiga's oeuvre: Ōoka and Kobayashi, eds. 1994, vol. 11.

Uragami Gyokudō (1745–1820)

58.

"Hidden Mountain Spring" by Li Bo

Edo period (1615–1868),
nineteenth century
Hanging scroll, ink on paper,
8⅞ × 12½ in. (22.5 × 31.8 cm)
Signed: Gyokudō Kinshi sho
Seal: Suikyo
Literature: Miyake 1956, vol. 2,
pl. 14; Addiss 1999, p. 100

The most striking aspect of this hanging scroll is the beautiful three-layered mounting (see appendix). The middle layer consists of gorgeously decorated printed paper imported from China, which is sandwiched between a layer of Indian chintz on the inside and a piece of green Japanese textile on the outside. Although the date of this mounting is uncertain, it is clear that this scroll was dressed with great care by someone profoundly affected by the calligraphy.

The mounting appears to be based on a deep understanding of the intellectual disposition of Uragami Gyokudō, the author of the calligraphy. Gyokudō was a member of an elite class of intellectuals during the early modern period who evinced a strong interest in classical Chinese learning. Living under the national policy of seclusion in effect during the Edo period, these intellectuals were highly alert to any information concerning the outside world that entered through the port of Nagasaki, at the time one of the few places connecting Japan and the rest of the world. Born in many cases into warrior families, figures such as Gyokudō were the products of a centuries-long period of relative tranquillity during which regional daimyos gradually shifted their emphasis from military concerns to such activities as the development of regional schools. In these establishments generations of privileged young Japanese studied a wide variety of classics, especially those in Chinese, and developed a wide appreciation for all branches of Chinese learning.

Gyokudō directly served a warrior-administrator who was both a retainer of the Ikeda family in Bizen province and the head of the Kamogata domain

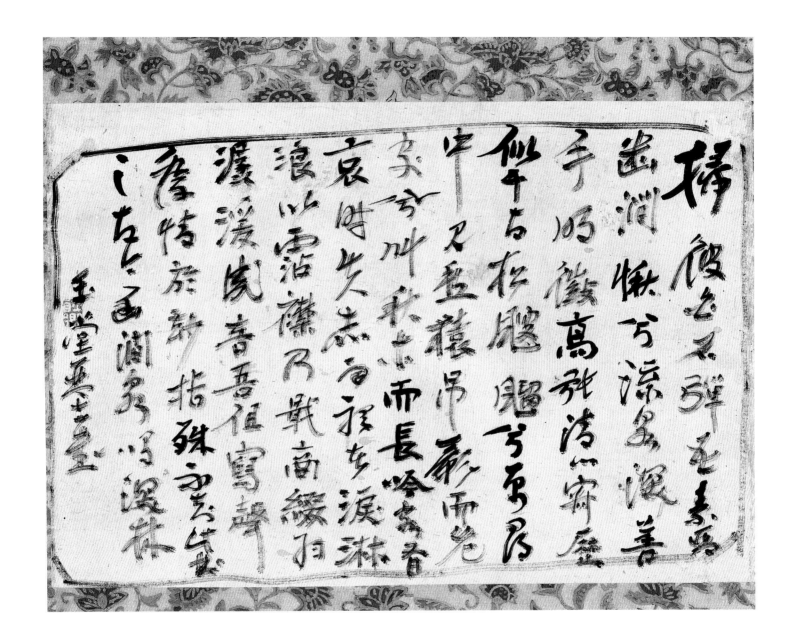

(both part of modern Okayama prefecture). Travel-ing with his lord back and forth from Edo to his home domain, Gyokudō developed a close relation-ship with members of the shogunate as well as with important artists in the capital, such as Tani Bunchō (1763–1840), a member of a samurai family with wide-ranging artistic interests. Bunchō had access to material entering from outside Japan and worked in a number of genres, including Chinese-style paint-ing (*kanga*), Japanese-style painting (*yamato-e*), and Western-style painting, never achieving a person-ally expressive brush style. In contrast, Gyokudō tirelessly pursued a unique style of representation. In 1793 he abruptly left his domain and the adminis-trative duties he held there. Traveling from province to province with his two sons, Shunkin and Shūkin, Gyokudō began to produce large numbers of paint-ings and works of calligraphy.

Hidden Mountain Spring was brushed sometime during this peripatetic period and transcribes a work by the Tang-period Chinese poet Li Bo (701–762):

> I brush off a white rock and play my unadorned
> *qin*—
> the hidden gully is melancholy, the flowing
> stream, deep.
> A touch of the fingers by the shining studs
> expresses noble purity
> and quiets the mind, as in a thousand ages past.

The wind sighs in the pines, ten thousand feet high, where sad gibbons can be seen, lonely in precipitous perches, crying out among the autumn trees, singing aloud. A traveler lamenting the season, heartsore, listens — his tears flow on and on, dampening his robe. Stringing together notes in *shang* and *yu* modes, forming a tune like bubbling water, I express only wordless sounds and emotion through this mysterious melody, not knowing whether this piece is old or new — a spring in a hidden gully sings through the deep woods.[1]

Within a casually drawn square frame, Li Bo's poem is brushed with energy-charged characters that appear flung onto the paper. This style of cal-ligraphy, in which characters are strung together into vertical columns bursting with rhythm, was unique to Gyokudō.[2] This small calligraphic work expresses not only the high regard in which Gyokudō held Li Bo but also as his own faith in the expressive potential of music that is the subject of the present lines. Gyokudō never traveled outside Japan, and here both China and Li Bo are products of his rich imagination.   Y Y

1. Addiss 1999, p. 100.
2. In 1956, Miyake Hisanosuke, a great admirer of Gyokudō, published at his own expense a large catalogue of Gyokudō's oeuvre, which contains this work. Miyake 1956, vol. 2, pl. 14.

APPENDIX

BIBLIOGRAPHY

INDEX

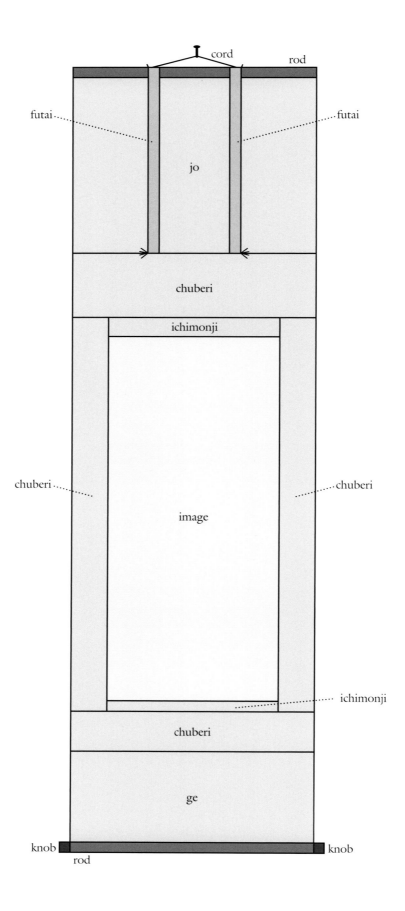

Mountings of Japanese Paintings and Calligraphies

SONDRA CASTILE

The mounting of a hanging scroll consists of all materials except the artwork itself. These materials are decorative papers or silks, various kinds of backing papers, top and bottom rods, knobs, hardware fittings, and cord.

The terms listed below are in general use to describe elements of Japanese style hanging scroll mountings. There are no one-word equivalents in English. The *shaku, sun, bu,* and *rin* units of measure are still used by the traditional mounter.

ichimonji: The elements of the mounting directly above, below, and sometimes on all sides of the art.

chuberi: The elements of the mounting attached above, below, and at the sides of the *ichimonji*. If there is no *ichimonji*, the material that surrounds the painting is called the *chuberi* when there is one other mounting section above and below it.

jo-ge: The top and bottom sections of a mounting attached to the two rods.

soberi: The framing of a *jo-ge* by strips on the left and right sides of the mounting.

futai: Narrow strips of the mounting attached to the top rod in some mounting styles. Below the rod, they either are pasted to the top section of the mounting or hang down freely.

hyoho: A style for Buddhist or Taoist figures and other religious subjects in which the mounting surrounds the painting or calligraphy in successive frames. The *chuberi* does not extend horizontally across the painting. Strips at the left and right of the *jo-ge* form the *soberi*.

rimpo: A style in which the mounting strips on the left and right of the painting are very narrow, usually no wider than 5 *bu* (approximately ⅝ in. [1.5 cm]).

2.
The Heart Sutra

Nara period (710–794), ca. 755
Handscroll mounted as a hanging scroll, ink on paper, 9½ ×
15⅛ in. (24.1 × 39.1 cm)
Literature: *Bessatsu Taiyō* 1999,
no. 25

This is a *hyoho,* or Buddhist-style mounting, that is used with some variations on other sacred or religious representations. Characteristic of this style is the manner in which the art is framed by sections of the mounting. The *chuberi* does not extend to the right and left sides but surrounds the calligraphy with a very narrow strip on right and left. The *jo-ge* also has strips on either side making another frame of one material called a *soberi*. Although three different materials are used consecutively, this style is not a three-level mounting, that is, one in which the *chuberi* extends from the right to left edges of the mounting. The material of the *ichimonji* and the *futai* are the same, a usual practice in *hyoho*.

The *ichimonji* and *futai* are a weft-patterned brocade of floral roundels on a blue ground. The *chuberi* is gold brocade with a pattern of chestnuts and leaves. The *soberi* is a figured twill with cloud

pattern. The roller knobs are gilded with fine-lined filigree of scrolling vine and lotus.

The calligraphy of this sutra fragment has been executed on decorated paper. The gold brocade of the middle section of the mounting subtly elaborates this richness of effect without overemphasis; the ground color is muted and balance with the gold is achieved here. The selection of the small cloud-patterned textile for the largest areas of the mounting makes a particularly favorable juxtaposition with the other two large-patterned textiles. Cloud patterns with great variation in size and form have long been used on mountings for Buddhist subjects. The gold brocade is used in a restrained manner at the side edges of the sutra and with slightly more emphasis at top and bottom, farther from the subject. The tones employed are subdued, and the overall effect of the mounting is heightened by the gold brocade.

Fig. 31. Overall of cat. no. 2

Fig. 32. Detail of cat. no. 2

12.

Section of "Peaceful Practices," with Canopy and Pedestal Decoration, Chapter 14 of the Lotus Sutra

Kamakura period (1185–1333), thirteenth century
Handscroll mounted as a hanging scroll, ink on paper, silver-ruled lines, one gold line, and silver-stamped decoration, 8¾ × 2¼ in. (22.2 × 5.7 cm)

This is an example of a *doho,* or banner mounting. The impact of this small calligraphic fragment is visually heightened by the placement of a larger light-colored and undecorated paper on all sides. The mounting is less likely to overwhelm something so small if the mounting's decorative elements are not contiguous to the calligraphy or painting. This style is common in Japanese mounting, but in Chinese practice these kinds of small elements or fragments are usually mounted as album leaves and only rarely as scrolls.

The *ichimonji* and *futai* are a gold brocade with pattern of single-vine small peony on a ground of indigo-dyed nested and tilted squares. The *chuberi* is a satin weave with changing colors and repeating weft patterns in the mounting strips at the left and right sides. In the top horizontal section of the *chuberi* above the *ichimonji,* young pine and facing cranes form scattered squares in a lattice pattern on a beige ground. The pattern changes to linked tortoiseshell hexagons enclosing flowers. The weave then follows with a lighter

brown section of large hexagons and smaller squares of floral design. These patterns of auspicious symbols repeat. The *jo-ge* is a Chinese figured satin in a pattern known as *shokko,* a rendering of a Chinese place-name. The knobs are ivory with many carved rings.

This is a mounting of refined taste. Its effect is realized to a great extent by the choice of patterns, their juxtaposition, and the variations of form, size, and color among them on this thin textile. The range of tone is beautifully conceived. The dyeing has employed overtones probably achieved with a thin ink wash. This has rendered the colors almost imperceptibly more subtle and subdued. The paper surrounding the sutra fragment itself has also been selected for its understated character. The surface is not quite smooth and regular as coarser fibers have been allowed to remain in the sheet with fine ones. The effect therefore is not one of an unsettling contrast but one of harmony with the mounting as a whole. The environment created by the relative sizes, tones, and patterns of the textiles achieves a remarkable balance with the sutra fragment.

Fig. 33. Overall of cat. no. 12

Fig. 34. Detail of cat. no. 12

Myōe Kōben (1173–1232)

29.
Letter to Jōjūbō

Kamakura period (1185–1333),
ca. 1221
Hanging scroll, ink on paper,
8¼ × 17 in. (21 × 43.2 cm)
Signed: Kōben

In this mounting style the *ichimonji* and the *futai* are of the same material. The textile is silver brocade with patterns of cloud and of facing deer on a rust ground. The *chuberi* is an embroidered-pattern gauze weave with large peonies, scrolling vines, and leaves. The thinness of the textile is visually countered by the large bold pattern and deep color. The *jo-ge* is indigo-dyed plain weave. The threads vary in width and have taken up the dye unevenly. The ivory knobs have been darkened to produce their present color.

The textiles of the *ichimonji, futai,* and *jo-ge* have been used in the direction of the weft, the warp going from left to right. Only the two side panels of the *chuberi* are used with the warp top to bottom. This was done to make the best use of the textile width and to gain greater lattitude in placement of the pattern. The mounter had considerable skill to make a stable mounting using the materials

in this way. Textiles do not shrink and stretch to the same degree in the directions of warp and weft. To complete this mounting, three textiles of different thickness and weave were used with the warps in two directions. The various paper backings, textiles with disparate characteristics, and another type of paper on which the calligraphy itself is written have all been joined into one stable object: the hanging scroll.

The large peony pattern in gold provides a decorative contrast to the rust of the *ichimonji-futai* and to the slightly coarse weave and subtle tone of the *jo-ge*. The silver on the rust-colored ground may have originally been brighter, but it now functions in a subdued manner. Because the pattern of gold is dispersed among vines and leaves instead of appearing as scattered individual flowers on a dark solid ground, the effect is less bold. Here more is rendered less to gain effectiveness.

Fig. 35. Overall of cat. no. 29

Fig. 36. Detail of cat. no. 29

Sen no Rikyū (1522–1591)

30.
Letter to Takigawa Katsutoshi
(1543–1610)

Momoyama period (1573–1615), dated April 21
Hanging scroll, ink on paper, 10⅞ × 15⅞ in. (27.6 × 40.3 cm)
Signed: Sōeki, with a cipher
Ex coll.: Takigawa Katsutoshi; Murakami Kōsuke
Literature: Komatsu 1985, no. 222; Komatsu 1996, no. 226; Komatsu 1999, no. 226

This *rimpo*-style two-level mounting has no *ichimonji* and has *futai* attached to the top section of the mounting. The *chuberi* is woven with coarse uneven threads, and the dye has therefore been absorbed unevenly. The color was probably achieved by dyeing yellow and then overdyeing with indigo.

The material of the *jo-ge* is crushed paper. During the Edo period there was great variety in this kind of paper. It was used extensively on sliding panels, walls, and screen backs. The paper was first brushed with a light ground color, over which a darker tone of the same or another color was applied. The paper was then crumpled or folded by hand in various ways to produce the desired effect. The pattern emerged in the creases where the undertone is revealed.

In this mounting a thin Japanese mulberry paper has been used. It has been brushed with a coating containing shell white or clay and slight pigment. Another deeper color was then applied. The paper was finished with a weak solution of persimmon tannin and ink. This produces a quiet tone and provides stability to the surface.

The *futai* are made of Chinese paper and are pasted to the top section of the mounting. To make these elements less stark, small scattered burn holes have been added. Probably made with an incense stick, they resemble insect holes.

The roller knobs are lacquered black and in the shape favored by, and probably first made and used by, the tea master Sen Sotan. This was a felicitous choice as Sotan was both a grandson and a great admirer of Sen no Rikyū, the writer of this letter and a famous man of tea.

The muted tones, achieved through both design and the passage of time, are complementary to the visual atmosphere of this calligraphy. The various elements achieve wholly appropriate proportions. Any potential harshness of line has dissolved in the carefully crafted imprecision.

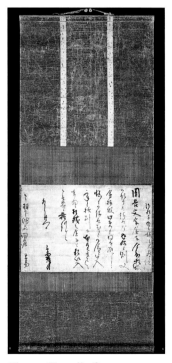

Fig. 37. Overall of cat. no. 30

Fig. 38. Detail of cat. no. 30

Gukyoku Reisai (ca. 1369–1452)

42.
Two Buddhist Maxims

Muromachi period (1392–1573)
Pair of hanging scrolls, ink on
paper; both: 36¼ × 8¾ in. (93.4 ×
22.2 cm)
Seals (on both): Fūgetsu shujin;
Gukyoku
Ex coll.: Nakamura Fujitarō,
Tokyo
Literature: Tamaya 1965, pl. 243;
Kyoto National Museum 1967,
pl. 142; Shimizu and Rosenfield
1984–85, no. 48

This pair of hanging scrolls is mounted in two-level *rimpo* style. They are mounted without *ichimonji*. The textile of the *chuberi* and the *futai* is gold brocade: a beige ground with interlocking key-fret pattern and a staggered dispersal of dragon roundels. The *futai* hang free from the top section of the mounting. The *jo-ge* is a dyed plain-weave silk.

Roller knobs are lacquered black in the *bachi* shape. There are several variant styles of this common form. The example on these scrolls has a slightly flared end to the knob. The elegant execution of these knobs is evident in the very discreet swell at the tip.

The mounting of these two hanging scrolls emphasizes the svelte character of single-line calligraphy.

The *jo-ge* section of the mounting, and therefore the *futai* as well, is elongated. The *futai* separate the *jo* visually into three equal parts, which is a device that encourages the eye to see the whole hanging scroll as long and slender. If there were an *ichimonji*, the horizontal elements would overwhelm this fluid line. The use of a pattern with roundels alternately executed presents enough gold to enhance the effect of the calligraphy but does not draw excessive attention (as would a geometrically opposed pattern). The gold is further mollified by the subdued tone of the *jo-ge*. The selection of materials and use of tone make these scrolls particularly well suited to be hung against the soft earth-toned walls of a tearoom alcove.

Fig. 39. Overall of cat. no. 42

Fig. 40. Detail of cat. no. 42 (hanging scroll at right in fig. 39)

Uragami Gyokudō (1745–1820)

58.
"Hidden Mountain Spring" by Li Bo

Edo period (1615–1868),
nineteenth century
Hanging scroll, ink on paper,
8⅞ × 12½ in. (22.5 × 31.8 cm)
Signed: Gyokudō Kinshi sho
Seal: Suikyo
Literature: Miyake 1956, vol. 2,
pl. 14; Addiss 1999, p. 100

This is an example of three-level mounting. An *ichimonji* of a twill-weave printed cotton with painted gold accent surrounds the calligraphy with two narrow strips at the sides. This floral pattern is cursive, and though it repeats, its free-hand gold work lends a somewhat informal and exuberant quality to this part of the mounting. The *chuberi* is a Chinese block-printed paper with flowers, vines, and scattered overlapping floral roundels on a yellow ground. The lines of the pattern are imprecise, indicating that an old worn block was probably used. The extreme smoothness of this prepared surface is in considerable contrast to the adjacent elements of the mounting. The *soberi* is a subtle tone of blue with irregular dye penetration and uneven thread size.

Narrow strips at the sides join the *jo-ge*. The roller knobs are undecorated ivory with rounded caps.

If taken individually, some materials combined with felicity in this mounting might not seem obvious choices. The *ichimonji* with its color and unrestrained and casual application of gold might seem out of character with a Chinese poem — or the deference usually paid by a Japanese mounting. However, the spirit of this small piece of textile — reduced to very narrow strips at the sides — leaves an impression of color, mostly red, and the glitter of gold that covers the floral edges and highlights with wide uncompromising strokes. The result of this application and the proportions of its exposure enlivens our perception of the calligraphy and establishes a resonance between the cadence of the characters and the tenuous ink line that borders them.

The yellow printed paper of the *chuberi* is a contrast whose tone is more refined. A smooth surface is essential for decorating paper with this technique, and in part it is this quality that usually gives this paper its formal quality. However, the imprecise lines of this printing dispel any tendency toward imbalance with the calligraphy. There is no consistent pattern to distract from the visual effect of the poem itself. The plain-woven, unaggressively dyed *soberi* produces a nuance of calm in the varying tone and thread thickness randomly exposed in the weave. This part of the mounting also has a grace that complements the other materials and elaborates the viewer's response to the calligraphy.

Fig. 41. Overall of cat. no. 58

Fig. 42. Detail of cat. no. 58

Bibliography

Addiss 1989
Stephen Addiss. *The Art of Zen: Paintings and Calligraphy by Japanese Monks, 1600–1925.* New York: Harry N. Abrams, 1989.

Addiss et al. 1999
Stephen Addiss et al. *The Resonance of the Qin in East Asian Art.* Exh. cat., New York, China Institute Gallery. New York, 1999.

Akiyama et al. 1972
Akiyama Terukazu et al. *Semmen Hokekyō no kenkyū* (Semmen Hokekyō: Twelfth-Century Genre Paintings Decorating Fan-Shaped Sutras). Tokyo: Kajima Institute Publishing Co., 1972.

Akiyama et al. 1980
Akiyama Terukazu et al. *Zaigai Nihon no shihō* (Japanese Art: Selections from Western Collections). Vol. 2, *Emakimono* (Narrative Scroll Painting). Tokyo: Mainichi Shinbunsha, 1980.

Ashton, ed. 1977
Dore Ashton, ed. *Picasso on Art: A Selection of Views.* 1972. New York: Penguin Books, 1977.

Asuka Historical Museum and Nara National Museum 1978
Tanaka Yoshiyasu. *Kodai no Tanjō Butsu* (Buddha at Birth from Ancient Times). Exh. cat., Asuka Historical Museum and Nara National Museum. Nara, 1978.

Ayscough 1921
Florence Ayscough. *Fir-Flower Tablets: Poems Translated from the Chinese.* Boston and New York: Houghton Mifflin Co., 1921.

Baskett 1980
Mary W. Baskett. *Footprints of the Buddha: Japanese Buddhist Prints from American and Japanese Collections.* Exh. cat., Philadelphia Museum of Art. Philadelphia, 1980.

Bechert, ed. 1991–97
Heinz Bechert, ed. *The Dating of the Historical Buddha/Die Datierung des historischen Buddha.* 3 vols. Abhandlungen der Akademie der Wissenschaften in Göttingen, Philologisch-Historische Klasse 3, nos. 189, 194, 222. Symposium zur Buddhismusforschung, 4. Göttingen: Vandenhoeck and Ruprecht, 1991–97.

Bessatsu Taiyō 1999
Yasuragi no Bukkyō bijutsu (Buddhist Art for Contemplation). *Bessatsu Taiyō*, no. 25 (July 1999). Tokyo: Heibonsha, 1999.

Bhikkhu and Bhikkhu 1995
Nanamoli Bhikkhu and Bodhi Bhikkhu, trans. *The Middle Length Discourses of the Buddha: A New Translation of the Majjhima Nikaya.* Boston: Wisdom Publications, 1995.

Birnbaum 1983
Raoul Birnbaum. *Studies on the Mysteries of Mañjuśrī: A Group of East Asian Mandalas and Their Traditional Symbolism.* [Boulder, Colo.]: Society for the Study of Chinese Religions, 1983.

Bokubi 1953
"Jiun Sonja sakuhin tokushū" (Special Issue on the Works by Monk Jiun). *Bokubi* 25 (June 1953).

Brinker and Kanazawa 1996
Helmut Brinker and Hiroshi Kanazawa. *Zen: Masters of Meditation in Images and Writings.* Translated by Andreas Leisinger. Artibus Asiae Publishers, Supplementum 40. Zurich: Artibus Asiae Publishers, 1996.

Brock 1990
Karen L. Brock. "Chinese Maiden, Silla Monk: Zenmyō and Her Thirteenth-Century Japanese Audience." In *Flowering in the Shadows: Women in the History of Chinese and Japanese Painting,* edited by Marsha Weidner, pp. 185–218. Honolulu: Hawaii University Press, 1990.

Brock 2001
Karen L. Brock. "'My Reflection Should Be Your Keepsake': Myōe's Vision of the Kasuga Deity." In *Living Images: Japanese Buddhist Icons in Context,* edited by Robert H. Sharf and Elizabeth Horton Sharf, pp. 49–113. Stanford: Stanford University Press, 2001.

Carpenter 1997
John Thomas Carpenter. "Fujiwara no Yukinari and the Development of Heian Court Calligraphy." Ph.D. diss., Columbia University, 1997.

Chang and Frankel, eds. 1995
Chang Ch'ung-ho and Hans H. Frankel, eds. *Two Chinese Treatises on Calligraphy.* New Haven and London: Yale University Press, 1995.

Chino 1991
Chino Kaori. "Kasuga-no no meisho-e" (Pictures of Famous Views of the Field at Kasuga). In *Akiyama Terukazu Hakase koki kinen Bijutsushi ronbunshū* (Festschrift for the Seventieth Birthday of Dr. Terukazu Akiyama), pp. 421–61, pls. 12–14. Tokyo: Benridō, 1991.

Chūgoku Sekkutsu 1980–82
Chūgoku Sekkutsu (The Grotto Art of China). *Tonkō Bakkōkutsu* (Dunhuang Mogao Caves). 5 vols. Tokyo: Heibonsha, 1980–82.

Cleary 1993
Thomas Cleary. *The Flower Ornament Scripture.* Boston and London: Shambhala, 1993.

Conze 1958
Edward Conze, trans. *Buddhist Wisdom Books, Containing The Diamond Sutra and The Heart Sutra.* London: G. Allen and Unwin, [1958].

Cunningham et al. 1998
Michael R. Cunningham et al. *Buddhist Treasures from Nara.* Exh. cat., The Cleveland Museum of Art. Cleveland, 1998.

Cuno et al. 1996
James Cuno et al. *Harvard's Art Museums: 100 Years of Collecting.* Cambridge, Mass., Harvard University Art Museums. New York: Harry N. Abrams, 1996.

Daizōkyō 1924–34
Takakusu Junjirō and Watanabe Kaigyoku, eds. *Taishō shinshū Daizōkyō* (The Taishō Edition of the Tripitaka). 100 vols. Tokyo: Taishō Issaikyō Kankōkai, 1924–34.

DeCoker 1988
Gary DeCoker. "Secret Teachings in Medieval Calligraphy: *Jubokushō* and *Saiyōshō.*" *Monumenta Nipponica* 43, no. 2 (Summer 1988), pp. 197–228; 43, no. 3 (Autumn 1988), pp. 259–78.

de Visser 1935
M. W. de Visser. *Ancient Buddhism in Japan: Sūtras and Ceremonies in Use in the Seventh and Eighth Centuries A.D. and Their History in Later Times.* 2 vols. Leiden: E. J. Brill, 1935.

Dunhuang Academy 1990
Dunhuang Academy (Tonkō Kenkyūin). *Ansei Yūrinkutsu* (The

Yulinku Grottoes). Chūgoku sekkutsu (The Grotto Art of China). Tokyo: Heibonsha, 1990.

Ebine 2000
Ebine Toshio. "Taiwa no Shōshi: Aru denshin ikka" (The Xiao Family of Taihe: A Family of Portrait Painters). *Kokka*, no. 1255 (May 2000), pp. 30–37.

Egami 1989
Egami Yasushi. *Sōshokukyō* (Decorated Sutra Copies). *Nihon no bijutsu* (Arts of Japan), no. 278 (July 1989). Tokyo: Shibundō, 1989.

Endō and Kasuga, eds. 1967
Endō Yoshimoto and Kasuga Kazuo, eds. *Nihon koten bungaku taikei* (Compendium of Japanese Classical Literature). Vol. 70. *Nihon Ryōiki*. Tokyo: Iwanami Shoten, 1967.

Etō 1973
Etō Shun. "Totō Tenjin zu: Kenkō Shōkei hitsu, Tokkō Shijun san" (Painting of Tenjin Returning from China: Painted by Kenkō Shōkei with Colophon by Tokkō Shijun). *Kobijutsu*, no. 42 (September 1973), pp. 145–46.

Fischer et al. 2000
Felice Fischer et al. *The Arts of Hon'ami Kōetsu, Japanese Renaissance Master.* Exh. cat., Philadelphia Museum of Art. Philadelphia, 2000.

Fister 1988
Patricia Fister. *Japanese Women Artists, 1600–1900.* Exh. cat., Spencer Museum of Art, University of Kansas, Lawrence; Honolulu Academy of Arts. New York: Harper and Row, 1988.

Fister 1994
Patricia Fister. *Kinsei no josei gakatachi* (Japanese Women Artists of the Kinsei Era: Arts and Gender). Kyoto: Shibunkaku Shuppan, 1994.

Fontein and Hickman 1970
Jan Fontein and Money L. Hickman. *Zen Painting and Calligraphy: An Exhibition of Works of Art Lent by Temples, Private Collectors, and Public and Private Museums in Japan.* Exh. cat., Museum of Fine Arts, Boston. Boston, 1970.

Foucher 1905–8
A. Foucher. *L'art Gréco-bouddhique du Gandhâra: Étude sur les origines de l'influence classique dans l'art bouddhique de l'Inde et de l'Extrême-Orient.* 2 vols. Paris: Imprimerie Nationale, 1905–8.

Foulk and Sharf 1993–94
T. Griffith Foulk and Robert H. Sharf. "On the Ritual Use of Ch'an Portraiture in Medieval China." *Cahiers d'Extrême-Asie: Bilingual Journal of the "École Française d'Extrême-Orient,"* no. 7 (1993–94), pp. 149–219.

Fu 1976
Shen [C. Y.] Fu. "Zhang Jizhi he tade zhongkai: Liang Song shujia dianjun Zhang Jizhi" (Zhang Jizhi [1186–1266]: The Last Great Calligrapher of the Sung and His "Medium-Regular" Script). *The National Palace Museum Quarterly* 10, no. 4 (Summer 1976), pp. 43–65 (English summary by Robert L. Thorp, pp. 21–39).

Fu et al. 1977
Shen C. Y. Fu et al. *Traces of the Brush: Studies in Chinese Calligraphy.* Exh. cat., New Haven, Yale University Art Gallery. New Haven, 1977.

Furuta 1959
Furuta Shōkin. "Jiun no sho ni tsuite" (On Jiun's Calligraphy). *Sansai* 112 (March 1959), pp. 58–69.

Furuta 1962
Furuta Shōkin. *Shoseki meihin sōkan* (Series of Masterpieces of Calligraphy). Vol. 76, *So Chō Sokushi, "Kongō Han'nyakyō"* (Song Zhang Jizhi, "Diamond Sutra"). Tokyo: Nigensha, 1962.

Furuya 1975
Furuya Minoru. "Kaishi no kenkyū: Shoshiki no seiritsu to hensen" (Study of the *Kaishi*: The Origins and Changes of Its Forms). In

Tokyo Kokuritsu Hakubutsukan kiyō (Proceedings of the Tokyo National Museum), vol. 11, pp. 153–215, pls. 1–7 (pp. 29–32). Tokyo: Tokyo Kokuritsu Hakubutsukan, 1975.

Girard 1990
Frédéric Girard. *Un moine de la secte Kegon à l'époque de Kamakura: Myōe (1173–1232) et le "Journal de ses rêves."* Paris: École Française d'Extrême-Orient, 1990.

Girard 1999
Frédéric Girard. "Remarques sur le fragment de Cambridge du *Journal des rêves* de Myōe (1173–1232)." *Bulletin de l'École Française d'Extrême-Orient* 86 (1999), pp. 377–84.

Gotoh Museum 1962
Emakimono to sōshokukyō tokubetsuten (Illustrated Hand Scrolls and Decorated Sutra Copies). Exh. cat., Tokyo, Gotoh Museum. Tokyo, 1962.

Gotoh Museum 1971
Kawase Kazuma. *Koshakyō* (Old Sutra Copies). Tokyo: Gotoh Museum. Tokyo, 1971.

Gotoh Museum 1991
Kunōjikyō to Kokyōrō (Gold Traces from a Man Who Loved Sutras). Exh. cat., Tokyo, Gotoh Museum. Tokyo, 1991.

Grapard 1992
Allan G. Grapard. *The Protocol of the Gods: A Study of the Kasuga Cult in Japanese History.* Berkeley and Los Angeles: University of California Press, 1992.

Graybill 1984–85
Maribeth Graybill. "The Immortal Poets." In Shimizu and Rosenfield 1984–85, pp. 96–111.

Guth 1992–93
Christine Guth. *Asobi: Play in the Arts of Japan.* Exh. cat., Katonah Museum of Art; San Antonio Museum of Art; Los Angeles County Museum of Art. Katonah. N.Y., 1992.

Gyōtoku 1994
Gyōtoku Shin'ichirō. "Suijaku-ga no kenkyū: Miya mandara o chūshin ni" (A Study of Shinto Paintings and Shrine Mandalas). *Kajima Bijutsu Zaidan nenpō* 11 (1994), pp. 240–57.

Haga 1963
Haga Kōshirō. *Sen no Rikyū.* Jinbutsu sōsho (Famous Personalities). Tokyo: Yoshikawa Kōbunkan, 1963.

Hagitani, ed. 1959
Hagitani Boku, ed. *Heianchō uta-awase taisei* (Records of *Uta-awase* of the Heian Period). Tokyo: Hagitani Boku, 1959.

Harrist and Fong 1999–2001
Robert E. Harrist, Jr., and Wen C. Fong. *The Embodied Image: Chinese Calligraphy from the John B. Elliott Collection.* Exh. cat., Princeton, N.J., The Art Museum, Princeton University; The Seattle Art Museum; New York, The Metropolitan Museum of Art. Princeton, N.J., 1999.

Härtel et al. 1982
Herbert Härtel et al. *Along the Ancient Silk Routes: Central Asian Art from the West Berlin State Museums.* Exh. cat., New York, The Metropolitan Museum of Art. New York, 1982.

Haruna 1979
Haruna Yoshishige. *Kohitsu daijiten* (Comprehensive Dictionary of the Calligraphy of Old Japan). Kyoto: Tankōsha, 1979.

Hasegawa, K. 2000
Kanae Hasegawa. "Report from Japan: Treasures of the Imperial Collections." *Oriental Art* 46, no. 2 (2000), pp. 87–89.

Hasegawa N. 1979
Hasegawa Nobuyoshi. "Sanjūrokkasen no seiritsu" (The Establishment of the Thirty-six Immortal Poets). In *Shinshū Nihon emakimono zenshū* (New Collection of Japanese Narrative

Handscrolls), edited by Tanaka Ichimatsu, vol. 19, *Sanjūrokkasen-e* (Paintings of the Thirty-six Immortal Poets), by Mori Tōru et al., pp. 40–47. Tokyo: Kadokawa Shoten, 1979.

Hayashiya et al. 1964
Hayashiya Tatsusaburō et al. *Kōetsu.* Tokyo: Daiichi Hōki, 1964.

Higuchi 1960
Higuchi Hideo. "Daiji shakyō no keifu: Ōjōmu ron" (Ojōmu). *Museum,* no. 113 (August 1960), pp. 20–23.

Hirata 1994
Hirata Hiroshi. *E-busshi no jidai* (Era of Buddhist Painters). 2 vols. *Shiryō hen* (Volume of Historical Material). Tokyo: Chūōkōron Bijutsu Shuppan, 1994.

Honda 1970
Honda H. H., trans. *The Shin Kokinshū: The 13th-Century Anthology Edited by Imperial Edict.* [Tokyo]: The Hokuseidō Press; The Eirinsha Press, 1970.

Horie 1977
Horie Tomohiko. *Kana. Nihon no bijutsu* (Arts of Japan), no. 130 (March 1977). Tokyo: Shibundō, 1977.

Hung 1952
William Hung. *Tu Fu, China's Greatest Poet.* Cambridge, Mass.: Harvard University Press, 1952.

Ide 2001
Ide Seinosuke. *Nihon no Sō-Gen butsuga* (Song and Yuan Buddhist Paintings in Japanese Collections). *Nihon no bijutsu* (Arts of Japan), no. 418 (March 2001). Tokyo: Shibundō, 2001.

Ienaga 1966
Ienaga Saburō. *Jōdai yamato-e nenpyō* (Chronology of Ancient Poems Related to Painting). Rev. ed. Tokyo: Bokusui Shobō, 1966.

Iijima 1975
Iijima Shunkei. *Shakyō tekagami: Murasaki no mizu* (Album of Sutra Copies Known as "Murasaki no mizu"). Tokyo: Akasaka Mitokō, 1975.

Iijima 1977
Iijima Shunkei. *Nihon no sho no bi* (Art of Japanese Calligraphy). Tokyo: Shogei Bunka Shinsha, 1977.

Iijima, ed. 1975
Iijima Shunkei, ed. *Shodō jiten* (Dictionary of Calligraphy). Tokyo: Tokyodō Shuppan, 1975.

Inagaki, H. 1994
Hisao Inagaki in collaboration with Harold Stewart. *The Three Pure Land Sutras: A Study and Translation from Chinese.* Kyoto: Nagata Bunshodō, 1994.

Inagaki Shin'ichi 1996
Inagaki Shin'ichi. "Edo jidai no moji asobi" (Play on Letters during the Edo Period). In *Moji-e to E-moji no keifu* (History of Writings as Pictures and Pictures in Writings), pp. 12–16. Exh. cat., Tokyo, Shibuyakuritsu Shōtō Bijutsukan. Tokyo, 1996.

Inagaki Susumu 1971
Inagaki Susumu. *Kodai no kawara* (Ancient Roof Tiles). *Nihon no bijutsu* (Arts of Japan), no. 66 (November 1971). Tokyo: Shibundō, 1971.

Ishida H. 1979
Ishida Hisatoyo. *Ryōkai mandara no chie* (Wisdom of the Two-World Mandalas). Tokyo: Tokyo Bijutsu, 1979.

Ishida M. 1972
Ishida Mosaku. *Tō: Tōba, Stupa* (Buddhist Towers: Pagoda and Stupa). *Nihon no bijutsu* (Arts of Japan), no. 77 (October 1972). Tokyo: Shibundō, 1972.

Ishida, M., et al. 1964
Mosaku Ishida, et al. *Japanese Buddhist Prints.* New York: Harry N. Abrams, 1964.

Itō 1970
Itō Toshiko. "Den Kōetsu utaibon to Kanze Kokusetsu" (A Book of *Utai:* Generally Ascribed to Kōetsu and Kokusetsu Kanze). *Kokka,* no. 922 (1970), pp. 91–120.

Izumi, ed. 1982
Izumi Motohiro, ed. *Jikkinshō: Honbun to sakuin* (A Treatise of Ten Rules). Tokyo: Kasama Shoin, 1982.

Izutsu 1992
Izutsu Nobutaka. "Kongōbuji denrai itabori Taizō mandara ni tsuite: Denrai to zuyō kara mita seisaku nendai" (Wood-Carved Mandala of the Womb World Owned by Kongōbuji: Dating Based on Provenance and Iconography). *Kanazawa Bunko kenkyū,* no. 289 (1992), pp. 17–37.

***Jūyō bunkazai* 1972–78**
Mainichi Shinbun Jūyō Bunkazai Iinkai Jimukyoku. *Jūyō bunkazai* (Important Cultural Treasures). 32 vols. Tokyo: Mainichi Shinbunsha, 1975.

***Kaikodo Journal* 2000**
Kaikodo Journal. Sale cat., New York, Kaikodo, Spring 2000.

Kakui 1964
Kakui Hiroshi. "Kengukyō 'Ōjōmu' shōkō" (An Essay on the "Ōjōmu"). *Museum,* no. 163 (October 1964), pp. 12–13.

Kameda et al. 1959
Kameda Tsutomu et al. *Nihon emakimono zenshū* (Japanese Handscroll Paintings), edited by Tanaka Ichimatsu. Vol. 1, *E-Ingakyō* (Illustrated Sutra of Past Causes and Present Effects). Tokyo: Kadokawa Shoten, 1959. Reprint, 1977.

Kaneko 1992
Kaneko Hiroaki. *Monju Bosatsuzō* (Images of the Bodhisattva Manjushri). *Nihon no bijutsu* (Arts of Japan), no. 314 (July 1992). Tokyo: Shibundō, 1992.

Kawamata, ed. 1928–38
Kawamata Keiichi, ed. *Shinkō Gunsho ruijū* (Collection of Essays, Newly Edited). 24 vols. Tokyo: Naigai Shoseki Kankōkai, 1928–38.

Kawamura 1981
Kawamura Tomoyuki. "Kasuga mandara no seiritsu to girei" (Emergence of the Kasuga Mandala and Its Ritual Background). *Bijutsushi,* no. 110 (March 1981), pp. 86–100.

Kikutake 1984
Kikutake Junji. *Bukkyō hanga* (Buddhist Prints). *Nihon no bijutsu* (Arts of Japan), no. 218 (July 1984). Tokyo: Shibundō, 1984.

Kikutake et al. 1984
Kikutake Junji et al. *Nihon kohanga shūsei* (Compilation of Japanese Old Prints). 2 vols. Tokyo: Chikuma Shobō, 1984.

Kinoshita 1973
Kinoshita Masao. *Tekagami* (Albums of Ancient Writings). *Nihon no bijutsu* (Arts of Japan), no. 84 (May 1973). Tokyo: Shibundō, 1973.

Kitamura 1995
Kitamura Intei. *Nihon zuihitsu taisei* (Compendium of Japanese Essays). New ed. Vol. 2, *Kiyū shōran* ([Essays on Music and Dance]). Tokyo: Yoshikawa Kōbunkan, 1995.

Kitanosha, ed. 1910
Kitanosha Shamusho, ed. "Ryōsei ki" (Records of Two Sages). In *Kitano shi* (History of Kitano Shrine), vol. 42. Tokyo: Kokugaku-in Daigaku Shuppanbu, 1910.

Koizumi 1987
Koizumi Haruaki. "'Kikai mondō' nishu honkoku" (Report on Two Documents Entitled "Kikai's Debate"). In *Shōwa rokujūichi nendo kenkyū hōkoku ronshū* (Collected Research Reports for 1986), edited by the Kōzanji Team, pp. 5–17. Tokyo, 1987.

Komatsu 1953
Komatsu Shigemi. "Fujiwara Sadanobu to sono jidai" (Fujiwara Sadanobu and His Times). *Museum*, no. 31 (October 1953), pp. 30–31.

Komatsu 1960
Komatsu Shigemi. "Sadanobu to kyōshi no tsuma" (Sadanobu and the Wife of a Sutra Copyist). *Museum*, no. 107 (February 1960), pp. 17–20.

Komatsu 1980
Komatsu Shigemi. *Kōetsu shojō* (Kōetsu's Correspondence). Vol. 1. Tokyo: Nigensha, 1980.

Komatsu 1985
Komatsu Shigemi. *Rikyū no tegami* (Rikyū's Correspondence). Tokyo: Shōgakkan, 1985.

Komatsu 1996
Komatsu Shigemi. *Zōhoban Rikyū no tegami* (Expanded Edition of Rikyū's Correspondence). Tokyo: Shōgakkan, 1996.

Komatsu 1997
Komatsu Shigemi. *Nihon shodōshi tenbō* (Development of Japanese Calligraphy). Komatsu Shigemi chosakushū (Writings of Komatsu Shigemi), vol. 18. Tokyo: Ōbunsha, 1997.

Komatsu 1999
Komatsu Shigemi. *Sen no Rikyū shojō kiso kenkyū* (Basic Study of Sen no Rikyū's Correspondence). Komatsu Shigemi chosakushū (Writings of Komatsu Shigemi), vol. 26. Tokyo: Ōbunsha, 1999.

Komatsu, ed. 1977a
Komatsu Shigemi, ed. *Genji monogatari emaki, Nezame monogatari emaki*. Nihon emaki taisei (Compendium of Japanese Narrative Handscrolls), edited by Sawa Takaaki, vol. 1. Tokyo: Chūōkōronsha, 1977.

Komatsu, ed. 1977b
Komatsu Shigemi, ed. *Shigisan engi* (Legends of Shigisan). Nihon emaki taisei (Compendium of Japanese Narrative Handscrolls), edited by Sawa Takaaki, vol. 4. Tokyo: Chūōkōronsha, 1977.

Komatsu, ed. 1978–80
Komatsu Shigemi, ed. *Nihon shoseki taikan* (Survey of Japanese Calligraphy). 25 vols. Tokyo: Kōdansha, 1978–80.

Komatsu, ed. 1981a
Komatsu Shigemi, ed. *Nihon no sho* (Japanese Calligraphy). Vol. 2, *Sanpitsu* (Three Great Brushes). Tokyo: Chūōkōronsha, 1981.

Komatsu, ed. 1981b
Komatsu Shigemi, ed. *Nihon no sho* (Japanese Calligraphy). Vol. 10, *Kan'ei sanpitsu* (Three Great Brushes of the Kan'ei Era). Tokyo: Chūōkōronsha, 1981.

Komatsu et al. 1989
Shigemi Komatsu et al. *Chinese and Japanese Calligraphy Spanning Two Thousand Years: The Heinz Götze Collection, Heidelberg*. Munich: Prestel-Verlag, 1989.

Kōzanji shiryō 1968–
Kōzanji tenseki monjo sōgō chōsadan (General Investigative Team for Kōzanji Books and Documents). *Kōzanji shiryō sōsho* (Compendia of Kōzanji Material). 23 vols. Tokyo: Tokyo Daigaku Shuppan, 1968– .

Kujō 1993
Kujō Kanezane. *Gyokuyō* (Jeweled Leaves). 3 vols. Tokyo: Meicho Kankōkai, 1993.

Kuno 1965
Kuno Takeshi. "Tanjōbutsu ni tsuite" (Buddha at Birth). *Kobijutsu*, no. 10 (September 1965), pp. 23–34.

Kurata 1973
Kurata Bunsaku. *Zōnai nōnyūhin* (Objects Inside Statues). *Nihon no bijutsu* (Arts of Japan), no. 86 (July 1973). Tokyo: Shibundō, 1973.

Kurata et al. 1980
Kurata Bunsaku et al. *Zaigai Nihon no shihō* (Japanese Art: Selections from Western Collections). Vol. 8, *Chōkoku* (Sculpture). Tokyo: Mainichi Shinbunsha, 1980.

Kurita 1988–90
Kurita Isao. *Gandhara Bijutsu* (Gandhāran Art). 2 vols. Tokyo: Nigensha, 1988–90.

Kuroda 1961
Kuroda Ryōji. "Rengetsu-ni nenpyō" (Chronology of the Nun Rengetsu). *Tōsetsu*, no. 102 (September 1961), pp. 36–38.

Kuwata 1971
Kuwata Tadachika. *Teihon Sen no Rikyū no shokan* (Standard Selection of Rikyū's Correspondence). Tokyo: Tokyodō Shuppan, 1971.

Kyoto National Museum 1967
Muromachi jidai bijutsu ten zuroku (Fine Arts of the Muromachi Period). Exh. cat., Kyoto National Museum. Kyoto, 1967.

Kyoto National Museum 1974
Takeda Tsuneo et al. *Heike Nōkyō* (Sutras Donated by the Heike). Exh. cat., Kyoto National Museum, 1972. Kyoto: Kōrinsha, 1974.

Kyoto National Museum 1990
Chion'in no Bukkyō bijutsu: Ugai Tetsujō Shōnin botsugo hyakunen kinen (Buddhist Art of the Chion'in Temple: A Commemoration of the Centenary of the Death of the Monk Ugai Tetsujō). Exh. cat., Kyoto National Museum. Kyoto, 1990.

Kyoto National Museum 1992
Kana no bi (Art of *Kana*-Letters). Exh. cat., Kyoto National Museum. Kyoto, 1992.

Kyoto National Museum and Bunkamura Za Myujiamu, Tokyo 2000–2001
Ryōkan-san: Botsugo hyakushichijūnen kinenten (Dear Ryōkan: Memorial Exhibition for the 170th Anniversary of His Death). Exh. cat., Kyoto National Museum; Tokyo, Bunkamura Za Myujiamu. Tokyo: Nihon Keizai Shinbunsha, 2000.

Ledderose 1972
Lothar Ledderose. (An Approach to Chinese Calligraphy). *The National Palace Museum Quarterly* 7, no. 2 (May–June 1972), pp. 1–14.

Lee 1955
Sherman E. Lee. "The Golden Image of the New-Born Buddha." *Artibus Asiae* 18, nos. 3–4 (1955), pp. 225–37.

Leidy and Thurman 1997–98
Denise Patry Leidy and Robert A. F. Thurman. *Mandala: The Architecture of Enlightenment*. Exh. cat., New York, Asia Society Galleries and Tibet House. New York, 1997.

Levine 2001
Gregory P. Levine. "Switching Sites and Identities: The Founder's Statue at the Buddhist Temple Kōrin'in." *The Art Bulletin* 83, no. 1 (March 2001), pp. 72–104.

Liaoning Provincial Museum 1962
Yang Renkai, ed. *Liaoning sheng bowuguan cang fashu xuanji* (Select Calligraphies from the Collection of the Liaoning Provincial Museum). Beijing: Wenwuchubanshe, 1962.

Link and Shimbo 1980–81
Howard A. Link and Tōru Shimbo. *Exquisite Visions: Rimpa Paintings from Japan*. Exh. cat., Honolulu Academy of Arts; New York, Japan House Gallery. Honolulu, [1980].

London Gallery, Tokyo 1995
Tajima Mitsuru, ed. *Kitsukin rakuseki*. Exh. cat., Tokyo, London Gallery. Tokyo, 1995.

London Gallery, Tokyo 2000
Tanabe Saburōsuke et al. *Nenge Mishō: Bukkyō bijutsu no*

miryoku/Buddha's Smile: Masterpieces of Japanese Buddhist Art. Exh. cat., Tokyo, London Gallery. Tokyo, 2000.

Machida City Museum of Graphic Arts 1994
Yamatoji no Bukkyō hanga (Buddhist Prints in the Nara Area). Exh. cat., Tokyo, Machida City Museum of Graphic Arts. Tokyo, 1994.

Makita 1955–59
Makita Tairyō. *Sakugen Nyūminki no kenkyū* (Study of Sakugen's Travels to Ming China). 2 vols. Kyoto: Hōzōkan, 1955–59.

Masaki 1965
Masaki Tokuzō. *Hon'ami gyōjō ki to Kōetsu* (Annals of the Hon'ami Family and Kōetsu). Tokyo: Chūōkōron Bijutsu Shuppan, 1965.

Masuda 1978a
Masuda Takashi. "Shōkadō Shōjō I." *Nihon bijutsu kōgei,* no. 482 (November 1978), pp. 48–54.

Masuda 1978b
Masuda Takashi. "Shōkadō Shōjō II." *Nihon bijutsu kōgei,* no. 483 (December 1978), pp. 52–58.

Masuda 1980
Masuda Takashi. *Kōetsu no tegami* (Kōetsu's Correspondence). Tokyo: Kawaide Shobō Shinsha, 1980.

Matsuhara 1990
Matsuhara Satomi. "*Shosetsu Fudōki* no 'Aruzu' to Daimitsu no taizōzu" (On the "Aru-Zu" in *Shosetsu-fudō-ki* and Garbhadhatu Mandalas in Tendai-Esoteric-Buddhism). *Bijutsushi kenkyū,* no. 28 (1990), pp. 25–44.

Matsuhara 1993
Matsuhara Satomi. "Daimitsu-kei ryōbu mandara no kenkyū" (Study of the Womb and Diamond World Mandalas of the Tendai Esoteric Sect). *Kajima bijutsu zaidan nenpō bessatsu,* no. 10 (1993), pp. 240–43.

Matsuhara 1999
Matsuhara Satomi. "Taizō shibutsu no haichi ni okeru Daimitsukei no tokuchō: Enchin ni yoru Genzukei haichi no kaihen" (The Character of the Configuration of Four Buddhas in Garbhakośa Mandalas of Tendai-Esoteric-Buddhism: The Alteration to Genzu-Lineage's Configuration by Enchin). *Bijutsushi kenkyū,* no. 37 (1999), pp. 99–116.

Matsui 1962
Matsui Joryō. *Shoseki meihin sōkan* (Series of Masterpieces of Calligraphy). Vol. 86, *So Chō Sokushi, "Ri Hakka boshimei"* (Song Zhang Jizhi, "Epitaph for Li Bojia"). Tokyo: Nigensha, 1962.

Matsumoto 1979
Matsumoto Yasuchiyo. *Yuasatō to Myōe* (The Yuasa Clan and Myōe). Wakayama: Uji Shoten, 1979.

Matsunaga and Matsunaga 1974–76
Daigan Matsunaga and Alicia Matsunaga. *Foundation of Japanese Buddhism.* 2 vols. Los Angeles and Tokyo: Buddhist Books International, 1974–76.

Matsuya 1967
Matsuya Hisamasa. "Matsuya Hisamasa chakai ki" (Record of M. Hi's Tea Ceremony). In *Chadō koten zenshū* (Compendium of Writings on the Tea Ceremony), edited by Sen no Sōshitsu, vol. 9. 1957. 2d ed. Kyoto: Tankō Shinsha, 1967.

Minegishi 1954
Minegishi Yoshiaki. *Uta-awase no kenkyū* (Study of Poetry Competitions). Tokyo: Sanseidō, 1954.

Mitsui 1986
Mitsui Atsuo. *Nihon no Bukkyō hanga: Inori to mamori no sekai* (Buddhist Prints: The World of Praying and Protecting). Tokyo: Ryūseisha, 1986.

Miya 1983
Miya Tsugio. "Sō-Gen hanpon ni miru Hokekyō-e (Jō)" (Frontispieces in Song and Yuan Printed *Lotus Sutra,* Part One). *Bijutsu kenkyū* no. 325 (September 1983), pp. 99–110, pls. VII–VIII; no. 326 (December 1983), pp. 131–46, pls. V–VI.

Miyake 1956–58
Miyake Kyūnosuke. *Gyokudō: Uragami Gyokudō shinsekishū* (Collection of Authentic Works by Gyokudō). 3 vols. Tokyo: Bijutsu Shuppansha, 1956–58.

Mori 1978
Mori Tōru. *Uta-awase-e no kenkyū* (A Study of Pictures of Poetry Competitions). 1970. Rev. ed. Tokyo: Kadokawa Shoten, 1978.

Mori et al. 1979
Mori Tōru et al. *Shinshū Nihon emakimono zenshū* (New Collection of Japanese Narrative Handscrolls), edited by Tanaka Ichimatsu. Vol. 19, *Sanjūrokkasen-e* (Paintings of the Thirty-six Immortal Poets). Tokyo: Kadokawa Shoten, 1979.

Morrell 1987
Robert E. Morrell. *Early Kamakura Buddhism: A Minority Report.* Berkeley and Los Angeles: Asian Humanities Press, 1987.

Morse and Morse 1996
Anne Nishimura Morse and Samuel Crowell Morse. *Objects as Insight: Japanese Buddhist Art and Ritual.* Exh. cat., Katonah Museum of Art; Museum of Fine Arts, Boston. Katonah. N. Y., 1995.

Murasaki 1987
Murasaki Shikibu. *The Tale of Genji.* Translated with an introduction by Edward G. Seidensticker. 1976. New York: Alfred A. Knopf, 1987.

Murase 1970
Miyeko Murase. "Farewell Paintings of China: Chinese Gifts to Japanese Visitors." *Artibus Asiae* 32, nos. 2–3 (1970), pp. 211–36.

Murase 1986
Miyeko Murase. *Tales of Japan: Scrolls and Prints from The New York Public Library.* Exh. cat., New York Public Library and traveled. New York and Oxford: Oxford University Press, 1986.

Murase 2000
Miyeko Murase. *Bridge of Dreams: The Mary Griggs Burke Collection of Japanese Art.* Exh. cat., New York, The Metropolitan Museum of Art. New York, 2000.

Nagazumi and Shimada, eds. 1966
Nagazumi Yasuaki and Shimada Isao, eds. *Nihon koten bungaku taikei* (Compendium of Japanese Classical Literature). Vol. 84, *Kokon chomojū* (Old and New Stories Read and Heard). Tokyo: Iwanami Shoten, 1966.

Nakabe 1993
Nakabe Yoshitaka. "Shōkadō Shōjō no kaiga sakuhin" (Paintings by Shōkadō Shōjō). In *Shōkadō Shōjō: Chanoyu no kokoro to hitsuboku* (Shōkadō Shōjō: His Tea Ceremony, Calligraphy, and Painting), edited by Yamato Bunkakan, pp. 2–6. Nara: Yamato Bunkakan, 1993.

Nakata et al. 1983
Yūjirō Nakata et al. *Chinese Calligraphy.* Translated and adapted by Jeffrey Hunter. A History of the Art of China. 1982. New York and Tokyo: John Weatherhill; Kyoto: Tankōsha, 1983.

Naniwada 1990
Naniwada Tōru. *Kyōzō to Kakebotoke* (Mirrors and *Kakebotoke*). *Nihon no bijutsu* (Arts of Japan), no. 284 (January 1990). Tokyo: Shibundō, 1990.

Nara National Museum 1983
Narachō shakyō (Sutra Copies from the Nara Period). Exh. cat., Nara National Museum, 1969. Nara, 1983.

Nara National Museum 1988
Hokekyō: Shakyō to shōgon (Lotus Sutra: Its Calligraphy and Decoration). Exh. cat., Nara National Museum, 1979. Tokyo: Tokyo Bijutsu, 1988.

Nezu Institute of Fine Arts 1994
Uemura Wadō. *Uemura Wadō Korekushon: Koshakyō* (Old Sutra Copies from the Collection of Uemura Wadō). Exh. cat., Tokyo, The Nezu Institute of Fine Arts. Tokyo, 1994.

Nihon Bijutsu Kurabu 1925
Maeda Kōshaku-ke onzōki nyūsatsu mokuroku (Marquis of Maeda Collection). Sale cat., Tokyo, Nihon Bijutsu Kurabu, 1925.

***Nihon kōsō iboku* 1970–71**
Nihon kōsō iboku (Calligraphy of Celebrated Monks of Japan). 3 vols. Tokyo: Mainichi Shinbunsha, 1970–71.

Nishigami 1999
Nishigami Atsushi. "Sumidera Shingyō no nazo" (Mystery of the Heart Sutra from Sumidera). In *Asahi hyakka: Nihon no Kokuhō* (Asahi Encyclopedia: National Treasures of Japan), vol. 5, p. 284. 12 vols. Tokyo: Asahi Shinbunsha, 1999.

Nishikawa et al. 1984
Nishikawa Kyōtarō et al. *Kokuhō* (National Treasures). Vol. 5, *Chōkoku* (Sculpture), vol. 2. Tokyo: Mainichi Shinbunsha, 1984.

Okuda 1978
Okuda Isao. *Myōe: Henreki to yume* (Myōe: Pilgrimages and Dreams). Tokyo: Tokyo Daigaku Shuppankai, 1978.

Okuda 1980
Okuda Isao. "Myōe Shōnin kankei tenseki no okugaki, shikigo ni tsuite: Tsuke Myōe Shōnin Yumenoki dai ju-jūhen sankan kō" (Concerning the Colophons and Inscriptions on Manuscripts Related to Myōe and Research on the Fragmentation of Book 10 of Myōe Shōnin's *Dream Record*). In *Kōzanji shiryō sōsho bekkan* (Studies of Kōzanji Material), pp. 165–79. Tokyo: Tokyo Daigaku Shuppan, 1980.

Onjōji, ed. 1978
Onjōji, ed. *Chishō Daishi zenshū* (Writings by the Monk Enchin). 3 vols. Kyoto: Dōhōsha, 1978.

Ono and Maruyama 1978
Ono Genmyō and Maruyama Takao, eds. *Busshō kaisetsu daijiten* (Great Compendium of Buddhist Texts). 1933–36. Rev. and enl. ed. 14 vols. Tokyo: Daitō Shuppansha, 1978.

Ōoka and Kobayashi, eds. 1994
Ōoka Makoto and Kobayashi Tadashi, eds. *Taiga*. Suibokuga no kyoshō (Masters of Ink Painting), vol. 11. Tokyo: Kōdansha, 1994.

Ōyama et al. 1987
Ōyama Jinkai et al. *Nihon no shakyō* (Hand-copied Sutras of Japan). Kyoto: Kyoto Shoin, 1987.

Pal 1988
Pratapaditya Pal. "An Infant Buddha from Kashmir." *Orientations* 19, no. 10 (October 1988), pp. 60–65.

Pal and Meech-Pekarik 1988
Pratapaditya Pal and Julia Meech-Pekarik. *Buddhist Book Illuminations*. New York: Ravi Kumar Publishers, 1988.

Perkins et al. 2000–2001
Larry David Perkins et al. *Intimate Rituals and Personal Devotions: Spiritual Art through the Ages*. Exh. cat., Gainesville, Fla., Samuel P. Harn Museum of Art. Gainesville, Fla., 2000.

Poster 1989
Amy G. Poster. "Religious Arts of Medieval Japan in The Brooklyn Museum." *Orientations* 20, no. 7 (July 1989), pp. 28–38.

Rengetsu 1980
Rengetsu. *Rengetsu-ni zenshū* (Complete Works of the Nun Rengetsu). 1927. Enl. ed., edited by Murakami Sadō. Kyoto: Shibunkaku Shuppan, 1980.

Richardson 1992–93
Brenda Richardson. *Brice Marden: Cold Mountain*. Exh. cat., New York, Dia Center for the Arts; Minneapolis, Walker Art Center; Houston, Menil Collection. Houston: Fine Art Press, 1992.

Rosenfield and Shimada 1970–71
John M. Rosenfield and Shūjirō Shimada. *Traditions of Japanese Art: Selections from the Kimiko and John Powers Collection*. Exh. cat., Cambridge, Mass., Fogg Art Museum, Harvard University; Seattle Art Museum; Princeton, N.J., The Art Museum, Princeton University. Cambridge, Mass., 1970.

Rosenfield and ten Grotenhuis 1979
John M. Rosenfield and Elizabeth ten Grotenhuis. *Journey of the Three Jewels: Japanese Buddhist Paintings from Western Collections*. Exh. cat., New York, The Asia Society. New York, 1979.

Rosenfield et al. 1973
John M. Rosenfield et al. *The Courtly Tradition in Japanese Art and Literature: Selections from the Hofer and Hyde Collections*. Exh. cat., Cambridge, Mass., Fogg Art Museum, Harvard University. Cambridge, Mass., 1973.

Ruppert 2000
Brian D. Ruppert. *Jewel in the Ashes: Buddha Relics and Power in Early Medieval Japan*. Cambridge, Mass., and London: Harvard University Asia Center, 2000.

Sano Museum and Shiga Prefectural Lake Biwa Cultural Center 1993
Tōrei no zen to sho: Nihyakunen onki kinen (Zen and Calligraphy Tōrei: Memorial for the Second Centenary). Exh. cat., Sano Museum and Shiga Prefectural Lake Biwa Cultural Center. Mishima-shi, 1993.

Sasaki 1985a
Sasaki Susumu. "Ōmi Ashiura Kannonji no ryōkai mandarazu: Daimitsukei Ryōkai mandara no ichi sakurei toshite" (Mandala of the Two Worlds of the Ashiura Kannonji in Ōmi Province: An Example of Ryōkai Mandala in the School of Tendai Sect of Esoteric Buddhism). *Ars Buddhica*, no. 163 (1985), pp. 63–82.

Sasaki 1985b
Sasaki Susumu. "Saimyōji no ryōkai Mandarazu ni tsuite" (Paintings of Two Worlds Mandalas Owned by Saimyōji). *Shiga Kenritsu Biwako Bunkakan kenkyū kiyō*, no. 3 (1985), pp. 13–17.

Sawa and Hamada 1983
Sawa Ryūken and Hamada Takashi. *Mikkyō bijutsu taikan* (Encyclopedia of Esoteric Buddhism). Vol. 1, *Ryōkai mandara* (The Two Worlds Mandalas). Tokyo: Asahi Shinbunsha, 1983.

Shanghai Museum 1964
Shanghai bowuguan cang lidai fashu zuanji (Selection of Calligraphies of Successive Periods from the Shanghai Museum). Beijing: Wenwu Chubanshe, 1964.

Shibayama 1974
Zenkei Shibayama. *Zen Comments on the Mumonkan*. Translated by Sumiko Kudō. New York: Harper and Row, 1974.

Shimatani 1985
Shimatani Hiroyuki. "Togakushigire" (Togakushi Fragment). *Museum*, no. 406 (January 1985), pp. 1–2.

Shimizu and Rosenfield 1984–85
Yoshiaki Shimizu and John M. Rosenfield. *Masters of Japanese Calligraphy: 8th–19th Century*. Exh. cat., New York, The Asia Society Galleries and Japan House Gallery; Kansas City, Missouri, The Nelson-Atkins Museum of Art; The Seattle Museum of Art. New York, 1984.

Shimizu and Wheelwright 1976
Yoshiaki Shimizu and Carolyn Wheelwright. *Japanese Ink Paintings from American Collections, The Muromachi Period: An Exhibition in Honor of Shūjirō Shimada*. Exh. cat., Princeton, N.J., The Art Museum, Princeton University. Princeton, N.J., 1976.

Shinbo 1983

Shinbo Tōru. "Narikane-bon Sanjūrokkasen-e" (Narikane Version of the "Handscroll Painting of Thirty-six Celebrated Poets"). *Bijutsu kenkyū*, no. 325 (September 1983), pp. 84–98, pl. VI.

Shinbo 1986

Shinbo Tōru. "Sanjūrokkasen-e no tenkai" (Evolution of the Thirty-six Immortal Poets Painting). In Suntory Museum of Art 1986, pp. 80–84.

Shirasu 1967

Shirasu Masako. *Toganoo Kōzanji Myōe Shōnin* (Monk Myōe at Kōzanji of Toganoo). Tokyo: Kōdansha, 1967.

Shirasu 1974

Shirasu Masako. *Myōe Shōnin*. Tokyo: Shinchōsha, 1974.

***Shodō zenshū* 1954–68**

Onoe Hachirō, Kanda Kiichirō, and Tanaka Shinbi, eds. *Shodō zenshū* (Compilation of Chinese and Japanese Calligraphy). 28 vols. Tokyo: Heibonsha, 1954–68.

Smith 1979

Mary Smith. "Journey of Three Jewels of Japanese Buddhism." *Art/World* 4, no. 2 (October 20–November 17, 1979), pp. 1, 7.

Snodgrass 1988

Adrian Snodgrass. *The Matrix and Diamond World Mandalas in Shingon Buddhism*. 2 vols. New Delhi: Aditya Prakashan, 1988.

***Song Jin Yuan shu fa* 1986**

Zhongguo mei shu quan ji (Complete Collection of Chinese Arts). *Shu fa zhuan ke bian* (Calligraphy and Seal Carving Series), edited by Shen Peng. Vol. 4, *Song Jin Yuan shufa* (Song, Jin, and Yuan Dynasties). Beijing: Renmin mei shu chubanshe, 1986.

***Songren juanji ziliao suoyin* 1974–76**

Chang Bide et al., eds. *Songren juanji ziliao suoyin* (Index to Biographical Materials of Song Figures). 6 vols. Taipei: Dingwen Shuju Yinhang, 1974–76.

***Song shi* 1977**

Tuotuo et al. *Song shi* (History of the Song Dynasty). 40 vols. Ershisi shi (Twenty-four Dynastic Histories). Beijing: Zhonghua shu ju, 1977.

Sotheby's, London 1994

Sotheby's, London. *Japanese Paintings, Prints and Works of Art*. Sale LN4356. June 16th and 17th, 1994.

Stone 1999

Jacqueline I. Stone. *Original Enlightenment and the Transformation of Medieval Japanese Buddhism*. Studies in East Asian Buddhism, vol. 12. Honolulu: University of Hawaii Press, 1999.

Sudō 1982

Sudō Hirotoshi. "Uesugi Jinja zō kindei Ryōkai mandala ni tsuite" (The Ryōkai Mandala [Painted in Gold] of Yonezawa's Uesugi Shrine). *Bijutsushigaku*, no. 4 (1982), pp. 30–44.

Suntory Museum of Art 1986

Sanjūrokkasen-e: Satake-bon o chūshin ni (Pictures of the Thirty-six Immortal Poets, with Special Emphasis on the Satake Version). Exh. cat., Tokyo: Suntory Museum of Art. Tokyo, 1986.

Suzuki H. 1995

Suzuki Hiroyuki. "Ōkan suru kaiga: jūgoseiki kanji bunkaken no naka no *kara-e* no igi" (Paintings Crossing Sea Borders: The Significance of *kara-e* in Fifthteenth-Century East Asia). *Bijutsu kenkyū*, no. 361 (March 1995), pp. 137–58.

Suzuki K. 1991

Suzuki Keiji. "Harima Kiyomizu-dera shozō no Tenpyō shakyō: Shinshutsu no daiji Hokekyō maki dai-go" ("Tenpyō Shakyō" Transcription of Sutra in the Harima Kiyomizu-dera: New Facts about the Hoke-kyō Sutra in Large Characters, vol. 5). *Museum*, no. 484 (July 1991), pp. 4–10.

Takeuchi 1964

Takeuchi Naoji. *Hakuin*. 2 vols. Tokyo: Chikuma Shobō, 1964.

Tamamura 1983

Tamamura Takeji. *Gozan zensō denki shūsei* (Collection of Biographies of Zen Monks from the Five Mountain System). Tokyo: Kōdansha, 1983.

Tanabe and Tanabe, eds. 1989

George J. Tanabe, Jr., and Willa Jane Tanabe, eds. *The Lotus Sutra in Japanese Culture*. [Papers presented at the first International Conference on the *Lotus Sutra* and Japanese Culture, University of Hawaii, 1984.] Honolulu: University of Hawaii Press, 1989.

Tanabe, G. 1992

George J. Tanabe, Jr. *Myōe the Dreamkeeper: Fantasy and Knowledge in Early Kamakura Buddhism*. Harvard East Asian Monographs, no. 156. Cambridge, Mass.: Council on East Asian Studies, Harvard University, 1992.

Tanabe, W. 1988

Willa J. Tanabe. *Paintings of the Lotus Sutra*. New York and Tokyo: Weatherhill, 1988.

Tanaka K. 1963

Tanaka Kaidō. *Nihon shakyō sōkan* (Compilation of Japanese Sutra Copies). Osaka: Sanmeisha, 1963.

Tanaka Yoshichika 1976–78

Tanaka Yoshichika. "Amida Nyorai zazō" (Statue of Seated Amida Buddha). In *Yamato koji taikan* (Comprehensive Study of the Old Temples in the Nara Area), edited by Ōta Hirotarō et al., vol. 7 (text), pp. 79–90. 7 vols. Tokyo: Iwanami Shoten, 1976–78.

Tanaka Yoshiyasu 1979

Tanaka Yoshiyasu. *Tanjōbutsu* (Buddha at Birth). *Nihon no bijutsu* (Arts of Japan), no. 159 (August 1979). Tokyo: Shibundō, 1979.

Tayama 1961

Tayama Hōnan. *Zoku Zenrin bokuseki* (Zen Calligraphy, Supplement). 2 vols. Tokyo: Zenrin Bokuseki Kankōkai, 1961.

Tayama 1965

Tayama Hōnan. *Zenrin bokuseki* (Zen Calligraphy). Tokyo: Zenrin Bokuseki Kankōkai, 1965.

ten Grotenhuis 1999

Elizabeth ten Grotenhuis. *Japanese Mandalas: Representations of Sacred Geography*. Honolulu: University of Hawaii Press, 1999.

Tokunaga 1980

Tokunaga Hiromichi. "Totō Tenjin zō to sono shakaiteki haikei: Santō Inshi san no zō ni kanren shite" (Totō Tenjin and Its Social Background with Special Reference to the Painting Inscribed by Santō Inshi). *Kokka*, no. 1032 (1980), pp. 7–13.

Tokyo and Osaka 1980

Ryōkan ten: Botsugo hyaku-gojūnen (150th Centenary Exhibition of Ryōkan). Exh. cat., Tokyo Mitsukoshi Museum; Osaka Mitsukoshi Museum. Tokyo: Mainichi Shinbunsha, 1980.

Tokyo National Museum 1980

Tokubetsuten zuroku Nihon no sho (Japanese Calligraphy: Commemorative Catalogue of the Special Exhibition). Exh. cat., Tokyo National Museum. Tokyo, 1980.

Tokyo National Museum 1985

Komatsu Shigemi. *Sōshokukyō* (Decorated Buddhist Scriptures). Exh. cat., Tokyo National Museum. Tokyo, 1985.

Tseng 1993

Tseng Yuho. *A History of Chinese Calligraphy*. Hong Kong: Chinese University Press, 1993.

Tsukamoto 1979

Tsukamoto Zenryū. *A History of Early Chinese Buddhism: From Its*

Introduction to the Death of Hui-yüan. Translated by Leon Hurvitz. 2 vols. Tokyo: Kōdansha, 1979.

Tyler 1990
Royall Tyler. *The Miracles of the Kasuga Deity.* New York: Columbia University Press, 1990.

Uchida 2000
Uchida Keiichi. "Shoson zuzō, darani to 'kokonoe no mamori' ni tsuite: Saidaiji-bon o chūshin to shite" (Various Iconographies, Dharani Sutra etc.: The Case of the Saidaiji Version). *Kanazawa Bunko kenkyū,* no. 305 (October 2000), pp. 1–19.

Uehara 1971a
Uehara Shōichi. "Futatsu no tanjōbutsu" (Two Statues of Buddha at His Birth). *Kobijutsu,* no. 33 (March 1971), pp. 95–97 and plates.

Uehara 1971b
Uehara Shōichi. "Kakebotoke santen" (Three Hanging Plaques with Buddhist Images). *Kobijutsu,* no. 35 (December 1971), pp. 121–23 and plates.

Wang 1999
Eugene Y. Wang. "The Taming of the Shrew: Wang Hsi-chih (303–361) and Calligraphic Gentrification in the Seventh Century." In *Character and Context in Chinese Calligraphy,* edited by Cary Y. Liu, Dora C. Y. Ching, and Judith G. Smith, pp. 132–73. Princeton, N.J.: The Art Museum, Princeton University, 1999.

Watson 1993
Burton Watson, trans. *The Lotus Sutra.* New York: Columbia University Press, 1993.

Yabe 1937
Yabe Ryōsaku, comp. *Sadō zenshū* (Collection of Writings on the Tea Ceremony). Vol. 5. Tokyo: Sōgensha, 1937.

Yabumoto 1980
Yabumoto Eitarō. *Jiun Sonja ihō* (Calligraphy of Jiun Sonja). 1938. 2 vols. Reprint with supplement edited by Yabumoto Sōshirō and Yabumoto Sōgorō. Tokyo: Nichibō Shuppansha, 1980.

Yamagishi 1965
Yamagishi Tokubei. "Heian jidai no shodō to Sadanobu" (Calligraphy of the Heian Period and Sadanobu). *Gekkan bunkazai* 17 (February 1965), pp. 4–8.

Yamasaki 1988
Taikō Yamasaki. *Shingon: Japanese Esoteric Buddhism.* Boston and London: Shambhala, 1988.

Yamazaki 2000
Yamazaki Shinji. *Chūsei kawara no kenkyū* (Study of Roof Tiles from the Medieval Period). Nara: Nara National Institute of Cultural Properties, 2000.

Yazaki 1974
Yazaki Itaru. "Shōkadō gajō' no Totō Tenjin zu" (Painting of the Totō Tenjin in the *Shōkadō Album*). *Nihon bijutsu kōgei,* no. 428 (May 1974), pp. 84–89.

Yoritomi 1991
Yoritomi Motohiro. *Mandara no kanshō kiso chishiki* (Introduction to Mandalas). Tokyo: Shibundō, 1991.

Yoshii 1959
Yoshii Seizō. *Kinsei kōsō ibokushū* (Calligraphy by Famous Monks of Recent Periods). Kyoto: Maria Shobō, 1959.

Zaitsu 1973
Zaitsu Eiji. *Tegami* (Correspondence). *Nihon no bijutsu* (Arts of Japan), no. 82 (March 1973). Tokyo: Shibundō, 1973.

Zenrin gasan 1987
Shimada Shūjirō and Iriya Yoshitaka. *Zenrin gasan: Chūsei suibokuga o yomu.* Tokyo: Mainichi Shinbunsha, 1987.

Zhongguo gudai shu hua tumu 1986–
Group for the Authentification of Ancient Works of Chinese Painting and Calligraphy. *Zhongguo gudai shu hua tumu* (Illustrated Catalogue of Selected Works of Ancient Chinese Painting and Calligraphy). Beijing: Wenwu chubanshe, 1986– .

Zhongwen da cidian 1973
Zhongwen da cidian (The Encyclopedic Dictionary of the Chinese Language). 10 vols. Taipei: Zhonghua xueshuyuan, 1973.

Zoku Gunshoruijū 1926
Zoku Gunshoruijū (Collection of Essays Continued). Vol. 13ge. 1907. Tokyo: Zoku Gunshoruijū Kankōkai, 1926.

Index